A Violent World

CRITICAL MEDIA STUDIES
Institutions, Politics, and Culture

Series Editor
Andrew Calabrese, University of Colorado

Advisory Board

Recent Titles in the Series

A Violent World

TV News Images of Middle Eastern Terror and War

Nitzan Ben-Shaul

ROWMAN & LITTLEFIELD PUBLISHERS, INC.
Lanham • Boulder • New York • Toronto • Oxford

ROWMAN & LITTLEFIELD PUBLISHERS, INC.

Published in the United States of America
by Rowman & Littlefield Publishers, Inc.
A wholly owned subsidiary of The Rowman & Littlefield Publishing Group, Inc.
4501 Forbes Boulevard, Suite 200, Lanham, Maryland 20706
www.rowmanlittlefield.com

P.O. Box 317, Oxford OX2 9RU, UK

British Library Cataloguing in Publication Information Available

Library of Congress Cataloging-in-Publication Data

Ben-Shaul, Nitzan S.
   A violent world : TV news images of Middle Eastern terror and war / Nitzan
Ben-Shaul.
      p.   cm. — (Critical media studies)
   INcludes bibliographical references and index.
   ISBN-13: 978-0-7425-3798-9 (cloth : alk. paper)
   ISBN-10: 0-7425-3798-6 (cloth : alk. paper)
   1. Terrorism—Middle East—Press coverage.   2. Arab-Israeli conflict—1993—
Press coverage.   3. Television broadcasting of news.   I. Title.   II. Series.
PN4784.T45B46   2006
070.4′4956053—dc22

                                                    2006009638

Printed in the United States of America

♾ ™The paper used in this publication meets the minimum requirements of
American National Standard for Information Sciences—Permanence of Paper for
Printed Library Materials, ANSI/NISO Z39.48-1992.

I dedicate this book
to my beloved wife, Daphna.

Contents

Acronyms

CNN	Cable News Network
EI	Electronic Intifada
EU	European Union
FLN	National Liberation Front
HRW	Human Rights Watch
IBA	Israel Broadcasting Authority
IDF	Israel Defence Force
IMF	International Monetary Fund
IMRA	Independent Media Review and Analysis
IPC	International Press Center
JCS	Jerusalem Capital Studios
MEMRI	Middle East Media Research Institute
PATV	Palestinian Authority Television
PBC	Palestine Broadcasting Corporation
PFLP	Popular Front for the Liberation of Palestine
PHRMG	Palestinian Human Rights Monitoring Group
PLO	Palestinian Liberation Organization
PMW	Palestinian Media Watch
PNA	Palestinian National Authority
PNGO	Palestinian Non-Governmental Network
WTC	World Trade Center

Preface

Like most people around the world I was struck by the suicide attacks on the Twin Towers in Manhattan on September 11, 2001. I could not get my eyes off the ongoing coverage of the event by CNN and by Israeli television. I began comparing the coverage of the two networks and realized how different it was. I then searched for the coverage of the event on Palestinian television and could hardly find it. The striking difference in the coverage of the event by these networks originated this study.

Being trained as a film scholar rather than in communication or television studies, I began an extensive reading of television news research by communication scholars and felt that their overall quantitative social science approach (embedded also in what the discipline terms *qualitative* approaches) and their verbal bias were not attuned to the qualities of televised audiovisuality. I therefore set out to study the coverage of terror events and constitutional violence through the qualitative approach and aesthetic sensibility developed in cinema studies. I hope the result presented here offers insights into the coverage of these events and will contribute to the general understanding of televised audiovisual articulations.

Although I take full responsibility for this study, I am dearly indebted to Dr. Amit Lavie-Denur for her encouragement and for introducing me to the concept of media frames. Her close reading of the manuscript helped me avoid some pitfalls.

I thank Hanania Rapaport, vice president of the Jerusalem Capital Studios (JCS), who helped me contact several media people; Mr. Liviu Carmeli, the director of the Film and Television Department Archive at Tel Aviv University, who gave me access to his recordings of Israeli television news; Mr. Ygal Carmon, president of the Middle East Media Research Institute (MEMRI), who kindly gave me free access to their unedited recordings of Palestinian television; Mr. Ilan Sztulman, head of the production unit of the Israeli Ministry of Foreign Affairs; and Mr. Radwan Abu Ayyash, chairman of the board of the Palestine Broadcasting Corporation (PBC), for his encouragement and for his sending me his own study of Palestinian television.

Many thanks go to my students at the various seminars I conducted on subjects related to this book in the Film and Television Department at Tel Aviv University, particularly to Noam Inbar, Elinor Davidov, Sigal Kiewe, and Adi Dror, who assisted me in the gathering and recording of reports used in this study.

Finally I wish to thank Rabab Nage Gebarah for her eloquent translations from the Arabic; Naomi Paz for her editing of the manuscript on short notice; and the editors at Rowman & Littlefield, Brenda Hadenfeldt and Erica Fast, who found my proposal interesting, encouraged its writing, and patiently awaited the delayed deliverance of the manuscript.

Introduction

The study presented in this book is set within the framework of a political-economic approach to globalization. It considers post-Fordism to be the dominant mode of production propelling globalization, and views the formation of a "new world order," led by U.S. core-elites, as a further expansion of the capitalist exploitation of the periphery. The violent acts undertaken by supranational movements (al-Qaeda), subnational movements (e.g., Hamas in the territories under the jurisdiction of the Palestinian National Authority, and the settler movement in Israel), and by states noncompliant with the core-elites' interests (e.g., former Afghanistan and Iraq, Iran, or Syria), disrupt this U.S. elites–led effort to expand and deepen the economic and geopolitical dependence of the peripheral Middle East on the U.S.-led core. Therefore, the reciprocal violent measures undertaken by the United States and by its dependent allies are ultimately aimed at sustaining and expanding this dependence system.

The study outlines the dominant ideologies that function to justify the interests of the elites in the United States and those of dependent elites in the periphery, focusing on the opposing dominant ideologies of elites in the State of Israel and in the Palestinian National Authority (PNA). It henceforth considers how these dominant ideologies are embedded in their mainstream television news and analyzes the resulting competing figurations of the escalating reciprocal terror and constitutional violence[1] that emanate from the U.S.–al Qaeda conflict and the exacerbation of the Israeli-Palestinian conflict evident in the al Aksa Intifada.

The coverage of these conflicts has been chosen because they exhibit a direct core-periphery conflict (U.S.–al Qaeda) and an indirect one (the al Aksa Intifada), allowing for the identification of different audiovisual frames exhibiting variations on a decentered-world ideological conception that facilitates the overall global divide-and-conquer U.S. core strategy through

1

which it subdues the periphery. This strategy is aided by the "double-talk" dominant ideology of core-dependent peripheral-state elites, legitimating their attempts to control the state apparatus that allows them a relative autonomy in a shaken state-based world system.

The analysis of television news as presented here stems from a critical media theory approach. It considers the ways in which mainstream television news frames events to be determined by dominant ideologies, offering a new model for the analysis of audiovisual formations so as to better deal with the coverage of terror events and war, where audiovisuals overwhelm the verbal commentary. It henceforth proposes an analysis of contemporary TV news that decodes the discursive television strategies peculiar to the different positions embedded in different dominant ideologies within the post-Fordist mode of production.

Within this framework, a comparative and relational analysis is conducted of the competing televised images of U.S. global Cable News Network (CNN) and of Israeli and Palestinian national mainstream television news that framed the violence emanating from the U.S.–al Qaeda conflict and from the al Aksa Intifada. These images respectively embedded U.S. core-elite global ideology and conflicting Israeli-Palestinian elite dominant national-peripheral ideologies.

Part I outlines the historical and theoretical background informing contemporary television news coverage of events: Chapter 1 outlines the political economy of globalization, focusing on its generation of the U.S.–al Qaeda conflict and on its exacerbation of the Israeli-Palestinian conflict. Chapter 2 outlines the ideological embedment of the specific interests of the U.S.-led core and that of the peripheral Israeli and Palestinian national elites. Chapter 3 offers a model for the analysis of television news' ideological audiovisual frames. Chapter 4 discusses the competing macro-frames of CNN and Israeli and Palestinian television news.

Part II offers an analysis of the way CNN and Israeli and Palestinian television mainstream news embedded their respective elite's dominant ideologies in their differing coverage of the terror and the reciprocal constitutional violence coming out of the conflicts dealt with. Chapters 5 and 6 analyze the television frames that have been developed by CNN and Israeli and Palestinian television news in their coverage of the U.S.–al Qaeda conflict and of the al Aksa Intifada.[2] Chapter 7 offers a summary discussion of these frames.

NOTES

1. There are many definitions of violence, terror, and state violence or state terror. See, for example, Alex P. Schmid, *Political Terrorism: A Research Guide to Concepts, Theories, Data Bases, and Literature* (New Brunswick, N.J.: Transaction Books,

1984); and Norbert Elias, *The Civilizing Process*, vol. 2, *State Formation and Civilization* (Oxford: Blackwell, 1982). Terror is understood here as political violence deemed illegal and criminal by international law and carried out by nonstate actors. Constitutional violence or "official violence" concerns violent measures taken by states. See on this Noam Chomsky and Edward S. Herman, *The Washington Connection and Third World Fascism: The Political Economy of Human Rights*, vol. 2 (Nottingham: Spokesman Books, 1979).

2. The extensive television coverage of the U.S.-led coalition war against Iraq merits a separate discussion though it generally follows the audiovisual frames detected here.

I

HISTORICAL AND THEORETICAL BACKGROUND

1

The Political Economy of Globalization

Following a period of uncertainty and confusion as to the general direction of world economy, politics, and ideology in the aftermath of the fall of the Soviet Union—a confusion evidenced in many writings on globalization and in the prominence of a widespread labyrinthine postmodern ideology—the contours of the emergent new world order are becoming clearer from one conflict to the next.

Contrary to theories of globalization that maintain that, while the colonial and neocolonial enterprises were intentional, globalization is unintentional,[1] diffuse,[2] and multifocal or multidetermined,[3] the explicit and effective economic-political deregulation policy of the U.S.-led G-7 core states and the military actions undertaken by U.S.-led coalitions testify to the core states' deliberate intent to enhance the periphery's dependence so as to better allow its exploitation.

The crumbling of the "second world" (the Soviet socialist bloc) has out-dated the first world–third world conceptualization of the colonial and neo-colonial world systems.[4] Also, the deterritorialized computer-based management of the post-Fordist mode of production, generating unprece-dented streams of migration and giving rise to several new economies, has outdated the conceptual geographical division of this new world system into a rich north and a poor south. This should not blind us, however, to the realities of interdependence between a rich world core-elite and a poor, dependent, and exploited world periphery.

This seems to be the case from the point of view of a political-economy approach that strives to embed a variety of economic, social, political, and cultural events within the totality of a period's dominant mode of produc-tion. Understanding these occurrences worldwide as instances of underlying

7

dominant modes of production predicated on inequality and exploitation has proved fruitful and led to prediction of what is currently termed globalization. Hence, according to Marx, the ever-expanding logic of capitalism was to lead, albeit in an exploitative and asymmetrical manner, to the global interdependence of all the forces of production in the process of procuring their means of subsistence.

Hence, the 1970s' gradual rise to dominance of what has been termed the "post-Fordist" or "flexible accumulation" capitalist mode of production, along with the crumbling of the Soviet Union and its East European satellite states, brought down the two-superpower-based world superstructure that was formed during the Cold War and was able to regulate a predominantly mass-oriented mode of production. The repercussions of this superstructural crumbling, which opened up new markets to post-Fordist capitalism and reawakened ethnic and religious conflicts (e.g., the disintegration of Yugoslavia), were felt worldwide. Of particular interest to this study are the conflicts exacerbated or inflamed by these processes within the Middle East region, notably the exacerbated Israeli-Palestinian conflict as evidenced in the al Aksa Intifada and the inflamed U.S.-led "War against Terror" following the September 11, 2001, al Qaeda terrorist attacks on U.S. soil.

Viewed within the totality of this period's dominant mode of production, the U.S.-led responses to these conflicts indicate the intentional mounting of a new, one-superpower-led superstructure aimed at "enlarging,"[5] integrating, and managing an exploitative post-Fordist global market economy.

POST-FORDISM

The mid-1970s' gradual rise to dominance of the flexible, computer-based, post-Fordist mode of production displaced the Fordist mode of production. Fordism is so-termed after Henry Ford's 1914 introduction of the five-dollar, eight-hour workday plan in his car assembly line, and broadly refers to a capitalist regime of accumulation based on rationalized corporate mass production for mass consumption. It is complemented by state regulation of intercapitalist competition and the generation of stable demand for Fordist production by public investment in infrastructures, by statist welfare plans, and by generally compliant large labor unions. This mode of production became dominant after the Second World War in Western capitalist countries and in Japan. It gradually expanded into third-world areas to which it promised modernization but actually continued their colonial exploitation as providers of cheap labor and as mass-consumption markets.[6] The end of the Second World War and the ensuing Cold War led to the rise of national liberation movements among third-world countries, which strove to attain a state apparatus that would allow them to organize and regulate production within. This was a process often supported by the Soviet Union, which strove to expand its influence and counter Western exploitation of these areas. In the Middle East, the West focused its efforts primarily on the oil-rich Gulf monarchies and on Israel, which it perceived mostly as a military strategic asset. Most of the other Middle East Arab states that attained independence, or were overtaken by nationalist movements after the Second World War, developed strong, state-regulated economies. This was the case in Middle East countries such as Egypt, Iraq, Syria, and Algeria. The state elites in these countries maneuvered between the two superpowers and managed in such a way to develop their relative independent economy, usually along Fordist-cum-state-socialist economic models.[7]

In a way, Fordism and state socialism, both predicated on mass production, conditioned the two-superpower-based superstructure that maintained a stable world production throughout the Cold War. However, the world-leading U.S. Fordist economy, predicated on highly organized modes of mass production and complemented by big labor unions and state regulation, began running into disarray during the mid-sixties and early seventies following mounting international competition—from Japan, Western Europe, and new industrialized nations—with which the rigid U.S. Fordist economy could not cope. This led to reduced corporate productivity and profit in the United States, resulting in accelerated inflation that eventually led to the dismantling of the Bretton Woods Agreement and devalued the dollar.[8] This volatile situation was further exacerbated by the embargo on oil imposed by the Arab world on the West following the Arab-Israeli War of 1973–1974. The Soviet Union for its part suffered from the 1970s on from a parallel deterioration of its economy due to its vast expenditure on armament; its support of poor third-world countries; and primarily due to its rigid, cumbersome, and ineffective economic centralization.

These parallel processes led in the United States to a period of stagflation that propelled new modes of production and technological innovation that came to be termed "post-Fordism," or what David Harvey has most aptly termed a "regime of flexible accumulation."[9] The Soviet Union at the time tried to revitalize its economy through measures that amounted to a contained liberalization of the market and cooperation with the West on international conflicts in order to obtain financial aid. Eventually, however, Mikhail Gorbachev's perestroika and glasnost policies got out of hand and led to the dismantling of the Soviet socialist bloc, the eventual infiltration of post-Fordism into these newly opened markets, and the actual demise of the Soviet Union as a balancing power to the West in the third world.[10]

Post-Fordism is predicated on rapid and flexible production and distribution of fast-changing and highly customized goods. It has accordingly changed the structure of the labor market, undermining the power of workers' unions—which depend on large concentrations of workers in factories—by its growing reliance on temporary work and subcontracting, which create a large, peripheral, insecure workforce surrounding small core groups of managerial tenured workers who enjoy abundant benefits and are expected to be sufficiently mobile and flexible to adapt to quick relocations. The growing detachment of a mobile core management from the location of production, along with the dispersed nature of post-Fordist production, eases the relocation of sites of production but with dire consequences to peripheral employees. However, although this spells insecurity and unpredictability for peripheral workers it does not mean that capitalism has become disorganized, as some have suggested.[11] On the contrary, post-Fordism indicates a tighter grip of the elites on an insecure, disorganized, and easily dispensable and exchangeable workforce, along with unprecedented efficiency in the maximization of profit. This is primarily achieved through the elite ownership of computer networks that allow the quick and effective coordination and structural control of the post-Fordist dispersed mode of production, as well as speedy adaptation to market fluctuations.

The flexible and nomadic nature of post-Fordist capitalist production strives by its very nature to expand its sites of production and distribution of goods. It has propelled a globalizing process made feasible through its reliance on computer networks that allow the coordination of its widespread, flexible, and dispersed activities. This globalizing process hastened the inner crumbling of the Soviet Union and its East European satellite states, given the latter's failure to restructure their deteriorating, centralized, mass-production oriented economy and match the flexible, "turbo-capitalist"[12] computer-based expansion of post-Fordism. This opened new markets to post-Fordist capitalism, which were not confined to the former Soviet Union and its satellites but also made inroads into China, which is cautiously and gradually incorporating post-Fordist strategies of production without foregoing centralized planning. Post-Fordism is also severely affecting the economies of underdeveloped peripheral states, mostly in ways that further their exploitation. This is because underdeveloped states that could earlier maneuver between the two superpowers and attain independent inner economic development cannot effectively counterbalance and halt the exploitative post-Fordist dynamic infiltration of their economies within a one-superpower-secured capitalist globalization process.[13]

For post-Fordism to flourish in such a way that it guarantees the accumulation of capital for the core-elites, it needs a structurally dominated "free flow" of money and information unimpeded by national barriers. Only in such a manner can the elites' private-finance and multinational corporations, through their global computerized infrastructures, manage their cheap-labor global production and the flexible distribution of their fast-changing and highly customized goods, as well as command the global, rapid, and simultaneous transfers of money and information. Thus, following a period of risky unpredictable "casino"-styled market economy[14] that evolved during the late seventies and intensified following the fall of the Socialist bloc, the core capitalist elites are now developing mechanisms to decrease peripheral state impediments to the expansion of capitalist post-Fordism and to orient the process of production. These processes amount to a new global superstructure.

THE NEW WORLD ORDER

The phrase "new world order" was used by the U.S. president George H. W. Bush when building the coalition against Iraq that led to the Gulf War of 1990–1991, following Iraq's invasion of Kuwait. The use of the phrase within this context should be seen as an expansion into military means of an ongoing post-Fordist-propelled economic-political alignment of the core capitalist states. This alignment aims at integrating and managing the complex global interdependence of the post-Fordist emergent world-system in such a way that the core capitalist elites maintain their economic and political upper hand and further the exploitation of the periphery.

Hence, globalization is an expansion of the colonial and neocolonial first world–third world or rich north–poor south phase of the capitalist world system. This new phase is better understood as a core-periphery division of labor,[15] since these latter terms imply the systemic, hierarchic, deterritorialized interdependence characteristic of globalization's post-Fordist mode of production. Hence, while there is still a geopolitical economic demarcation between core states and peripheral states, post-Fordism has blurred these boundaries and engendered a global exploitation irrespective of geographic location. This is evidenced in the post-Fordist replication of the core-periphery exploitative division of labor among core states' citizens (but also toward the globalization-propelled large communities of alien immigrants from peripheral states); in its inclusion within core-elites of some peripheral state–located financiers and elites (Saudi Arabia has been invited to sit on the board of directors of the International Monetary Fund, or IMF);[16] and in the opportunity-based geographic relocation of economic elites. While these geographic relocations have led some to maintain that globalization is unintentional, diffuse, and multifocal or multidetermined, the explicit and effective economic-political policy of the world core-elites testifies to their deliberate intention to enhance the world periphery's dependence so as to better allow its exploitation.

Nevertheless, this new phase of the capitalist exploitative division of labor, characterized by the flexible, territorially detached mode of management of private, global financiers and multinational corporations, still needs the support of the core capitalist state apparatuses in the protection of their structurally controlled "free flow" of money and information to maximize their profits. This support is primarily implemented through the regulation of deregulation policies by the core states' managed global financial institutions such as the World Bank and the International Monetary Fund, which pressure peripheral states to deregulate and privatize their markets, opening them up to unfair competition, from which their constituencies often fall prey to multinational corporations.[17] This expansion of the market economy to peripheral states and their consequent integration through deregulation into the world economy facilitates the vast accumulation of capital for core-elites because it eases, through deregulation, their unimpeded, computer-based structural control of global and flexible, rapid and simultaneous flows of money, goods, and information. Furthermore, the primary implementation of deregulation policies through loans (often granted on the condition that peripheral states deregulate their economy and privatize national assets) furthers the economic-political dependence of peripheral states on the core states and the core-elites since they supply most of the funds for these loans.[18]

These pressures of globalization emanating from the core, which hastened the fall of the Soviet Union along with its function as a balancing power to the present one-superpower-led capitalist globalization process,[19] weaken the legitimacy and bargaining power of core-dependent, peripheral governments. Since the latter cannot efficiently monitor the elite-controlled global capital flow, it diminishes their effectiveness in maintaining through legitimate coercion their interests, and paradoxically, through their needed cooperation, the interests of the elites. This weakening and destabilization often devastates peripheral economies and generates miserable economic-political conditions. It leads to heavy migration from peripheral to core states and to awakening dominance of ethnic and religious frames of reference earlier subsumed under the dominant ideologies of nation-states. These miserable conditions and awakened awareness often translate into violent challenges—by radical subnational and supranational movements and by states noncompliant with elite interests—to the core's dependent-peripheral-state system. This leads to reciprocal constitutional violence from the core states and their dependencies. This globalization-propelled violence is particularly evident in the exacerbation of Middle East conflicts.

U.S.-LED GLOBALIZATION AND TWO MIDDLE EAST CONFLICTS

The Israeli-Palestinian Conflict in the Wake of the New World Order

The one-hundred-year-old peripheral conflict between the State of Israel and the Palestinian people took an unprecedented violent shift following the institution of the Palestinian National Authority.[20] This violence, evidenced during the al Aksa Intifada through Palestinian terrorist suicide bombings and Israel's air raids, closure measures, and harsh incursions, is due to a large extent to processes of globalization. The fall of the Soviet Union diminished the importance of Israel as a strategic military asset for the United States because it opened the way for the U.S. elites to forward their interests in the region without proxies like Israel. Israel, which had earlier checked Soviet influence in the region, as was the case in its wars against Soviet-backed Egypt, Syria (in the 1967 and 1973 wars), and Iraq (through its air raid against Iraq's nuclear facility in 1981), began to be seen as a liability in the first Gulf War, since it threatened the support and participation of the Gulf monarchies and Egypt in the U.S.-led coalition against Iraq. Thus, during the first Gulf War, despite Saddam's sending scud missiles against Israel in order to break the coalition against him, following U.S. pressure the Israeli right-wing government, headed at the time by Prime Minister Moshe Shamir, abstained from any retaliation. Furthermore, following the first Gulf War the United States began pressuring Israel, whose economy is totally dependent on American aid, to reach a solution to the Israeli-Palestinian conflict by convening the Madrid Conference in 1991. This was the catalyst to the secret Israeli-Palestinian negotiations in Oslo that led to the Oslo Accords signed in Washington in 1993 and which established the Palestinian National Authority (PNA) after the Palestinian Liberation Organization (PLO) recognized Israel. The PNA was perceived as able to align with other peripheral, core-dependent states (e.g., Egypt, Jordan) and to disengage from noncompliant Arab states (e.g., Syria and prewar Iraq). It was believed that the conflict would be resolved while expanding the core's dependent-peripheral-state system.

However, contrary to initial expectations, the prolonged conflict between the predominantly Jewish State of Israel and the nationally dispossessed Palestinian people took a violent turn. This was mostly due to the rise of non-constitutional violent activism on the part of subnational groups driven by radical religious ideologies in Israel and the PNA-held territories. These groups reawakened due to the shaky foundations of the PNA and the destabilization of the Israeli government (brought about by core-elites' political pressures and by Israel's economic deterioration following its implementation of deregulation policies and enhanced privatization of national assets). They garnered the support of those destitute by the integration of the Israeli economy and of the PNA elites to the market economy, effectively pressuring the legitimate leaders to refuse any compromise. Hence, the subnational, religious settler movement in Israel pressured the Israeli government to dismantle the PNA and claim the occupied territories while it forcefully resisted attempts made by the government to block the expansion of Jewish settlements in the West Bank and Gaza Strip. Ariel Sharon's core-pressure-derived implementation in August 2005 of a very limited "disengagement" plan that led to the dismantlement of tiny settlements in the Gaza Strip and in the West Bank encountered violent opposition from the settler movement that threatened civil war and was the primary factor in Sharon's unprecedented decision to leave the Likud Party,[21] establish the new party Kadima, and set a date for general elections. It seems that this violent opposition will escalate in any future attempts to dismantle settlements (as happened in the January 2006 forced dismantlement of nine illegal houses in the West Bank settlement of Amona, where over 250 policemen and settlers were wounded). Likewise, several radical subnational Islamist movements such as Hamas and Islamic Jihad effectively pressured the PNA to join them in a relentless terror war against Israel so as to bring about its destruction, while they forcefully resisted attempts by the terror-implicated PNA to curb them.[22] The growing support of Hamas by destitute Palestinians led to its sweeping victory in the January 2006 Palestinian Legislative Council elections. The results of these core-pressure-derived elections (which urged the PNA elites to democratize) backfired on the core. It remains to be seen how the conflict will develop now that the PNA president Mahmoud Abbas (elected in January 2005 following Arafat's death) faces a legislative council dominated by Hamas. In face of these radical groups whose mode of operation often transcends legitimate venues of change, the PNA and the Israeli government will find it hard to implement the core states' desired two-state solution to the conflict. The murder of the Israeli prime minister Yitzhak Rabin by a settler in 1995, the eruption in 2000 of the violent al Aksa Intifada, and the victory of Hamas in the 2006 Palestinian Legislative Council elections are salient expressions in the context of the Israeli-Palestinian conflict of the destabilization of the core's dependent-peripheral-state system in the region.

Al Qaeda and the U.S.-Led "War against Terror"

Due to processes of globalization, and facilitated through its networks (which allow the untraceable traffic of money and information through different venues such as off-shore financial centers and the Internet), nonconstitutional-type violence, difficult to contain, spreads across the globe and backlashes into the core states with unprecedented scope and nondiscrimination. The establishment of the al Qaeda organization by Osama bin Laden is exemplary of such repercussions. Formed within the confines of the last and anachronistic Cold War conflict between the United States and the Soviet Union over control of Afghanistan, the radical Islamists that gathered in Afghanistan and eventually formed al Qaeda actively reawakened the notion of a pan-Islamic revolution aimed at ousting the core states' presence from the Middle East region, dismantling the region's core-dependent governments, and establishing a pan-Islamic nation (*Ummah*) based on

Sharia law. Mostly funded by the United States and Saudi Arabia to fight their war by proxy against the Soviets, these "Afghan Arabs" sensed the weakening of the peripheral-state-based superstructure that had earlier effectively repressed these movements and confined their pan-Islamism to Islamo-nationalisms (e.g., the Muslim brotherhood movement in Egypt, Algeria, or Palestine).[23]

This reawakening was due to their belief in the feasibility of their revolution following the success of the Iranian Islamist revolution that ousted the core-dependent shah, their own successful ousting of the Soviets from Afghanistan followed by the collapse of the Soviet Union, and the widespread popular support for their actions. This support was based on the resentment long felt by many poor Muslims toward the "heathen West," which they viewed as responsible for the deformation of Islamic cultures, the rise to power of corrupt governments, and the choking of Islamic nations under the burden of colonialism and neocolonialism. This resentment was heightened by the economic destabilization of the Middle East dependent-peripheral-state system following core-state pressures on them to "democratize" or rather deregulate their economies (e.g., Egypt, Jordan, Algeria, etc.),[24] a process that brought further destitution to poor Muslims both within Arab states and within the constantly growing, poor Muslim immigrant communities in core states. This support grew further toward the Gulf War, following the unprecedented massive positioning of U.S. troops in Saudi Arabia, which many poor Muslims perceived as an act of blasphemy on the part of the United States and the Saudi regime "in charge" of protecting Islam's holiest sites.

Thus, this group of neofundamentalist radical Islamists headed by bin Laden and fueled by his vast economic resources, turned against their former U.S. and Saudi "benefactors" and designed their supranational murderous actions, using global computer networks to gather and channel the money and information needed for their loosely structured, hard to pinpoint, global-reaching terror network.[25] This network has been instrumental in aiding the Muslim Bosnians against Serb expansionism, the Muslim Chechens against Russian occupation, and the Muslims in Somalia against American intervention (in Mogadishu, 1993). Beyond these, al Qaeda has attacked U.S. military targets in the periphery such as the U.S. barracks in Dhahran, Saudi Arabia (1996), and the suicide attack on the *U.S.S. Cole* in Aden, Yemen (2000), as well as attacks on U.S. embassies in Nairobi, Kenya, and Dar-es-Salaam, Tanzania (1998). They have also killed thousands of core-state civilians both in peripheral states (such as the bombs in the tourist resort of Bali that were carried out by groups linked to al Qaeda) and within core states (such as the spectacular destruction of the Twin Towers in New York and the coordinated bombing of trains in Spain).

The U.S.-led response to these atrocities, entitled the "War against Terror," has also been violent and indiscriminate. This is due in general to the unwillingness of core states to relieve the post-Fordist economic pressures that generate the grounds for support of the al Qaeda network, and to the difficulty in tracing a supranational weak-linked organization that inspires rather than directs its spread affiliates. Hence, in their somewhat futile attempt to pinpoint al Qaeda and deter further challenges, core governments, particularly in the United States, have been curtailing civil liberties and harassing Muslims within, while the U.S.-led coalition against terror indiscriminately unleashed its immense firepower on Afghanistan, one of the world's poorest countries.[26]

To sum up, the spreading indiscriminate violence from the Middle East is reciprocated by global and extremely violent constitutional responses, as evidenced in the U.S.-led "War against Terror" and in its campaign against weapons of mass destruction. This has also given license to core-dependent peripheral states like Israel to harshly retaliate in response to local Palestinian terror warfare. One main objective of these actions is to maintain and expand the global dependence system. U.S.-led military actions against "terror hosting states" (e.g., Sudan and former Afghanistan) and against "noncompliant" states (e.g., former Iraq), aim to maintain the stability of dependent peripheral states (e.g., Kuwait, Saudi Arabia) and allow through military means the expansion of the market economy by seeking to institute core-compliant governments.

CONCLUSION

This chapter outlines how post-Fordism has become the dominant mode of production propelling capitalist globalization and how the U.S.-led core-elites' formation of a new world order is a further expansion of the core's capitalist exploitation of the periphery, instantiated in the discussion of the "War against Terror" and of the al Aksa Intifada in the wake of the new world order. The next chapter outlines the dominant ideologies that function to justify the global interests of the U.S. elite and those ideologies aimed at justifying the interests of dependent elites in the periphery, focusing on the opposing dominant ideologies of elites in the State of Israel and in the Palestinian National Authority.

NOTES

1. John Tomlinson, *Globalization and Culture* (Cambridge, U.K.: Polity, 1999).
2. Roland Robertson, *Globalization: Social Theory and Global Culture* (London: Sage, 1992).

3. Arjun Appadurai, *Modernity at Large: Cultural Dimensions of Globalization* (Minneapolis: Minnesota University Press, 1996).

4. Immanuel Wallerstein, *The Politics of the World Economy: The States, the Movements, and the Civilization* (Cambridge, U.K.: Cambridge University Press, 1984).

5. The term was used by the U.S. president Bill Clinton to describe his post-Fordist-propelled expansionist policy couched in terms of the expansion of democracy and freedom. See Richard Crockatt, *America Embattled: September 11, Anti-Americanism, and the Global Order* (London: Routledge, 2003), 142.

6. A good exposition of the shift from Fordism to post-Fordism can be found in David Harvey, *The Condition of Postmodernity* (Cambridge, U.K.: Blackwell, 1991), 125–172.

7. Paul Marantz and Brenda S. Steinberg, eds., *Superpower Involvement in the Middle East: Dynamics of Foreign Policy* (Boulder, Colo.: Westview, 1995); Baghat Korany and Ali E. Hillal Dessouki, eds., *The Foreign Policies of Arab States: The Challenge of Change* (Boulder, Colo.: Westview, 1991).

8. The Bretton Woods Agreement of 1944 was designed to regulate the international financial system and was based on state regulation and control. It also fixed the exchange rates in relation to the dollar. See James Curran, *Media and Power* (London: Routledge, 2002), 176. The dismantling of the Bretton Woods system of regulation is an index of the reduced power of states in the control of the global financial system.

9. Harvey, *Condition of Postmodernity*, 121–200.

10. Richard Sakwa, *Gorbachev and His Reforms, 1985–1990* (New York: Prentice Hall, 1991), 65–125, 268–349.

11. Scott Lash and John Urry, *The End of Organized Capitalism* (Oxford: Oxford University Press, 1987).

12. The term was first used by the economist Edward Luttwack as reported in Hans-Peter Martin and Harald Schumann, *The Global Trap* (London: Zed Books, 1997), 9.

13. Martin and Schumann, *Global Trap*, 12–39; Raymond Hinnebusch, "The Politics of Economic Liberalization: Comparing Egypt and Syria," in *The State and Global Change: The Political Economy of Transition in the Middle East and North Africa*, ed. Hassan Hakimian and Ziba Moshaver (Surrey: Curzon, 2001), 111–135.

14. Susan Strange, *Casino Capitalism* (New York: St. Francis Press, 1996).

15. Wallerstein, *Politics of the World Economy*.

16. Baghat Korany and Ali E. Hillal Dessouki, "The Global System and Arab Foreign Policies: The Primacy of Constraints," in *Foreign Policies of Arab States*, 35.

17. Mustapha al-Sayyid, "International and Regional Environments and State Transformation in Some Arab Countries," in Hakimian and Moshaver, *The State and Global Change*, 168–169. For an account of specific measures taken by these institutions (and by Saudi Arabia) against the Egyptian economy see Ali E. Hillal Dessouki, "The Primacy of Economics: The Foreign Policy of Egypt," in *The Foreign Policies of Arab States*, 162.

18. For an account of the dependence generated by these debt policies in the case of Iraq, see Korany and Dessouki, "The Global System and Arab Foreign Policies," in *The Foreign Policies of Arab States*, 42–43.

19. Although there are sporadic rifts among the elites in core capitalist states (e.g., the divisions between Germany or France and the United States over the war against Iraq), these cannot develop into opposing spheres of influence given their interlocking interests in the exploitation of the periphery, earlier opposed by the Soviet bloc.

20. For a good general account of the Israeli-Palestinian conflict see Mark Tessler, *A History of the Israeli-Palestinian Conflict* (Bloomington: Indiana University Press, 1994). See also a brief outline of the conflict in chapter 2, and in particular see chapter 2, note 28. For a discussion of the conflict in the wake of the new world order see Noam Chomsky, *Fateful Triangle: The United States, Israel, and the Palestinians* (Cambridge, Mass.: South End Press, 1999); Edward W. Said, *Peace and Its Discontents* (New York: Vintage Books, 1999); Naseer H. Aruri, *Dishonest Broker: The U.S. Role in Israel and Palestine* (Cambridge, Mass.: South End Press, 2003); Baruch Kimmerling, *Politicide: Ariel Sharon's War against the Palestinians* (New York: Verso, 2003); Jeremy Pressman, "The Primary Role of the United States in Israeli-Palestinian Relations," *International Studies Perspectives* 4, no. 2 (2003): 191–194; Pressman, "The Second Intifada: Background and Causes of the Israeli-Palestinian Conflict," *The Journal of Conflict Studies* 23, no. 2 (2003): 114–141; Alan Dowty, "Impact of the Aqsa Intifada on the Israeli-Palestinian Conflict," *Israel Studies Forum* 19, no. 2 (2004): 9–28.

21. Mostly due to the mounting opposition to Sharon coming from settler-supporting members within the Likud Party.

22. See the October 2001 Hamas-sponsored protests in Gaza, where a crowd of thousands of demonstrators consisting mostly of Islamic students chanted, "Long live Palestine, long live Afghanistan, long live Islam," and "Hail bin Laden!" The Palestinian police opened fire on the demonstrators, killing three of them. Following this the demonstrators stoned and fire-bombed PNA police stations and burned other PNA buildings. Over two hundred demonstrators were wounded in the riots, and many policemen were also injured.

23. John Downey and Graham Murdock, "The Counter-Revolution in Military Affairs: The Globalization of Guerrilla Warfare," in *War and the Media: Reporting Conflict 24/7*, ed. Daya Kishan Thussu and Des Freedman (London: Sage, 2003), 70–86.

24. Korany and Dessouki, "The Global System and Arab Foreign Policies," in *The Foreign Policies of Arab States*, 25–48.

25. Yossef Bodansky, *Bin Laden: The Man Who Declared War on America* (Roseville, Calif.: Prima, 2001), 313–316. Al Qaeda has cooperated with other local Islamo-nationalist movements such as the Abu Sayyaf group in the Philippines. See, for example, James Lutz and Brenda Lutz, *Global Terrorism* (London: Routledge, 2004), 85.

26. These radical Islamists or "neofundamentalists" have also been supported by "rogue" states, like the former Iraq and Iran, "noncompliant" with core states' interests. On Iraqi support see Bodansky, *Bin Laden*, 343–346; and John Cooley, *Unholy Wars: Afghanistan, America, and International Terrorism* (London: Pluto Press, 1999), 207. On Iranian support see Bodansky, *Bin Laden*, 208–209; and Cooley, *Unholy Wars*, 81–85. These noncompliant states tried (Iraq) or are trying (Iran) to expand their regional influence through different measures (including the develop-

ment of weapons of mass destruction) and to further destabilize core-dependent governments (e.g., Egypt, Jordan, and the Gulf monarchies). This is what led George H. W. Bush to mount an international coalition against Iraq following Saddam Hussein's miscalculated invasion of Kuwait. This invasion, presumed by Hussein to be feasible in face of the vacuum created by the fall of the Soviet Union and his presumption that the United States would tolerate such an act, was critical to the United States, since it threatened to destabilize beyond Kuwait all the core-compliant Gulf monarchies along with their oil resources. This is also what led George W. Bush to reenact his father's war. This time, however, based on the pretext of Iraq's presumed development of weapons of mass destruction, Bush not only curbed potential Iraqi aggression but conquered Iraq altogether and is now trying to rebuild this oil-rich, destroyed nation as a core-compliant state in the region. Thus, the "new world order" is being forcefully implemented in Iraq and potentially expanded, since Iraq is also a base to counter and perhaps topple the Iranian and Syrian noncompliant-state elites. In such ways the U.S.-led core is expanding "democracy and freedom," which are ideological buzz words for the expansion of the post-Fordist free market economy.

2

U.S. Global Ideologies and Israeli/ Palestinian National Ideologies

MODES OF PRODUCTION AND DOMINANT IDEOLOGIES

Within the framework of the political-economic approach underlying this study, dominant ideologies are defined as widespread ideas about the world that function to justify elite interests within specific economic and geopolitical configurations of power, and which are propagated through modes of communication that are dependent on the elites (e.g., mainstream media). These dominant ideologies are derived from, and are symptomatic of, the dominant mode of production that benefits the ruling elites, and are ultimately aimed at justifying the mode of production's continuation and its attendant privileges for these elites. Dominant ideologies conduct such justification by presenting the particular interests of the elites as benefiting everybody.[1] These ideologies are presently determined by the dominant post-Fordist mode of production and by the globalization processes it engenders.[2]

The next sections critically discuss the post-Fordist-derived dominant post-structural/postmodern ideology in the core and the dominant "double-talk" ideology in the periphery, focusing on U.S. core-elite dominant ideologies in respect of the periphery and on the opposing dominant ideologies of Israeli and Palestinian ruling elites.

THE CORE POST-STRUCTURAL/POSTMODERN DOMINANT IDEOLOGY

Just as Fordism found in structuralism and modernism its dominant ideological modes of cultural production, expressed through tropes such as coherence, centeredness, depth, affectivity, and attention, so post-structuralism and postmodernism are the dominant ideological cultural expression of the post-Fordist mode of production. Their characterizing tropes of decentered-ness, segmentation, depthlessness, lesser affectivity, disorientation, split identity,[3] "cyborgization,"[4] and "simulacrization"[5] replicate and forward on the cultural level the underlying flexible, constantly shifting and relocating mode of post-Fordist production. Post-structuralism and postmodernism, in their perception of a boundless decentered textual universe, a notion initially propelled by a radical desire to shatter the structural hierarchies and bound-aries of the modernist text and implying textual freedom and equality, did not lead to real extratextual economic-political freedom and equality. In fact, the post-structural apparent democratic cultural expression and legitimating of marginalized voices (mostly in core countries) effaces the real core-elites' structural cultural domination. It does so in its leveling of marginalized posi-tions with various other positions, particularly in the presentation of the economic-political potent positions as culturally even positions among oth-ers. Such leveling strategy, detaching culture from economy (or conceiving of economy as just another cultural discourse),[6] in being backed by potent economic infrastructures, structurally dominates an apparent dispersed and multiple cultural discourse, replicating on the level of culture the core-elites' structural domination of the post-Fordist dispersed mode of production. On the textual level this post-structural strategy is evident in the theory of inter-textuality, whereby texts are rather intertexts implicated in a boundless tex-tual net and generating polysemous meanings, a strategy echoed in the production of postmodern texts. Post-structuralism does not deconstruct nor reveal the post-Fordist capitalist configurations of power but rather stems from post-Fordism and helps its propagation by the effacement of its configurations of power.[7]

GLOBAL-TO-LOCAL DOMINANT IDEOLOGIES OF THE U.S. ELITES

As mentioned, the political-economic reality of globalization processes is cloaked in core states' dominant globalization ideologies that obscure the core-elites' structural domination of the post-Fordist process of production and the expanding dependence system needed to sustain this process. These ideologies present as universal the particular interests of core-elites in a glob-alizing post-Fordist capitalism requiring "free flow" of capital unhindered by local state interests, peripheral threats to the dependence system, or local-turned-global violence.

Simulacrum and *glocalization* post-structural and postmodern theories, which often figure in discourses on global news communication networks (see Ingrid Volkmer's glocal position discussed in chapter 4), are the most salient U.S. elites' global ideological discourses. Their overall claim is inclusionist, offering a "global perspective" (i.e., a core perspective) on local peripheral issues, perceived as being included within an abstract and decentered global sphere either through simulacra *cloning* or multicultural democratic *equalizing*.

The virtual abstractions of reality[8] in simulacrum theory elaborate a far-fetched computer-derived human perception, which has been characterized by nonlinear thinking, quantified information, waning of affect, and surrounded by hyper-real simulacra.[9] This technology-determined perception is attributed to global, technologically decentered communication networks. It obscures in its apparent decenteredness and in its idealist abstract perception of reality the concrete global cloning of branches belonging to core elites' multinational corporations, structurally dominated by the computer networks through which core-elites monitor their capital flow and propagate their detached idealist ideologies.

This simulacrum-derived ideological notion of a global decenteredness also supports the core and U.S. elites' divide-and-conquer military strategy. Hence, whenever the core interests are directly threatened by peripheral supranational groups (e.g., al Qaeda), or by peripheral "rogue totalitarian states" (former Iraq), the ideological notion of global decenteredness is used to isolate, decontextualize, and single them out while the rest of the decentered world is expected to either join the "coalition of the willing" or stay disinterested and disconnected, abstaining from intervention while the intruder is eradicated. These isolated intruders are also presented as difficult to contain because of the decentered nature of globalization. Thus, noncompliant Afghanistan, one of the world's poorest nations, was singled out for invasion based on the claim that in this decentered world, where there is no direct access to the globally menacing (i.e., core-menacing) yet evasive clandestine al Qaeda, state sovereignty is no longer sacred. Likewise, the singling out, targeting, and consequent invasion of the noncompliant Iraqi state, presumed to be an inherently expansionist totalitarian "rogue" state, was justified as global caring in face of global decenteredness, given that the weapons of mass destruction it may have strived to develop, its human rights violations, and its environmental abuses had no borders and could easily spread. Under such latter banners, which in and of themselves may be commendable, massive killing and destruction of the peoples and infrastructure of Iraq was undertaken by the U.S. elites.[10]

Decenteredness also supports the U.S. core divide-and-conquer diplomatic strategy in the case of violent conflicts that do not directly impede core interests, as in the case of the Israeli-Palestinian conflict. In such cases decenteredness justifies military nonintervention in presenting the conflict as a sporadic, independent, and contained violent eruption that does not threaten to spread, while legitimating a diplomatic divide-and-conquer strategy vis-à-vis the warring parties in presenting the U.S. core as a political-economic disconnected entity that is morally engaged as "honest broker," offering to help the warring parties by presenting both Israelis and Palestinians to be in the wrong and itself in the right.

Simulacrum ideology also generates a dynamic of its own in the conception of what it means to be human in our present world. To borrow Walter Benjamin's words, this perception furthers humankind's "self-alienation . . . to such a degree that it can experience its own destruction as an aesthetic pleasure of the first order."[11] This spreading far-fetched perception of reality and of the human as *Cyborg*,[12] elaborated in many writings and cultural productions that promote the idea of the body as mere flesh that can be transcended and transmuted (as in the emblematic figure of Neo, played by Keanu Reeves in the *Matrix* film trilogy), is also specifically used to obscure the very real corporeal violent action taken by the core against those who directly impede its interests. Hence, influenced by simulacrum ideology, the notions of a "revolution in military affairs" (RMA) and the development of "future combat systems" (FCS) heralded by the Pentagon present the use of computer-guided "smart bombs," surveillance systems, and digital combat simulations as leading to "cleaner" wars with fewer casualties[13] (perhaps true only for core armies), obscuring through sophisticated army-controlled TV coverage the widespread and indiscriminate killing and mutilation of peoples along with the destruction of civil infrastructures at the receiving end of these bombs, as was the case in Afghanistan and Iraq.[14]

According to glocalization ideology,[15] differing communities or lifestyles, particularly peripheral ones, in their subjectivist perceptions of the world are perceived as different-yet-even[16] in relation to core-elite communities. This global-reaching multicultural democratic perception expedites the obscuring of the economic-political dependence of peripheral communities on the core-elites by detaching culture from political economy. One particularly effective and proliferating variation of this ideology is that of glocal consumerism. This latter ideology supports post-Fordist locally customized consumerism (e.g., McDonalds has particular menus responding to local food cultures, such as hot and spicy hamburgers in Middle East countries). The occasional fashionable challenge of notions of cultural imperialism made by glocal ideologies, since denuded of political-economic determinants, actually supports customized post-Fordism. This is because this detached cultural protest presumes a set of cultures whose ethnic varieties are economically and politically neutralized by their presumed "even" and "legitimate" cultural variety. Therefore, these "other" cultures can coexist as cultures within a post-Fordist mode of production that can cater to their distinctive cultural preferences. In other words, the glocal legitimating of peripheral communities allows them to express their culture so as to alleviate the post-Fordist denial of their economic-political interests.

Glocalism also legitimates and justifies the core-elite's nonintervention in bloody peripheral conflicts that do not directly impede their interests (e.g., the Israeli-Palestinian conflict), since in attributing conduct to culture and in perceiving cultural differences as even, there is no justification for intervention. Conversely, glocalism also legitimates and justifies the core-elite's violent intervention when their interests are impeded (e.g., Afghanistan, Iraq) by criminalizing the opponent's culture and by obscuring through the different-yet-even claim the opponent's vast economic-political and military disadvantage. Hence, studies such as those of Bernard Lewis or Samuel P. Huntington[17] justified U.S. violence against Afghanistan and Iraq in their being a response to global threats motivated by essentialist cultural attributes exclusively found respectively in "radical Islam" or in "rogue totalitarianism." The problem with such studies, which take, glocal style, cultural ideas to be the major explanation for violent acts, is not only in their selectivity,[18] but more so in their failure to explain how ideas that have been around for a long time have not always led to violent acts (as, conversely, U.S. ideas on world peace often lead to war).[19]

Thus, in the name of simulacrum, glocalism, and multiculturalism (the post-Fordist versions of the U.S. core-elites' traditional ideological notions of freedom and democracy), the peoples of the periphery are divided and conquered by the core, often leading to the massive destitution of peoples and the destruction of peripheral infrastructures.

THE PERIPHERY'S DOUBLE-TALK CHARACTERISTIC OF ITS DOMINANT IDEOLOGIES

The political-economic reality of globalization processes is cloaked in peripheral dependent states by statist ideologies used to support the interests of the national elite.[20] While claims about statist ideologies as dominant have lost currency in analyses of core-elite states, they are particularly relevant to peripheral states because in peripheral economically and politically dependent countries, control of the state apparatus is the main source for maintaining the elite's economic privileges. Through it, the core loans that keep the state's economy afloat (and further the state's dependence on the core-elites) are channeled.

Hence, statist ideologies by definition perceive the "global" as external to their respective internal state affairs. This ethnocentric view is aimed at representing the interests of their elite as being exclusively relevant to all their respective peoples so as to establish their prominence over emergent subnational and supranational peripheral voices contesting the national imagined community.[21] This is because the challenging voices focus their religious, ethnic, or racial rhetoric on the state elite's compliance with foreign economic and political interests as against the interests of their imagined communities (e.g., radical Islam claims against secular Arab governments' alliance with the "heathen" West). However, given the peripheral state elite's economic and political dependence on and pressures from the core-led globalization process, peripheral dominant national ideologies are led to incorporate alongside their exclusive statist internal-external rhetoric, a local-to-global rhetoric. This is aimed at representing the interests of their elite as being at one with the core-elites' globalizing interests. This internal-to-global double-talk reflects the stranded position in which elites in dependent peripheral states find themselves. This stranded position also aids the overall global divide-and-conquer U.S. core strategy, in that the survival strategy of dependent peripheral elites is confined to their control of their state apparatus to the exclusion of their intervention in conflicts that seemingly do not affect them directly (unless of course "asked" to participate in some core-led "coalition of the willing").

This understanding of peripheral dominant ideologies is quiet different from postcolonial theories, which, while noticing the mixture characteristic of peripheral state rhetoric, view this as an undifferentiated multidetermined amalgam characterizing peripheral identities, thus confusing rather than clarifying the double-bind determination of this rhetorical mixture. The postcolonial notion of hybridity, developed by its most prominent advocate Homi K. Bhaba[22] and used to analyze the peripheral situation and its cultural production, actually replicates and embraces postmodernism while presenting this rhetorical mixture as a subversive or progressive strategy on the part of the periphery. Likewise, Bhaba's postcolonial/postmodern notion of the mimicry of core-elite discourses performed by peripheral people, while aptly describing an aspect of the periphery's double-talk aimed at catering to core interests, is misleadingly presented as a destabilizing subversive strategy that constantly dismantles the core-elites' attempts to consolidate their ideologies. In fact, Bhaba's postcolonial discourse simply mimics the core's postmodern dominant ideology. Rather than promoting subversion, Bhaba's discourse partakes in the postmodern leveling, neutralization, and ultimate subduing of any potential subversion to the interests of the core-elites. Rather than an indiscernible, shifting, allusive, destabilizing amalgam, as implied in Bhaba's colonial-determined hybrid peripheral identity, the peripheral elite's characteristic double-talk is a discernable cultural composite or admixture, resulting from clear internal and external political-economic pressures.

INTERNAL-TO-GLOBAL DOMINANT
IDEOLOGIES IN ISRAEL AND PALESTINE

The dominant statist ideologies of Israel's state elites and of the Palestinian National Authority elite are exemplary cases of threatened peripheral states' internal-to-global double-talk. This is symptomatic of the respective Israeli and Palestinian (opposing) ruling elites' weakened legitimacy and bargaining power. This weakening has been brought about by the political economy of globalization, leading to an intensified mutual struggle to attain (Palestinians) or maintain (Israelis) a state apparatus allowing these peripheral elites a relative autonomy in a shaken state-based world system. This double-talk is aimed at enlisting the superpower to their side (despite the detrimental effects of globalization) alongside a dominant national ideology aimed at overcoming competing subnational and supranational contesting trends.

Siege and Democracy in Israeli Dominant State Ideology

Israel's state elite dominant national siege ideology seeks internal enlistment through the perpetuation of a self image of Israelis as a besieged, victimized collective.[23] The notion of Israel as a persecuted nation is based on historical experiences and religious traditions. It draws on Israelis' experiences of conventional war and terror warfare, as well as from sporadic condemnations of Israel by world organizations. These experiences are used to evoke for Israeli Jews the long history of anti-Semitism culminating in the Holocaust, a history constituting traumatic past experiences both for the individual and the collective. This history evokes deeply ingrained biblical Jewish religious tenets having to do with Jews being a chosen people (*Am Nivchar*), alone among the nations (*Am Levadad Yshkon*), with no one but God Almighty and their own resources to protect them in a hostile world seeking their destruction. As has been shown, Israel's dominant state ideology has used the collective remembrance of the past atrocities inflicted on the Jewish people to maintain the idea that the world is against Israel because it is a Jewish state.[24] Hence, the Israeli secular elites (which include both center-right and left parties), by representing themselves as the most capable in dealing with security matters, and by threatening that contesting their power will lead to a destabilization of the state and henceforth its destruction given the hostile world surrounding them, have traditionally tried to secure their benefits against contesting classes and ethnicities. Notwithstanding other factors, it was this position that facilitated the stronghold held by the left Labor Party elite over the state apparatus for the first thirty years of Israeli statehood (1948–1977) given the Israeli army's successful defeats of combined Arab armies in what Israelis term the 1948 War of Independence and in the

Six Day War in June 1967, as well as Israel's "successful" repression of Palestinian insurgence throughout the years. However, it was this very same position that facilitated the ascendance to power of the right-wing Likud Party in the 1977 elections, following their challenging of Labor's ability to secure Israel after a series of successful terror attacks by Palestinian organizations against Israeli targets within Israel and abroad, and following the October 1973 war, referred to in Israel as the Yom Kippur War (since it began on Yom Kippur, the Jewish day of atonement and holiest day of the year on the Jewish religious calendar)—in which Egypt and Syria initiated a surprise concerted attack from south and north leading to heavy casualties on the Israeli side. Although the 1973 war was eventually won by Israel, which reestablished its pre-1973 cease-fire borders, the price paid in human lives was unprecedented for Israelis.

However, the state elites' security-oriented national unification ideology, effective throughout Israeli history in maintaining the legitimacy of elite power vis-à-vis other power groups within Israel, as well as toward the West, with which it completely aligned from the mid-fifties on, has somewhat lost its currency for the Israeli state elites. It has lost its currency toward the U.S. and Western European elites who, driven by their own interests and views of the situation in the region, have reached the conclusion that Israel does not face destruction, contrary to what is claimed by its state elites. The core-elites claim this based on the fall of the Soviet Union, the signing of relatively stable peace accords between Israel and its neighboring countries Egypt and Jordan, the destruction of Iraq along with its support of the Palestinians, and the U.S. presence deterring Syria and Iran. The dominant siege ideology has also lost currency for the Israeli state elites within because the core state pressures on Israel to reach a solution to the Israeli-Palestinian conflict and the advances made by Israeli left and right governments on this subject is seen as contradicting their dominant siege ideology in face of Palestinian terror warfare. Furthermore, the siege ideology is being capitalized on by the settler subnational movement, which has incorporated the religious underpinnings of this ideology into its messianic religious dictum to hold onto the whole "promised land" irrespective of geopolitical configurations, and accuses any government that considers handing out territories as betraying God's will.

The stranded position of the Israeli government generates its double-talk. Hence, Israel's main dominant ideology aimed toward enlisting the superpower to its side has shifted to emphasize the affinities between Israel and the traditional superpower's ideological notions of democracy, freedom, law, and order. It henceforth consists primarily in representing the conflict as being one between Israeli democracy, freedom, law, and constitutional order as against what the Israeli government presents as the tyranny, corruption, lawlessness, and brutal violence characterizing the Palestinian National

Authority's nature and mode of struggle, a conflict presented as replicated in the global sphere (i.e., Arafat is like bin Laden).[25] However, these strategies of enlistment also work against Israeli elite interests since some of Israel's actions and measures are internationally considered illegal. Such are the cases of the West Bank and Gaza Strip settlements, Israel's claim of sovereignty over the Old City of Jerusalem, and its measures against the Palestinians, which consist of destroying the houses of suicide bombers' families and the preemptive killing of terrorist group activists and leaders such as the March and April 2004 assassinations of Hamas leaders Ahmed Yassin and Abed el-Aziz Rantisi. The laudation of these latter forms of conduct, however, forms part of the Israeli elite dominant siege ideology through which it seeks internal enlistment by exploiting Palestinian terror to perpetuate its self-image of a besieged victimized collective. This ideology, however, competing with its co-optation by the settler movement, is devoid of the Jewish religious undertones that accompanied its earlier articulation and is now constrained to its national security aspect. These internally contradicting components of Israeli state elite double-talk dominant ideology, and their being challenged from both the core-elites and the subnational settler movement are symptomatic of the destabilization of the Israeli state governing elites.

Martyrdom (Shahada) and Human Rights in the Palestinian National Authority Dominant Ideology

The Palestinian National Authority (PNA) elite dominant Shahada ideology seeks internal enlistment through the perpetuation of a self-image of the dispersed Palestinians as a betrayed collective, resolute to attain on their own a just national liberation of their land. This through the collective and personal holy sacrifice to the cause, implemented in guerrilla and terrorist forms of struggle. This was the dominant ideology of the PNA evolved during the course of the second Intifada and until PNA President Yasser Arafat's death in November 2004.[26] It compiled the secular version traditional to the Palestinian Liberation Organization (PLO), with a co-optation of religious components taken from the radical Islamist movement Hamas. Hence, in a speech before a large audience in Ramallah, Arafat called for millions of shahids (martyrs) for the sake of Jerusalem and prayed that he himself will become a shahid for Jerusalem.[27] This dominant ideology was based on Palestinians' historical experiences and on religious tenets. It drew on the West-supported ongoing expansion of the Zionist project culminating in the constitution of the State of Israel on account of the Palestinians, and on the harsh treatment accorded to them by several Arab state elites.[28]

The co-optation of Hamas' Shahada ideology, however effective in the mobilization of the Palestinian people toward the second Intifada that broke out in 2000, dragged the PNA elites into a form of struggle that often went beyond their control. Hence, this Intifada, aptly termed al Aksa given its religious undertones,[29] differed from the previous one in its being armed, suicidal in its nature, extremely violent, and often propelled by radical Islamism and personal vengeance beyond the control of the PNA. While the notion of a relentless terror war against Israel and the co-optation of religious tenets characterized the PLO leadership since its inception (e.g., the religious notion of *Jihad* or holy war was often used by Yasser Arafat to legitimate the Palestinian struggle), the co-optation of the notion of Shahada as collective and personal sacrifice legitimated by religion eventually lost its inward currency for the PNA elite. This was because the Shahada's underlying totality of struggle against Israeli occupation and the harsh Israeli reprisals against the Palestinians during this Intifada have given credence to the Hamas and Islamic Jihad accusations that the PNA has betrayed the Palestinian cause in its acceptance of a two-state solution. These accusations led Arafat to both (unsuccessfully) try and curb these groups,[30] as well as to accommodate the PNA position with radical claims by insinuating inwardly that the acceptance of a two-state solution by the PNA conforms to the PLO's 1974 Phased Plan,[31] whereby the Palestinians will form a state in any portion of the land given to them, so that the two-state solution is just a temporary phase in the ongoing struggle to liberate all of Palestine.

However, the sporadic renouncement by PNA officials of shahids who committed suicide bombings,[32] the core-pressure-derived "democratization" of the PNA system of governance (in their election of a prime minister in January 2005), and their insinuations that they might make concessions on the cardinal Palestinian issue of the right of return to Palestinians living outside Palestine[33] delegitimated their co-optation of the Shahada ideology. Outwardly, the Shahada ideology severely damaged the PNA's position vis-à-vis the core-elites for opposite reasons. Hence, the core-elites identified this co-opted ideology and the type of suicidal terror it legitimates with the radical Islamism of al Qaeda, which has directly compromised their own interests. Therefore, the PNA's dominant ideology aimed toward enlisting the superpower to its side incorporated, alongside the ongoing claim of the Palestinians right to self-determination, the appeal to the core-elite's traditional dominant ideology of human rights. By emphasizing the victimization of the Palestinians by the Zionist state, the PNA claims that only international military intervention will curb the aggressions and human rights violations of the State of Israel. Nevertheless, the terror associated with the PNA has also damaged its human rights violation claim in the eyes of core-elites. These internally contradicting components of the PNA core-dependent elite double-talk dominant ideology challenged from both the core-elites and by Hamas and Islamic Jihad, resulted in the core-dependent elite loss of partial control over the PNA after the Hamas won the core-pressure-derived elections to the Palestinian Legislative Council in January 2006.

CONCLUSION

Chapters 1 and 2 analyze the political economy of the post-Fordist propelled globalization and its resulting dominant ideologies. It has been claimed that the U.S. core-elite ideologies support, through the notion of a decentered world, the divide-and-conquer strategy used to subdue the periphery. This strategy is aided by the double-talk characteristic of the opposing dominant ideologies of the Israeli and Palestinian core-dependent peripheral state elites, a double-talk aimed at legitimating their respective attempts to maintain or attain a state apparatus that allows them a relative autonomy in the post-Fordist shaken state-based world system.

The next chapter considers how mainstream news, a major venue for the embedment and propagation of dominant ideologies, audiovisually frames terror and war events.

NOTES

1. See Antonio Gramsci, *Selections from Prison Notebooks* (London: Lawrence and Wishart, 1971); Louis Althusser, "Ideology and Ideological State Apparatuses," in *Lenin and Philosophy* (New York: NLB, 1971), 127–186; Noam Chomsky and Edward S. Herman, *Manufacturing Consent* (New York: Pantheon, 1988).

2. See Fredric Jameson, *Postmodernism; or, The Cultural Logic of Late Capitalism* (London: Duke University Press, 1991); David Harvey, *The Condition of Postmodernity* (Cambridge, U.K.: Blackwell, 1991).

3. Jameson, *Postmodernism*.

4. Donna Haraway, *Simians, Cyborgs, and Women: The Reinvention of Nature* (London: Free Association Books, 1991).

5. Jean Baudrillard, *Simulations* (New York: Semiotext(e), 1983).

6. This position is clearly evident in Jean Baudrillard's *For a Critique of the Political Economy of the Sign* (St. Louis, Mo.: Telos, 1981).

7. See also Jameson, *Postmodernism*; Harvey, *The Condition of Postmodernity*.

8. Mark Wolf, *Abstracting Reality* (Lanham, Md.: University Press of America, 2000).

9. E.g., Baudrillard, *Simulations*; Donna Haraway, "Manifesto for Cyborgs: Science, Technology, and Socialist Feminism in the Late Twentieth Century," in *Simians, Cyborgs, and Women*, 149–181; Nick Perry, *Hyper-Reality and Global Culture* (London: Routledge, 1998); and Paul Virilio, *Open Sky* (New York: Verso, 1995).

10. It should be pointed out, however, that while the noncompliant secular totalitarian state of Iraq may have strived to expand its influence, abuse the environment, and develop weapons of mass destruction, this mode of conduct is, as is well-known, widely shared by nontotalitarian states like the United States. Moreover, allegations of human rights violations as grounds for targeting Iraq is somewhat disturbing given the U.S. alliance with Saudi Arabia, one of the worst human rights violators. Finally, the current selective targeting of al Qaeda and Iraq does not sit well with their earlier

perception by the U.S. elites, who supported the radical Islamists that formed al Qaeda during their fight against the Soviet invasion of Afghanistan and who supported Saddam's Iraq in its war against Iran. See John Cooley, *Unholy Wars: Afghanistan, America, and International Terrorism* (London: Pluto Press, 1999).

11. Walter Benjamin, "The Work of Art in the Age of Mechanical Reproduction," in *Illuminations*, ed. Hannah Arendt (New York: Shoken Books, 1969), 242.

12. Haraway, "Manifesto for Cyborgs."

13. Daya Kishan Thussu and Des Freedman, "Introduction," in *War and the Media: Reporting Conflict 24/7* (London: Sage, 2003), 7.

14. The ultimate simulacrum-styled obscuring of the realities of war was suggested by Baudrillard in his claim that the first Gulf War never happened, see Jean Baudrillard, *The Gulf War Did Not Take Place* (Bloomington: Indiana University Press, 1995).

15. E.g., Roland Robertson, "Glocalization: Time-Space and Homogeneity-Heterogeneity," in *Global Modernities*, ed. Mike Featherstone, Scott Lash, and Roland Robertson (London: Sage, 1995), 25–44; John Tomlinson, *Globalization and Culture* (Cambridge, U.K.: Polity, 1999).

16. Nitzan Ben-Shaul, "Different yet Even: The Effacement of Power in Post-Structuralism: The Case of *Seinfeld*," *Third Text*, Special Issue 51, (Summer 2000): 75–84.

17. Bernard Lewis, *What Went Wrong: Western Impact and Middle East Response* (New York: Oxford University Press, 2001); Samuel P. Huntington, *The Clash of Civilizations and the Remaking of World Order* (New York: Simon & Schuster, 1996).

18. While Hamas, Islamic Jihad, al Qaeda, Hizbolla, or other terror acting groups share a radical murderous Islamist ideology inspired or "hosted" by noncompliant states such as Iran and formerly Afghanistan, indiscriminate terror or suicidal terror acts have been carried out elsewhere by non-Islamic states (e.g., Japanese Kamikaze) or by non-Islamic groups "hosted" by non-Islamic states as in Northern Ireland. On suicidal terror in Northern Ireland, see Bethami A. Dobkin, *Tales of Terror* (London: Praeger, 1992), 48.

19. As suggested here, economic-political factors are needed to explain when and under what circumstances cultural ideas gain support and lead people to act on them.

20. Althusser, "Ideology"; Gramsci, *Prison Notebooks.*

21. See Benedict Anderson, *Imagined Communities: Reflections on the Origins and Appeal of Nationalism* (New York: Verso, 1991); Roland Axtmann, "Collective Identity and the Democratic Nation State in the Age of Globalization," in *Articulating the Global and the Local*, ed. Ann Cvetkovich and Douglas Kellner (Boulder, Colo.: Westview, 1997), 33–54.

22. Homi K. Bhaba, "DissemiNation," in *Nation and Narration*, ed. Homi K. Bhaba (London: Routledge & Kegan Paul, 1990), 291–322; Homi K. Bhaba, *The Location of Culture* (London: Routledge, 1994).

23. Several scholars have considered this notion in relation to Israeli society using somewhat different terms and methods. See Nitzan Ben-Shaul, *Mythical Expressions of Siege in Israeli Films* (Lewiston, N.Y.: The Edwin Mellen Press, 1997); Daniel Bar-Tal and Dikla Antebi, "Siege Mentality in Israel," *International Journal of Intercul-*

tural Relations 16 (1992): 251–275; Conor Cruise O'Brien, *The Siege* (New York: Simon & Schuster, 1986); Michael Brecher, *Decisions in Crisis: Israel, 1967 and 1973* (Berkeley: University of California Press, 1980); Meron Benvenisti, *The Sling and the Club* [in Hebrew] (Jerusalem: Keter, 1988); Charles Liebman and Eliezer Don Yehiya, *Civil Religion in Israel* (Berkeley: University of California Press, 1983); Yehoshafat Harkaby, *Facing Reality* [in Hebrew] (Jerusalem: Van Leer Foundation, 1981).

24. Liebman and Don Yehiya, *Civil Religion in Israel.*

25. For example, in April 10, 2002, in the midst of Israel's extensive incursion into Palestinian territories termed "Operation Defensive Shield," the former Israeli prime minister Benjamin Netanyahu, speaking on behalf of the Israeli government before a group of U.S. senators, drew parallels between the U.S. battle against terrorism in the wake of September 11 and Israel's response to a series of Palestinian suicide bombings. He added that the United States could undermine its war on terrorism and encourage terrorist attacks if it does not support Israel's military campaign in the Palestinian territories.

26. After Arafat's death and the ascendance of his successor, Mahmoud Abbas (who won the presidential elections in January 2005), the PNA ideology underwent a gradual process of secularization. Since the January 2006 victory of Hamas in the elections to the Palestine Legislative Council, a stark ideological and political split is evolving within the PNA between President Mahmoud Abbas, who represents a secularized version of the original position of the PNA in favor of a two-state solution, and the religious fundamentalism of Hamas, which rejects the existence of Israel. For earlier discussions of Palestinian dominant ideologies see Mohamed E. Selim, "The Survival of a Non-State Actor: The Foreign Policy of the Palestine Liberation Organization," in *The Foreign Policies of Arab States: The Challenge of Change*, ed. Baghat Korany and Ali E. Hillal Dessouki (Boulder, Colo.: Westview, 1991), 260–309; Rashid Khalili, *Palestinian Identity: The Constitution of Modern National Consciousness* (New York: Columbia University Press, 1988); Dov Shinar, *Palestinian Voices: Communication and Nation Building in the West Bank* (Boulder, Colo.: Rienner : 1987).

27. Aired on Palestinian TV on January 26, 2002, and again on March 29, 2002, when Arafat's headquarters in Ramallah were surrounded by Israeli tanks, Al Jazeera television interviewed him by telephone and he said, "They either want to kill me, or capture me, or expel me. . . . I hope I will be a martyr in the Holy Land. I have chosen this path and if I fall, one day a Palestinian child will raise the Palestinian flag above our mosques and churches."

28. The Palestinian plight began with the waves of Jewish immigration into Palestine (1889; 1904–1914; 1930–1940; 1945–1948) and the organized spreading of Jewish settlements, mostly on lands purchased by the Zionists from landholders residing outside Palestine who betrayed the Palestinian inhabitants. These actions, which led to sporadic ethnic clashes between Jews and Arabs in Palestine over the acquisition of land and labor (1921; 1929; 1936–1939), helped consolidate the Palestinians as a distinctive entity (as opposed to their initial self-perception as belonging to southern Syria) and were colored by national aspirations, particularly following the shifting British mandate policy toward this evolving conflict (most clashes on an organized

level were carried out following British policy statements issued in support of a national Jewish entity). The Palestinians' first major dispersion occurred during Israel's War of Independence in 1948, referred to by the Palestinians as *al nakba*—the catastrophe. In this war, which immediately followed Israel's declaration of independence, the Palestinians fought Israel aided by the armies of several Arab states. This aid was mostly achieved due to the Palestinian leaders' success in representing their case as a pan-Arab concern, thus catering to the Arab governments' interest in creating a pan-Arab movement (whose underlying political-economic interests gelled into the ideological conception of the Zionist enterprise as an intrusion of the imperialist West into Arab lands). Israel's military victory in this war resulted in the expansion of Israel's territories beyond the UN partition decision of 1947, the fleeing and expulsion of six hundred thousand Palestinians mainly into the West Bank and Gaza Strip territories, and the signing of cease-fire agreements with the Arab states participating in the war, thus maintaining a state of suspended war. The second failure of the Arab nations to aid the Palestinians occurred during what Israelis term the "Six Day War" in June 1967, when Israel initiated what most Israelis at the time perceived as a preemptive strike against the Egyptian, Syrian, and eventually the Jordanian armies. For an extensive analysis of the cognitive factors—such as what the writer terms the "Holocaust Syndrome"—leading to the Israeli government decision to open war in 1967 and its abstention from a preemptive strike during the October war in 1973, see Brecher, *Decisions in Crisis*. This brief war resulted in the expansion of Israel's territories beyond the cease-fire borders established after the War of Independence. From that time, Israel occupied the West Bank of the Jordan River and the Gaza Strip with its million Palestinian inhabitants and post-1947 refugees (who subsequently became subject to Israeli military rule), the Egyptian Sinai desert to the Suez Canal, and the Syrian Golan Heights. The 1967 war led to intensified guerrilla and terrorist actions against Israel on behalf of different Palestinian organizations, operating mainly from Jordan and the occupied territories of the West Bank and Gaza Strip. During the 1970s and 1980s intermittent and internationally escalating guerrilla and terror activities on behalf of Palestinian organizations, particularly those carried out by the PLO (created in 1964 and dominated by the Fatah movement, whose founder Yasser Arafat was appointed leader of the PLO in 1969, a position he held until his death in 2004), consolidated the dominant ideology of the PLO as a national liberation movement resolute to attain a just national liberation of their land through guerrilla and terror warfare. This ideology attained wide international legitimacy within the context of the Cold War and the anticolonial struggles for national liberation in the third world. Hence, the widespread acceptance of terror as a legitimate venue for national liberation struggles—see Frantz Fanon, *The Wretched of the Earth* (New York: Grove Press, 1968)—along with the success of the guerrilla and terror warfare of the National Liberation Front (FLN) in Algeria (which ousted the French and gained independence to Algeria) led most of the world to recognize the Palestinians' plight and to recognize the PLO as the semiofficial representative of the Palestinian people, as symbolized in its acquisition of an observer status in the UN. However, the national liberation activities of these Palestinian groups were often carried out without consulting the governments of their Arab host countries, since the Palestinians felt they could not rely on their help. These activities, harshly reciprocated by the Israeli army, enraged some of their Arab host countries, who viewed their actions and their military presence as threatening their sovereignty. King Hussein of Jordan, for example, expelled in 1971 the Palestinian organizations from Jordan following a bloody battle that became known as Black September, while other Arab states like Lebanon, to where the Palestinians fled after their expulsion from Jordan, refused to grant the dispersed Palestinians citizenship and kept them within refugee camps. The Palestinians' sense of being betrayed by the West and by their Arab brothers was exacerbated following the Egyptian president Anwar Sadat's signing of a peace treaty with Israel in 1979. This U.S.-brokered peace treaty, which allowed Sadat to gain back Egypt's Sinai Peninsula, conquered by Israel in 1967 and reconquered in 1973, while including future provisions to solve the Palestinian issue was somewhat rightly perceived by the Palestinians (as well as by radical Islamists in the Arab world) as a betrayal of their cause and led to Sadat's assassination by radical Islamists in 1981. (This feeling of betrayal persists through this day. Hence, in a demonstration in Gaza aired on Al Hara TV on March, 30, 2003, Palestinians burned coffins carrying the inscriptions "The Arab League" and "The Arab Summit" in contempt of the Arab states' incompetence concerning the Palestinians' plight.) In a sense, this peace treaty, which neutralized Egyptian armed intervention in respect of the Israeli-Palestinian conflict, eased Israel's invasion of Lebanon in 1982, following the Palestinian organizations' constant shelling of northern Israel from that country. The invasion was primarily aimed at destroying the Palestinian military infrastructure and killing or dispersing the Palestinian leadership in Lebanon so as to better deal with Palestinians within the occupied territories of the West Bank and Gaza Strip. However, contrary to Israeli expectations, the main consequence of this invasion was the arousal in 1989 of the entire Palestinian population in the occupied territories against Israeli occupation in what came to be known as the first Intifada (Arabic for "shaking off"). This first popular uprising, carried out with sticks and stones, further consolidated the Palestinians as a people. However, Israel's killing and dispersal of the Palestinian leadership in Lebanon created a leadership vacuum. This, along with the further destitution of the Palestinians during the Intifada, enhanced the power and influence of radical Islamist groups within the occupied territories, particularly through the latter's provision of material aid and religious education to widening sections of the devastated population. The radical Islamism propelling groups such as Hamas and Islamic Jihad, along with the growing destitution of the people supporting them, translated into a new form of terror warfare against Israel. Based on the religious notion of Shahada (martyrdom), these groups called for personal martyrdom through suicide bombings. These terrorist acts, to be rewarded in heaven, are aimed at avenging the wrongdoings of the heathen Jews, at liberating all of the holy land of Palestine from the Zionist occupation, and at establishing an Islamic regime. (Aziz Rantisi, the leader of the radical Islamist Hamas movement assassinated by Israel after Israel's assassination of Hamas founder and leader Ahmed Yassin, stated this ideology in many interviews. For example, in an interview on Katari TV on December 12, 2003, Rantisi said, "The Hamas will continue its Jihad and Shahada until the liberation of Palestinian lands and the return of the last refugee to Palestine and the liberation of the holy places and of the prisoners in the Zionist enemy's prisons and the expulsion of the invaders from our land and the cleansing of the land from their filth." The return in

1993 of the PLO leadership to the occupied territories through the institution of the Palestinian National Authority under the leadership of Yasser Arafat, a return resulting from the Oslo Accords, led to a clash between Hamas and the PNA over control of the territories under the PNA jurisdiction and over the aims of the struggle against Israel. While Hamas called for a relentless suicidal terror war against Israel so as to seek its destruction, the PNA officially renounced terror and maintained that the struggle for national liberation should focus on the establishment of an independent Palestinian state confined to the territories of the West Bank and the Gaza Strip conquered by Israel in the war of 1967. This official position of the PNA, brought about by Israeli and core-elite pressures, led Hamas to accuse the PNA of betrayal of the Palestinian cause, an accusation that reverberated in the minds of the Intifada-devastated Palestinians and led to their massive voting for Hamas in the January 2006 elections for the Palestine Legislative Council.

29. Al Aksa is the name of the mosque provocatively visited by Sharon, a visit maintained by Palestinians to have sparked this Intifada. See Radwan Abu Ayyash, *Broadcasters' Obligations towards Their Audience in Times of Crisis (The Palestinian Intifada as an Example)* (master's thesis, Center for Mass Communication Research, Leicester, U.K.: Leicester University, 1992), 51.

30. Arafat made several attempts to arrest militants belonging to competing organizations following suicide bombings, usually also following U.S. pressures. For example, on October 18, 2001, Palestinian security forces arrested two members of the Popular Front for the Liberation of Palestine (PFLP) leadership, and on June 9, 2002, Palestinian security forces arrested two senior leaders of the Palestinian Islamic Jihad in Gaza. Another index of the tension between the PNA and these subnational radical Islamist groups was the July 24, 2001, night demonstrations organized by Hamas movement members, which led to the burning of the house of PNA Brigadier General Musa Arafat, Yasser Arafat's relative.

31. The plan was adopted at the twelfth session of the Palestinian National Council in Cairo, June 9, 1974. Arafat and other Palestinian leaders have sometimes termed the agreements reached in Oslo as implying *Hudna* (an Islamic term roughly meaning "cease-fire") rather than peace. This position was also stated on September 1, 2000, by the Israeli-Arab member of the Israeli parliament, Abd al Malek Dahamshe, when interviewed on Palestinian Authority Television (PATV). In response to a viewer who called the studio and said, "Our problem with Israel is not a problem of borders but a problem of existence," he responded, "We are exaggerating when we say 'peace' . . . we are talking about 'Hudna' " (noted by Palestinian Media Watch (PMW), at www.pmw.org.il.)

32. For example, on June 2, 2001, the Palestinian National Authority president Yasser Arafat condemned a suicide bomb attack that killed eighteen people. He said, "I repeat our condemnation of this tragic operation and to all operations that result in the killing of civilians, Israelis or Palestinians. . . . We will now exert our utmost efforts to stop the bloodshed of our people and the Israeli people and to do all that is needed to achieve an immediate and unconditional, real and effective cease-fire." Also on December 21, 2001, following intensive pressure from the United States, Arafat declared on PATV, "We would like to reiterate again here today that all sorts of armed activities should be stopped and there should be no more attacks, especially

the suicide and bombing attacks that we have always condemned. And we will arrest all those who planned these attacks. And we will stop all those who have no other mission but to give excuses to further Israeli attacks against our land, against our people, against our women. Any violation of this decision will be seen as a trespass of our supreme national interest of our people and of our Arab nation, and will be dealt with accordingly. Those who violate this decision will be penalized firmly and strongly, because this is our credibility in order to restore quiet and calm and to achieve and implement the recommendations of Mitchell and to return to the table of negotiations, which forms, and has to form, the only and the sole means for a settlement."

33. In an interview given by Nabil Sha'at to Almanar Television on August, 15, 2003, he promised the return of Palestinian refugees to their homes in Palestine, but concerning their return to Israel he said that that should be negotiated.

3

Television News Audiovisual Ideological Frames

The present analysis of television news stems from a critical media theory approach.[1] Contrary to a widespread conservative liberal "freedom of the press" ideological conception of television news as striving toward an achievable objectivity, and contrary to the neoliberal postmodern recouching of this conception through the notion of television news as indeterminate "associational flows" that "open" the news to whatever viewers want to read into it, this study considers the ways in which mainstream television news effectively audiovisually frames events[2] (in particular terror and war events where audiovisuals overwhelm the verbal commentary) to be determined by dominant ideologies.[3] Hence, Stuart Hall has persuasively argued that in the striving of mainstream television news to forge consensual conceptions and in its reliance for information on the ruling elites, "in the moment of news production, the media stand in a position of structured subordination to the primary definers."[4]

Following a critique of the conservative and the postmodern versions of the freedom-of-the-press perspective, a countermodel based on contained associations and headline shots is offered for the analysis of how mainstream television news effectively embeds dominant ideologies in its audiovisual coverage of terror and war.

CRITIQUE OF FREEDOM-OF-THE-PRESS PERSPECTIVES

The importance of the study of how television news embeds dominant ideologies comes forth once we consider the fallacies of a widespread approach

among communication scholars, newspeople, and audiences from what may
be termed a freedom-of-the-press perspective. According to this view, television networks in democratic countries independently set the agenda of news
in an overall objective presentation, that is, free of ideology. They presume
that the media has autonomous power that often influences governments and
the elite. Thus, freedom-of-the-press perspectives on the coverage of terror
events tend to explain the extensive coverage of these events as a result of the
independent agenda setting of networks, derived primarily from the inherently telegenic (i.e., audiovisually attractive) aspect of such events.[5] Consequently, some who criticize the press from this perspective claim that the
undue extensive and event-oriented coverage of terrorist violent acts leads by
definition to an obscuring of the reasons for terrorism. This focuses attention on terror's indiscriminate violence and may support terrorist aims
because it confers high status on terrorists, while their figured indiscriminate
violence may arouse public panic.[6]

Such perspective considers television news coverage of terror events irrespective of the ideological framework orienting the selection of the event to
be covered and the textual forms of its embedding. This approach presumes
the highly unlikely presupposition that television newsmakers do not offer
a sociopolitical point of view when covering highly significant sociopolitical
events or that the events "speak for themselves." A closer look shows that
while the amount of coverage may confer undue importance on terror, just
as it may confer importance on any other event, why and when an event is
made important can hardly be considered in objective telegenic terms. Thus,
while terror may be telegenic, not all terror events are treated equally. As has
been shown, while Middle Eastern terrorist acts are given extensive coverage,
South American ones are hardly covered at all. This can scarcely be related
to technical issues of accessibility, as Michael Delli Carpini and Bruce A.
Williams suggest.[7] Not only is accessibility also ideologically determined, as
studies on the global spread of reporters indicate,[8] but high coverage of inaccessible sites is also found when it is ideologically warranted. Hence, Robert
Picard, who shares this freedom-of-the-press perspective, has claimed that
the hijacking of the cruiser *Achille Lauro* in mid-sea made it inaccessible to
the media, only to point out that the hijackers failed in their violent "communication."[9] However, this event, despite its nonaccessible setting, was
extensively covered. This shows that the consideration of what terror event
is to be extensively covered is not determined by telegenic considerations.

Moreover, among reports on Middle East terror extensive coverage is variable and selective, following ideological directives. For example, contrary to
the early and somewhat successful attempts to suppress the airing of bin
Laden's taped communications, the U.S. secretary of state Colin Powell
drew the attention of Western news to a forthcoming airing on the Qatar-
based Al Jazeera network of bin Laden's address to the Iraqi people.[10]

Powell's suggestion and the extensive coverage that followed cannot be explained solely on the grounds that bin Laden is telegenic or that his tapes were readily available (they were not so easily acquired), but because it served the administration's interest in associating bin Laden with Iraq in order to legitimate its planned war against Iraq. This regenerated in Western television news an intensified framed coverage of bin Laden's terror, reemphasizing his association with weapons of mass destruction, and by implication, with Saddam's Iraq. This is clearly a case whereby, as stated by Hall, "in the moment of news production, the media stand in a position of structured subordination to the primary definers."

Furthermore, while analysts are right in their claim that event-oriented reports do not usually provide explanations of the wider processes leading to the events, this does not mean, as claimed by freedom-of-the-press proponents, that the events covered are henceforth perceived as reasonless by their makers or their viewers.[11] Hence, perceptions of event-oriented coverage as reasonless derive more from the way the event is figured and from the ideological function embedded in this figuration, and less from the fact that reasons are provided or not. Hence, puzzling or questioning event-oriented figurations may enhance search for reasons among viewers, whereas there are figurations that "fix" events and may block viewers' search for reasons.[12] Moreover, while most reports on terror are event-oriented they are also reasoned ad nauseam in newsroom commentaries and expert debates. What this may indicate is not that these reports are neutral or perceived as reasonless but rather that the audiovisual imaging of the event overwhelms its verbal couching. This overwhelming, however, does not mean, as these studies contend, that event-orientation on terrorist violence presents ipso facto terrorist acts as irrational, accentuates nondiscrimination, and generates panic. In fact, the presumed ideologically neutral perception of television coverage as ipso facto carrying its own implications ultimately uses television's apparent objectivity to naturalize this ideologically driven perspective on terror.

Contrary to this ideology-free freedom-of-the-press perspective, it should be clear that there is no inherent and ipso facto conception of terror in event-oriented coverage. This becomes clear in comparative analyses of event-oriented reports on the same event. Hence, differently figured events imply different conceptualizations. Thus, as will be detailed below, Israeli mainstream television event-oriented coverage of the Twin Towers destruction was audiovisually panicky, whereas that of CNN was detached. Likewise, Israel's panicky figuration of Palestinian suicide bombers contrasts with their martyred-styled figuration in Palestinian television. Hence, events are not inherently telegenic but are turned telegenic by the way they are relayed. This crafted telegenicity audiovisually frames events in different ways, and this diversity is highly determined by ideological points of view. As Hall, quoting George Gerbner remarks, "Representations of violence on TV screens 'is not violence but messages about violence.'"[13]

Therefore, a more sophisticated approach to television news is needed—one that takes into consideration its forms of figuration and the ways these are oriented by ideologies.

CRITIQUE OF THE POSTMODERN "TV NEWS AS ASSOCIATIONAL FLOWS" PERSPECTIVE

Differing from traditional freedom-of-the-press oriented studies, which are on the whole content bound and do not seriously consider the ways figurations form events nor how these formations embed ideologies, postmodern approaches do focus on these aspects. However, postmodern approaches, which as stated above are the dominant ideology of the post-Fordist mode of production, in their notion of television news as polysemic associational flows, engender a methodological labyrinth that ends up neutralizing any meaningful understanding of ideological embedment and effectiveness, resulting in a new, neoliberal version of the freedom-of-the-press perspective.

The post-structural/postmodern approach evolved out of attacks on the problematic structural notion of textual boundaries, claiming these are ultimately unjustifiable, henceforth also collapsing the structural-derived notion of a deep, central, determining, static, or essential feature underlying a given text.[14] This approach found in television an emblematic text. As Nick Browne writes, "The 'television text' as a concept and as a practice is very different from the discreet unity of film. Its phenomenology is one of flow, banality, distraction, and transience: its semiotic complex, fragmentary and heterogeneous. The limits of the text 'proper' and its formal unity—apt to be broken at any moment by an ad or a return of the dial—are suspect."[15]

These general characteristics were also found to specifically inhere in television series, serials, and news, which were perceived, in principle, as open endless chains of episodes or events with no closure (except for the arbitrary closure of seasonal cycles or of newscasts).[16]

However, while post-structuralists and postmodernists shook certainties maintained by structuralists, the post-structural perception of a boundless decentered textual universe generated a theoretical and practical labyrinth in comparison to which the structural problems pale.[17] This labyrinth emerges when the impulse that led to deconstruction attempts to reconstruct the concepts it earlier dismantled. Such is the case with the post-structural/postmodern notion of television. Any perception of television as constantly shifting configurations of variables is self-contradictory in that it cannot do away at every given point with determining invariables, simply because you cannot specify a difference unless you have something constant against which to measure it. Indeed, although such approaches always posit some such invariable, given their basic premises they have no good reason to justify their choice (actually, textual boundlessness and decentralization are themselves unjustified invariables).

Hence, the central post-structural television metaphor of flow and the concept of polysemy, along with the segmented nature of television programming and reception,[18] have led to self-contradicting and unjustifiable psychoanalytic and ideological interpretations of television in general and of television series and news in particular. Beverle Houston, for example, offers a post-structural Lacanian reading of television as "contradiction between flow and interruption,"[19] whereby flow implies an imaginary plenitude disturbed yet replicated in a symbolic interminable polysemous concatenation of signs. Based on this post-structural notion of television's "super text," Houston presumes that television's interrupted flow invariably coerces any viewer to the subject position of a consumer, "which it promotes by shattering the imaginary possibility over and over, repeatedly reopens the gap of desire."[20] However, she also presumes that "the strategies of the television institution, enunciation, and apparatus . . . put all its spectators in situations . . . [where] multiple positions are occupied simultaneously by actual subjects."[21] Since both contradicting conclusions derive from the same problematic premise (interrupted flow), her postulation—of the invariable subject positioning as consumer over other positioning presumed to be variable— seems arbitrary and unwarranted.

Houston's problematic post-structural approach to television's "super text" gets further complicated when it is applied to specific discreet television programs. This for example happens with John Fiske's post-structural conception of series and news as polysemous texts.[22] According to Fiske, television series and news, given their interminable intertextual references, allow a variety of gender, class, and ethnic differentiated subjects to read practically anything from a given text. Given Fiske's "semiotic democracy,"[23] it is strange that he ventures to decipher in a discrete series (e.g., *Cagney and Lacey*) and in his analysis of TV news,[24] what he calls ideologically dominant readings in relation to which he dissects other readings. This is because transferring the question of determining invariables from the television series or TV news to presumed solid extratextual ideologies either turns the series or the news broadcast into a nonsignificant pretext for predetermined ideological decoding, or, if the series signifies, his approach is redundant for these ideological potentialities are "in" the series or the news. In the latter case, it is practically impossible according to Fiske's approach to determine which combination of polysemic features relates to which ideology except by reverting to the nonsignificant occurrence of the series in the act of its viewing. Furthermore, the transfer of invariability to extratextual ideological readings in order to maintain the notion of series or news as polysemic, raises the question of the polysemous nature of ideologies, for are not ideologies polysemous texts by Fiske's own definition?

Given this theoretical labyrinth and the concomitant effacement of concrete configurations of power promoted by post-structuralists and postmodernists, it seems that a countertextual strategy is called for, one that resists incorporation and allows for a clear critique of the current state of affairs.

TELEVISION NEWS AUDIOVISUAL IDEOLOGICAL FRAMES

Stuart Hall, followed and expanded yet ultimately degenerated by Fiske's postmodern position, developed a powerful and comprehensive semiotic textual approach to news whereby events were placed "within a range of known social and cultural identifications."[25] Showing that television news is structurally oriented to rely on the opinions of the elite, both Hall and Fiske tried to explain how television news textually encodes the dominant ideology relayed by elite opinion, since "formal characteristics . . . bear the brunt of the ideological work."[26] In what Fiske describes as a "claw back" strategy, television news dominant ideologies were understood as being relayed through a top-to-bottom chain of verbal commentary that frames the audiovisuals of reports. Hence, starting from the apparently neutral and objectively perceived newsroom anchor who usually does not speak his own thoughts but rather those of the elite, down to newsroom experts, field reporters, and interviewed eyewitnesses, the audiovisual figurations of events are made to conform to the elite-dependent conception of the event. At the same time, the perceived as transparent audiovisual figurations authenticate and naturalize the conception relayed from the studio. Thus, according to Fiske, the encoding of inherently "polysemic" audiovisuals is carried out mainly through the event's couching in verbal poetics and narrative.[27] Following this line of inquiry were Bethami A. Dobkin's melodramatic approach or Jack Lule's mythical approach, which offered interesting decipherments of ideological encoding in the verbal poetic story structuring of televised terror events such as the hijacking of TWA flight 847 and the hijacked cruise ship *Achille Lauro* in 1985. These and other studies showed how such coverage by U.S. and European television news replicated governmental ideology.[28] For example, Dobkin's interesting study of ABC's construction of the terrorist threat outlined how the U.S. government and ABC positioned the concept of terror against that of freedom and how their presentation of terror as irrational supported U.S. military retaliation against Libya as a "terror hosting state."

While my approach is in line with these earlier approaches to television news and their analyses of the coverage of terror events, I reject their main focus on thematic categorizations and the formal properties of verbal commentary in television news, which treats the reports' audiovisual configurations as simple and incidental authentications of the ideology embedded in relayed verbal commentaries. Hence, despite some theoretical claims made regarding audiovisual configurations, these studies tend to treat the audiovisual aspect of television news as secondary or subservient to verbal poetics and narrative devices.[29] Their main focus is on how verbal narrative lends coherence to images and drives their selection, exclusion, or emphasis. This bias recurs in textual studies of reports on terror events. Hence, Dobkin's extensive analysis of the ideology embedded in the verbal narration of covered events only briefly and incidentally analyzed their moving audiovisual framing over two pages in her book. Leaving this framing untapped often results in an emphasis on the reality reference aspect of these images. This conception of images is particularly self-defeating when it comes to analyses of television news on terror, since the overwhelming power of such images and sounds often renders irrelevant the detailed analysis of their narrative verbal couching. This analytic neglect is strange, given that audiovisual articulations are the major factor that turns television news into the world's most prominent and widespread source of information. Some even claim that verbal commentaries are subordinate to audiovisual configurations rather than the other way around.[30] Thus, while I accept the general approach of these media frame theorists, a more comprehensive approach to audiovisual configurations is called for.

While accepting the claim of textual analysts within the critical media approach whereby dominant ideologies are primarily embedded in formal configurations, this study is not predominantly of the verbal poetics or narrative formations of news reports as is characteristic of these analysts.[31] Rather, it is on television news audiovisual formations, whose analysis is generally neglected in these studies. In what follows I argue that television news offers distinct audiovisual formations that ideologically frame the events covered, often in consonance with but independently from their verbal couching. In discussing these issues, focus is mostly on the coverage of terror and war events, where audiovisuals overwhelm the verbal commentary. The failure of current analyses to come to terms with this type of coverage reveals more general lacunae in television news analyses as far as its audiovisual formations go. Since it is audiovisual formations that turn mainstream television news into the main source of information for people on the actual world they live in, failure to come to terms with such formations obscures our understanding of the powerful ideological workings of mainstream television news.

AUDIOVISUAL MICRO-FRAMES: HEADLINE
SHOTS AND ASSOCIATED SHOT CLUSTERS

The reductive or incidental approach to audiovisual figurations in television news may derive from the fact that, contrary to the explicit stylization of fictional films and most documentaries, television news reports are peculiar textual formations consisting of scattered, mostly documentary shots accompanied by verbal commentaries. However, the fact that shots are scattered and that verbal commentary often coincides with what is shown, does not mean that shots are invariably subservient to verbal poetics and narrative commentary, that there are no coherent audiovisual formations, or that ideology is mostly embedded in verbal articulations. It is often the case that verbal commentary, narrative or not, follows from available shots, contradicts them, or is simply unrelated to them. Actually, as will be discussed below, scattered sounds and images in news reports are structurally resistant to verbal poetics and narrative devices. This verbal-oriented dominant approach to television news neglects serious consideration of its audiovisual framing. This may be due to the verbal bias among communication researchers or to the scattered nature of audiovisual news report formations.

On the other hand, there are several researchers with a cinematic bias that unduly impose ideological decoding on minute audiovisual poetic details found in scattered news shots. This is particularly problematic when reports on terror events are analyzed. Much is made in these latter studies of the lighting pattern in a given shot, the angle and distance from which it was taken, its foreground to background layout, its typecast characters, the audiovisual narration pattern, or its causal ideologically determined ordering. This approach conveniently overlooks the fact that most televised news reports are not carefully preplanned stylized films. The search for cinematic audiovisual poetics and narrative devices also counters the peculiar formation of news reports. Reporters do not set out with preplanned shooting scripts. Gathered shots forming reports are often haphazardly taken and are constrained by event, location, and time pressures. Likewise, report editors cannot seriously impose cinematic audiovisual narrative continuity on reports. Even if they try, they will never be able to meet deadlines. This constraint on audiovisual newsgathering is further enhanced in live or deadline-constrained event-oriented reports. Attempts to impose cinematic poetic and narrative devices on such reports are therefore highly suspect. Actually, television news reports from this perspective are bad films.

To sum up, verbal or cinematic poetics and narrative formations are difficult to impose on the scattered shots comprising news reports. This does not mean, however, as Fiske ended up claiming, that television news reports effectively evade the structural impositions of dominant ideologies given their images' uncalculated capture of reality or their explicit intertextual nature due to their shot scattering.[32] The fact that the audiovisual aspect of reports evades verbal and cinematic narrative and poetic impositions does not mean that they are therefore open to whatever viewers want to read into them. It probably means that the analytic tools used to decode their audiovisual embedding of ideology do not fit. Television news is a powerful ideological tool precisely because of its loosely knit, perceived as reality referential, scattered shots. Its structural resistance to explicit verbal narrative ordering, rather than opening them up to indeterminate meanings, lends power to its audiovisual modes of ideological encoding. While verbal commentary may, arguably, often try to turn audiovisual figurations into coherent wholes through narrative formations, these are more often made coherent through nonnarrative and nonsequential audiovisual strategies, better fitted to their scattered nature. It seems that the more the attempt is made to turn scattered shots of news reports into coherent wholes through verbal or cinematic narrative sequential devices, the more these audiovisual figurations evade verbal commentary.

Television news reports, as Fiske contended, are indeed intertextual in that they are constituted by scattered quotations taken from various sources (primarily shot and recorded events, but also formal conventions and themes taken from television formats, literature, cinema, the plastic arts, history texts, etc.). This does not mean, however, that the meaning of a given report inheres in some predetermined meaning imposed by viewers or in the predetermined meaning quoted texts, reality referential or not, import into the composed report. Rather, the meaning often inheres in their particular nonnarrative and non-causally-sequential horizontal interdependence. That is, in what is compositionally or figuratively shared by the selected portions of the different quoted texts. This is usually based on metonymical relations such as in simple reports on floods, often composed of shifting overlapping views from various angles of an overflowing river. What is shared encodes the dominant ideological perspective that drove the selection process to begin with. Hence, in our example, focus in adjacent shots may be on the gushing waters, encoding the ideological notion of nature's strength. These shared portions shift the meaning of the various incorporated quotations away from the meaning they had within their texts of origin to that generated by their ideologically determined interdependence within the given report. Thus, a shot of a tank overturned by the gushing waters could have evoked the idea of an end to arms, but that notion cedes in favor of the aforementioned dominant interrelation between shots.

Hence, scattered shots in reports are rarely arranged according to narrative and causal-sequential directives. They are clustered wholes horizontally interrelated through contained association. This interrelation can be seen in Israeli television news reports on suicide bombings. These use overlapping warm colors and shaky compositions, nervous narrative commentary, and jumpy disorienting editing of unstable hand-held camera movements surveying the site, as well as figuring close shots of mutilated bodies; spread body parts; confused victims, soldiers, policemen, and paramedics; and stressed witnesses running around in despair. These audiovisual panicky configurations evoke a notion of indiscriminate persecution, resonating for Israeli Jews the long history of persecution of the Jewish people, which translates into their feeling of being a besieged nation, an ongoing theme in Israeli culture.[33] They are also ideologically aimed at internal enlisting, by representing the particular interests of Israel's state elite in Jewish, secular, and security-oriented national unification, as pertaining to all Israelis. Such coverage, as will be discussed further on, sharply differs from the coverage of suicide bombings in other national or global networks.

This interrelated audiovisual containment of meaning across scattered images is usually enhanced and refined through their formal or figurative association to carefully chosen headline shots.[34] Headline shots, given salience in recurrent trailers and often inserted within reports, attract attention to their ideologically formal encoding and the consequent meaning attributed to what they figure, forming a form-content blend. They thus semantically frame thematically related images by drawing attention to what the latter's horizontally articulated shared portions have in common with the headline shot (though this sharing can be simply vertical in spaced-apart or isolated images addressing the headline shot's theme). This association to headline shots extends to audiovisual segments that replicate only the headline shots' dominant composition, which bears with it the meaning of its figures. Thus, although a nondominant and nonrecurring image may include different (theme related) figures, these new figures will be comprehended just as the figure in the headline shot is. Hence, replicating in an audiovisual segment figuring Saddam Hussein's foreign minister the headline shot's composition of Hussein imparts on the foreign minister the headline shot's attribution of meaning to Saddam. This association also extends to shots replicating only the headline shot's dominant figures. These figures, by "bearing the brunt" of the headline shot's formal composition, turn the different composition of the same figures in the nondominant shot into an inconsequential factor.

Hence, placing Saddam within a different composition in a nondominant shot will not change the meaning he carries with him in the headline shot. Like prototypes, headline shots comprise the center in relation to which other audiovisual segments are grouped (e.g., the sparrow is the prototypical bird in relation to whose properties other birds are grouped). For example, one of CNN's recurrent headline shots figuring Saddam Hussein shows him from a low angle, wearing a modern black suit, drawing a sword and waving it in the air. This formation encodes in CNN newscasts the U.S. dominant ideology perception of Hussein as a dangerous (the low-angle shot imparting menace), backward barbarian (he waves a sword) in modern appearance (he wears a western suit). The low-angled shot also encodes a discourse of exposure ("below" the modern suit hides a dangerous barbarian). This headline shot semantically dominates and groups other available nondominant scattered images that figure in reports on Iraq. This association is clarified, for example, in a somewhat differently composed shot of Saddam, where we see him from a high angle, wearing a military uniform and shooting a rifle. Although this image includes other figures (a rifle, a military uniform) and a different composition (Saddam is shot from a high angle), other compositional features and figures that resemble the headline shot dominate the incidental shot, and encode by association the rest of its features according to the headline shot's meaning. Hence, the fact that the subservient audiovisual segment replicates the figure of Saddam as well as of his posture in the headline shot (here, too, he holds a weapon to the sky and waves it), causes the different features to be understood as nonconsequential substitutions. Thus, the rifle merely exchanges the sword, the uniform the suit, and the low angle the high one. Saddam, however, still retains his "barbaric menace below his apparent modernity" meaning in this shot. Thus, news reports embed dominant ideologies through the metonymical interrelation of scattered images and through their association to carefully selected headline shots. The spreading semantic coloring of headline shots ideologically frames audiovisual spaces characterizing places, events, or people. Thus, notions of *Iraqiness* spread from Saddam's headline shot figurations.

AUDIOVISUAL MACRO-FRAMES:
AESTHETIC FABRICATIONS OF FLOW

While on the micro-level of reports associations are delimited by headline shots, on the macro-level these delimiting strategies inhere in the aesthetic fabrication of television flow. This fabrication does not follow Fiske's conflation of flow with the presupposed intertextual and apparent indeterminate extreme segmentation and constant mix of news, generating thus a notion of associational flows. While this conflation may be pertinent to music videos, as Fiske points out, it is hardly relevant to news.[35] Rick Altman offers a more interesting conception of flow. His claim is that television flow, designed through thematic scheduling and promotional strategies (such as "lead in" programs, hammocking weaker programs in between strong ones, and inserting promos for later shows) fuses the many transitions among segments to counter the threat of zapping so as to generate loyal consumers.[36] However, while Altman's notion of fusion is instructive, scheduling and promotion hardly comprise the extent of the economic-political driven interests that dominant ideologies aim to justify, nor the primary audiovisual strate-

gies that embed these ideologies. What viewers are asked to consume in television infotainment, and how they are asked to consume this, cannot be
located solely in their theme groupings or overall calculated scheduling and
promotions. It may more so inhere in their specific audiovisual flow suturing
strategies: in the aesthetic audiovisual strategies (cinematic, graphic, digital,
or photographic) forming the television news overall "look" through floating logos, promos, newsroom sets, and ritualistic audiovisual repetitions. It
is this aesthetic that embeds dominant ideologies in differently configured
flows and in their reconfiguration of micro-level reports. These aesthetic
strategies, used to suture television fragments and relay dominant ideologies,
differ in different places and according to different dominant ideologies.

Hence, CNN International, in its overall digital-graphic aesthetics and
overall news-relaying formats, implies simultaneity and synchronicity, and
appears decentralized in its nonlinear and nonnarrative flow. This specific
flow embeds its core globalizing ideology, whereby it looks from above and
from nowhere at everything all the time, obscuring the true loci of power
whose interests it projects on the world.[37] It thus reconfigures its micro-
frame reports, or reports quoted from other television news, by placing
them as a frame within a frame, by enclosing them through running written
commentary on the bottom of the screen, or as a frame among others on the
screen. This results in the distancing of reports, in distracting attention away
from them and in their abstraction. Consider, for example, CNN's reconfiguration of Saddam Hussein's headline shot discussed above. Framed
within CNN's digital multimedia macro-frame aesthetics, Saddam's barbarian menace is diminished, distanced, and ridiculed.

On the other hand, Israeli and Palestinian television news, for example,
which at times seem like CNN, do not simply clone or replicate CNN, but
transform and recontextualize its quoted aspects within their own largely
cinematic oriented macro-frame aesthetic flow. This flow counters CNN's
digital aesthetic macro-frames evoking simultaneity, synchronicity, and sterile detachment, with frames that evoke linearity, diachrony, and warm
attachment through narrative audiovisual cinematic strategies. Through this
flow they embed their respective (and opposing) peripheral, dominant
national ideologies. This recontextualization occurs even when CNN
reports are quoted, either on the micro-level reshuffling of the quoted CNN
report shots, offering instead other headline shots, or in their embedding
within their respective cinematic aesthetic macro-frames. Hence, CNN's
headline shot of Saddam, unframed or "stripped'" of CNN's macro-framing
retains its menace (Israel) or heroism (Palestine) respectively.[38]

A good example of recontextualization can be seen in a comparative analysis of CNN and Israeli Channel 2 News coverage of the Twin Towers destruction, evidencing their respective ideological audiovisual frames. CNN's
headline shot and consequent framing of nondominant shots is characterized

by calm monotonous reporting showing, through lengthy and long shots taken from afar, spectacular beautifully framed images of the towers engulfed in smoke or of the planes slowly approaching the buildings and crashing into them. These headline shots accentuate by association the articulate and calm tone of onlookers or survivors that were interviewed in other reports. Likewise, it accentuates the orderly, calm, and efficient actions and movements of police, firefighters, or paramedics. CNN's reports are characterized by avoidance, detachment, and aesthetic sterilization of the horrific event and are aimed to convey the unshakable power of the United States. Conversely, in a report prepared by Israel's leading Channel 2 television station, material gathered by CNN and other networks is edited together according to the station's fashioning of suicide bombings in Israel. Thus, its headline shot is one that caught from an oblique angle the moment the plane approaches and crashes into the building, accentuating the moment of impact. This recurring shot is edited in fast pace with various other shots showing from different angles the moment of the crash. This editing is aimed at creating a shocking and panicking effect. Other reports gather together bits of hysterical reactions by survivors or onlookers, and select from the various tracking shots the few hand-held and unstable portions. These shots, figuring survivors, policemen, firefighters, and paramedics running, are edited together so that shift in direction and locale is emphasized, aiming at creating troubling disorientation and a sense of chaos. This panic-arousing report projects Israel's siege-typed audiovisuals briefly discussed in the previous section.

FORM AND IDEOLOGY

Another problem recurring in economic-political oriented textual analyses of television news concerns a certain confusion of textual codes with ideological codes whereby it is often claimed that a given formal configuration always implies a similar ideology. Hence, it should be pointed out that there is no predetermined and fixed correspondence between dominant ideologies and their figurations. It is therefore impossible to start analysis of formal configurations from their presupposed inherent codes, as do many. Although, as Fiske claims, it seems to be the case that "formal characteristics . . . bear the brunt of the ideological work," in and of themselves, formal configurations may embed different ideologies. Thus, cinematic or digital fashioning of television flows in and of themselves do not import any inherent meaning. What a particular formal configuration means depends on the specific dominant ideology orienting the figuration and can be better understood in relation to other forms of figurations oriented by other ideologies. In order to understand a given formal configuration, one needs to start from the study of the dominant ideology of the elite informing such configuration, and what functions it aims to fulfill for this elite within specific economic and geopolitical situations.

Hence, similarly figured events may embed different ideological functions. Thus, the Israel Broadcasting Authority's (IBA) panicky report of the Twin Towers destruction, which Americans might have considered sensationalist, was a projection on the U.S. tragedy of Israel's dominant siege ideology. This does not mean, however, as Fiske contends, that textual configurations, given their intertextual qualities, open reports to a variety of legitimate meanings. The fact that texts are sometimes differently understood implies that some of those understandings misinterpret the text at hand. This often occurs when researchers (or viewers for that matter) have no knowledge of the dominant ideology that oriented the textual configuration to begin with. Hence, such readings impose their own preconceptions and miss the specific address of the text at hand.

Also, economic-political oriented textual analyses of television news often tend to overlook the particular functioning of a particular ideology orienting the news' formal configurations and embedded in them. Thus, the studies mentioned earlier, which note the replication of governmental ideology by U.S. and European television news, imply a conception of ideology that does not consider its function of forwarding specific elite interests and strategies. For example, Dobkin's otherwise interesting study of the ABC television network lacks explanation of the underlying U.S.-first-world elite interests that forged the oppositions of terror and freedom that she notices so well; nor does she offer an explanation for why the United States attacked Libya. She seems to imply that the United States, somewhat in response to public opinion forged by television, attacked Libya because it sought revenge and narrative closure after a series of terror attacks.[39] However, the U.S. doctrine of isolating and targeting "hosting terror states" is better understood as aimed at maintaining the periphery's economic-political dependence on the first world through a divide-and-conquer strategy, a dependence that "rogue" states like Iraq or North Korea, and "terror hosting states" like Libya in the eighties and Taliban-led Afghanistan in the nineties, threatened. That is why states are usually targeted separately and that is also why only noncompliant "terror hosting states" are targeted, whereas compliant states that have funded terror (e.g., Saudi Arabia) are not targeted. These interests and strategies, which derived dominant ideologies aim to justify, have to be taken into account when analyzing their embedding in television news. They forge the very categorization and opposition of terror to freedom and the ways these figure in news reports.

CONCLUSION

Countering liberal and neoliberal postmodern approaches to television news, and differing from the verbal bias of ideological, textual analyses of television news, this study considers the analysis of audiovisual formations to be of uttermost importance if we are to understand the ideological work embedded in television news. The analysis of audiovisual formations in television reports and in the overall aesthetic audiovisual look of news broadcasts shows that television news audiovisually embeds dominant ideologies in ways that differ from written, oral, or cinematic modes of embedding. The containment of audiovisual association in news reports and the audiovisual aesthetic fabrication of the flow of news are powerful and distinct venues for dominant ideologies to be transmitted.

The next chapter considers how the post-Fordist-propelled dominant ideologies of the U.S. core-elites and of the Israeli-Palestinian periphery elites discussed so far are embedded in each party's respective mainstream television news macro-frames.

NOTES

This chapter is a revised version of my paper "TV News: Visual Ideological Frames and the Coverage of Terror Events," *Third Text* 73, vol. 19, no. 2, (March, 2005): 145–153.

1. See reviews of this approach in James Curran, *Media and Power* (London: Routledge, 2002).

2. One of the first to have used the concept of "frame" was Erving Goffman, who said that while everyone uses frames to organize and comprehend the complex world we live in there are several power groups (e.g., politicians or journalists) whose frames influence others. See Ervin Goffman, *Frame Analysis: An Essay on the Organization of Experience* (New York: Harper & Row, 1974). Tuchman, Gamson and Modigliani, Entman, and Gitlin developed the concept of "media frames." See Gaye Tuchman, *Making News: A Study in the Construction of Reality* (New York: The Free Press, 1978); William A. Gamson and Andre Modigliani, "Media Discourse and Public Opinion on Nuclear Power: A Constructionist Approach," *American Journal of Sociology* 95, no. 1 (1989): 1–37; Robert Entman, "Framing: Toward Clarification of a Fractured Paradigm," *Journal of Communication* 43, no. 4 (1993): 51–58; and Todd Gitlin, *The Whole World Is Watching: Mass Media in the Making and Unmaking of the New Left* (Berkeley: University of California Press, 1980). As defined by Gitlin, "Media frames are persistent patterns of cognition, emphasis interpretation, and presentation, of selection, and exclusion, by which symbol-handlers routinely organize discourse, whether verbal or visual" (*The Whole World Is Watching*, 6).

3. As mentioned, dominant ideologies are understood as ideas on the world that function to justify elite interests within specific economic and geopolitical configurations, propagated by elite-dependent modes of communication. See Antonio Gramsci, *Selections from Prison Notebooks* (London: Lawrence and Wishart, 1971); Louis Althusser, "Ideology and Ideological State Apparatuses," in *Lenin and Philosophy* (New York: NLB, 1971), 127–186; and Noam Chomsky and Edward S. Herman, *Manufacturing Consent* (New York: Pantheon, 1988). These ideologies are presently determined by processes of globalization. See Fredric Jameson, *Postmod-*

ernism; or, The Cultural Logic of Late Capitalism (London: Duke University Press, 1991); David Harvey, *The Condition of Postmodernity* (Cambridge, U.K.: Blackwell, 1991).

4. Stuart Hall, Charles Critcher, Tony Jefferson, John Clarke, and Brian Robert, *Policing the Crisis: Mugging, the State, and Law and Order* (Bakingstoke, U.K.: Macmillan Education Ltd., 1978), 60.

5. See Robert Picard, *Media Portrayals of Terrorism* (Ames: Iowa State University Press, 1993).

6. See David L. Paletz, Pewter Fozzard, and John Z. Ayanian, "The IRA, the Red Brigades, and the F.A.L.N. in the 'New York Times,' " *Journal of Communication* 32 (1982): 162–171; Yonah Alexander, "Terrorism, the Media, and the Police," *Journal of International Affairs* 32, no. 1 (Spring–Summer, 1978): 101–113; Gabriel Weinman, "The Theatre of Terror: Effects of Press Coverage," *Journal of Communication* 33, no. 1 (1983): 38–45. For a critical discussion of such "contagion" hypotheses, albeit from a freedom-of-the-press perspective, see Picard, *Media Portrayals of Terrorism*. In any case, even if we accept the notion of contagion, we must also take into account that such coverage may also support state repression or retaliation as suggested by A. Bethami Dobkin, *Tales of Terror* (London: Praeger, 1992).

7. Michael Delli Carpini and Bruce A. Williams, "Terrorism and the Media: Patterns of Presentation and Occurrence, 1969 to 1980," *Western Political Quarterly* 40, no. 1 (1987): 45–64.

8. Jaap Van Ginneken, *Understanding Global News* (London: Sage, 1998).

9. Picard, *Media Portrayals of Terrorism*.

10. On February 5, 2003, Secretary of State Colin Powel addressed the UN, where he used electronic intercepts, satellite photographs, and other intelligence sources to convince the Security Council that Iraq was actively working to deceive UN weapons inspectors and had links to al Qaeda. He stated that "this nexus between terrorist and states that are developing weapons of mass destruction can no longer be looked away from and ignored." The week after, he drew attention to an upcoming bin Laden tape calling on Iraqis to resist the U.S. invasion (aired on February 11, 2003).

11. Weinman, "Theatre of Terror," 44.

12. Dobkin, *Tales of Terror*, 57–58.

13. Stuart Hall, "The Question of Cultural Identity," in *Modernity and Its Futures*, ed. Stuart Hall, David Held, and Tony McGrew (Cambridge, U.K.: Polity Press, 1992), 131.

14. Jacques Derrida tackled this problematic notion in referring to the term *genre*, claiming that the very term *genre* implies a nonjustifiable boundary and origin or center, which immediately spreads and leads to a search for wider boundaries and further origins in an endless chain. Therefore, Derrida rejected the term *genre*. See Jacques Derrida, "The Law of Genre," *Critical Inquiry* 7 (Autumn 1980): 55–81.

15. Nick Browne, "The Political Economy of the Television (Super) Text," in *American Television: New Directions in History and Theory*, ed. Nick Browne (Langhorne, Pa.: Harwood Academic Publishers, 1994), 71.

16. Jane Feuer discusses the implications of these forms. See Jane Feuer, "Melodrama, Serial Form, and Television Today," in *Television: The Critical View*, ed. H. Newcombe (Oxford: Oxford University Press, 1984), 87–101.

17. An interesting discussion of the problematic relativism implied in dominant notions of intertextuality is discussed by John Frow. See John Frow, "Intertextuality and Ontology," in *Intertextuality: Theories and Practices*, ed. Judith Still and Michael Worton (Manchester, U.K.: Manchester University Press, 1990), 45–55.

18. A brief critical survey of these notions can be found in Daniel Dayan and Elihu Katz, *Defining Media Events: The Live Broadcasting of History* (Cambridge, Mass.: Harvard University Press, 1992).

19. Beverle Houston, "Viewing Television: The Metapsychology of Endless Consumption," in Browne, *American Television*, 81.

20. Houston, "Viewing Television," 82.

21. Houston, "Viewing Television," 88.

22. John Fiske, "Television Polysemy and Popularity," *Critical Studies in Mass Communication* 3 (1986): 391–408.

23. John Fiske, *Television Culture* (London: Methuen, 1987), 236.

24. John Fiske, "*Cagney and Lacey:* Reading Character Structurally and Politically," *Communication* 19 (1987), 399–426.

25. Hall et al., *Policing the Crisis*, 55.

26. Fiske, *Television Culture*, 301–302.

27. Fiske, *Television Culture*, 281–301.

28. Dobkin, *Tales of Terror*; Jack Lule, "The Myth of My Widow: A Dramatic Analysis of News Portrayals of a Terrorist Victim," in *Media Coverage of Terrorism*, ed. A. Odasuo Alali and Kenoye Kelvin Eke (Newbury Park: Sage, 1991): 86–111; Susan L. Carruthers, *The Media at War* (New York: St. Martin's Press, 2000).

29. While Fiske mentions Barthes's verbal poetic rhetorical strategies of exnomination, inoculation, and metaphorization, he does not address Barthes's image analyses of news photographs, and considers verbal rhetorical strategies as subservient to narrative story structuration. Fiske, *Television Culture*, 290–296.

30. Martin Esslin, *The Age of Television* (San Francisco: Freeman, 1982).

31. See also Peter Golding and Philip Elliot, *Making the News* (London: Longman, 1979); Hall, "The Question of Cultural Identity"; Hall et al., *Policing the Crisis*.

32. Fiske, *Television Culture*, 301–308.

33. Nitzan Ben-Shaul, *Mythical Expressions of Siege in Israeli Films* (Lewiston, N.Y.: The Edwin Mellen Press, 1997). See also the discussion of the siege dominant ideology in chapter 2.

34. The idea of clustering and the concept of the headline shot are closely akin to Dobkin's "ideographic clusters" and "nominalized images." See Dobkin, *Tales of Terror*, 6–8, 63. However, Dobkin's bias toward narrative and story structure, unwarranted in news' audiovisual figurations, searches for story clusters (e.g., melodramatic plots) rather than the more apt nonnarrative clustering by association. Also, what she terms "nominalized shots" are considered primarily in their fixing of meaning for consequent narrative development.

35. In fact, Fiske's overall postmodern perception of television as fragmented flow, offering an "open" text allowing viewers to read into it various meanings and resist dominant ideologies, forms part of the widespread idea of a television-made global interconnected and decentered community. It helps to efface the very clear first-world loci of power and the global dependence system they feed on. See also

Ben-Shaul, "Different yet Even: The Effacement of Power in Post-Structuralism: The Case of *Seinfeld*," *Third Text*, Special Issue 51 (Summer 2000): 75–84.

36. See Rick Altman, "Television/Sound," in *Studies in Entertainment: Critical Approaches to Mass Culture*, ed. Tania Modelsky (Bloomington: Indiana University Press, 1986), 39–54. Nevertheless, while it seems feasible that first-world global networks aim at positioning their viewers as consumers through calculated scheduling and promotion strategies, within the current post-Fordist economy, loyalty is secured through more diverse strategies catering to specific inclinations of targeted communities and individuals than those delineated by Altman.

37. See the discussion of U.S. core-elite ideology in its relation to post-Fordism in chapter 2.

38. Many Western-ethnocentric studies of television news derive their conclusions about television news from Western networks, which they consider cloned in the periphery. As this example implies, relational comparative analyses offer different perspectives.

39. Dobkin, *Tales of Terror*, 38, 78–80.

4

Competing Macro-Frames

THE POLITICAL ECONOMY OF CNN

The core-elites' need to coordinate and command the complex globalizing post-Fordist mode of production led to the enhanced development of computerized communication technologies resulting in the field of mass communications in digital broadcasting through global satellite and cable networks. The Cable News Network (CNN) is the major news network resulting from and ideologically promoting post-Fordist-propelled globalization. Founded in 1980 by Ted Turner, as post-Fordism aroused to dominance, CNN is now a division of the Turner Broadcasting System owned by Time Warner. CNN, which introduced the concept of 24-hour global news coverage, broadcasts primarily from its headquarters at the CNN center in Atlanta, Georgia, and has become the most watched 24-hour news network in the world, globally available to more than 1.5 billion people in over 212 countries and territories. The political economy of CNN is emblematic of post-Fordism in its being a privatized global satellite network owned by a huge core-elite corporation that merges media, computer, and telecommunications industries.[1] Its fluid and flexible globally cloned presence through world-spread offices, reporters, and broadcasts in other languages (e.g., Spanish, German, Turkish), while ideologically imparting a notion of decenteredness, is actually coordinated and structurally directed by its core-located U.S. headquarters. CNN's 24-hour "rolling-news" broadcasts position the network as a corporate and technologically driven core-elite global agent.[2]

CNN GLOBAL MACRO-FRAMES

Several studies of CNN uncritically consider its replication of core-elite ideology. Hence, Ingrid Volkmer's extensive study entitled *News in the Global*

Sphere: A Study of CNN and Its Impact on Global Communication, offers a glocal, freedom-of-the-press-perspective driven description of CNN.[3] She lauds CNN's different-yet-even core-elite ideology and the rhetorical strategies used to articulate it. Hence, in her noncritical appraisal of CNN, Volkmer considers the network to have global democratizing effects resulting from its technological innovations, its journalistic initiative, and its ideology-free "objective" coverage. Dazzled by the time-space compression brought about by global communication networks, she ascribes to CNN's global flow the power to bring about

> new forms of global political communication . . . affecting political action on many levels and on a worldwide scale. By *extending* political communication globally, CNN has *reshaped* the conventional agenda of international and "foreign" news and created a platform for worldwide communication. This *journalistic initiative* has altered the focus of global news in an interrelationship of changing political centers and peripheries, and has given a new meaning to news, journalistic values, *the setting of a global agenda.*[4]

Furthermore, following Roland Robertson's glocal perspective[5] Volkmer claims that "this switch to global determinants builds worldwide political structures through new demand for the integration of political action into a *new worldwide consensus of democracy which includes the co-existence of diverse realities and values*" (all italics mine). She then claims that through new stylistic devices such as " 'sound bite' semiotics, 'fact journalism,' [and] 'breaking news' stories instantaneously and simultaneously transmitted around the globe via 24-hour satellite," the overall objective view offered by CNN helps "spread" a global consensual democracy. This occurs, according to Volkmer, not only because of CNN's widespread vast constituency of viewers and its superior news-gathering facilities, but even more so because it is cloned in national stations. This, she says, is due to various types of "global" and "local" reciprocity—"defined as effects of re-broadcasting national political issues from a global viewpoint back into the political framework where they originated."[6] Finally, Volkmer presents a case study of CNN's *World Report* program, where CNN "hosts" "unedited" reports submitted by "local" stations around the world, which she takes to exemplify this democratic process.

While Volkmer uncritically identifies CNN's glocal core-elite ideology, the effects she ascribes to CNN are questionable. Thus, her presumption about the influence of CNN whereby, given its widespread flow and intense coverage of events, it sets the global agenda and influences governments' decisions and actions, has been convincingly shown to be wrong. This is the case, for example, in the often cited cases of CNN's coverage of human suffering, which are presumed by Volkmer and others to ipso facto bring forth democratic human sentiments (naturalizing thus their ideology of consensual democracy). Hence, as Susan Carruthers and others have shown, in all the humanitarian crises often cited as leading to intervention following global media attention, such as the coverage of the refugees that fled Rwanda in the wake of the 1994 massacres, the "ethnic cleansing" acts by Serbs in former Yugoslavia, and the starvation in Somalia, CNN and other core-elite global news networks followed governmental decisions rather than the other way around.[7] Moreover, while Volkmer cites such instances to exemplify how a shared humanitarian driven action was generated in face of television's imaging of human suffering, Carruthers shows that selective coverage of human suffering conforms to selective intervention, often driven by interests other than human democratic sentiments.

Likewise, Volkmer's claim that CNN's global network views dominate and are cloned within local TV stations given "various types of reciprocity," runs counter to other findings. Hence, in a study of how European networks treat material from global networks, Michael Gurevitch, Mark Levy, and Itzhak Roeh have shown how the same news is differently domesticated in each country.[8] As has been claimed earlier (chapter 3), although national networks often use material from global networks, this material is transformed within the national context according to the latter's elite interests rather than the core-elite interests. More interesting, however, is Volkmer's uncritical laudation of the democratizing effects of CNN's program *World Report*. Actually, what *World Report* ideologically embeds in this neutralizing ghetto of mostly peripheral reports on nonpolitical events is their perception as apparently "equal" or "even" to first-world perceptions. The mere constant reminder by the CNN anchor that these reports are subjectivist and do not present CNN views implies CNN's apparent "objective" and "neutral" hosting role, thus overvaluing CNN's core-elite ideology.

Hence, CNN, the most prominent U.S. core-elite global network, rather than offering objective, independent agendas, implements in its audiovisual macro-frame aesthetic configurations, dominant global-to-local ideologies, particularly those of the U.S. elites. CNN's aesthetic presents as universal these ideologies through a macro-level digital graphic designed flow, which implies simultaneity, synchronicity, and sterile detachment. It thus offers an apparent decentered, nonlocalized "global perspective" on local issues, perceived as being "included" within a decentered globality. It evokes simultaneity and synchronicity through swift, live, on-air shifts to CNN's "globally" spread reporters, and through constant use of split frames figuring different localities and running written reports on ongoing events at the bottom of the screen. It thus offers a notion of its being everywhere at once, thereby lending credibility to its selective coverage as being what's really important out of what there is around. Furthermore, CNN's overloading of the screen with digital graphics and coloring generates sterile detachment and distraction, thereby removing events away rather than bringing them closer. This aesthetic embedding of CNN's global-to-local perspective finds explicit expression in its many self-promoting bits, repeatedly aired in-between and within each of its programs.

CNN's representation of core-elite interests as universal is expressed in one such promotion bit as follows: The earth is shown slowly turning in dark space half lit, then the opposite side is lit and finally the whole globe is bathed in light. In voice-over we hear, "We cover the world from every perspective. Be the first to know on your TV, PC, or mobile." The two latter sentences in their broad-to-narrow-cast presentation (from TV to mobile) and in their personal address ("Be the first to know") verbally reinforce CNN's global-to-local reach. Another trailer advertising CNN's non-English broadcasts, embeds the locally cloned global perspective characteristic of post-Fordist customized capitalism with a tracking shot from above of a series of different items (a computer screen, a watch, a soccer ball) while in voice-over we hear, "Get a local view on global issues." Cloning through appropriation is another CNN strategy, exemplified in the aural use of English voice-over dubbing of any foreign-language speaking interviewee, whose voice is still heard in the background. This recurs, for example, in its program *World Report*, where reports offered by indigenous networks are aired. CNN's anchorwoman in this program significantly speaks English with a non-Western English accent. Moreover, as discussed above, this program embeds first-world ideology of glocalizing through equalizing, by presenting the alien reports as "unedited," emphasizing the subjectivist yet "equally" legitimate position of these reports.

THE POLITICAL ECONOMY OF THE OPPOSING PERIPHERAL ISRAELI AND PALESTINIAN NATIONAL MAINSTREAM TELEVISION NEWS

Israeli mainstream television news (the Israel Broadcasting Authority's Channel 1 television news and Israeli Channel 2 television news) and their opposing Palestinian Authority Television news (PATV) are exemplary cases of the political economy of mainstream communication networks in post-Fordist threatened peripheral states. I have chosen these stations for my study because, despite news broadcasts by other local and global channels, most Israelis watch the news on Channel 1 and Channel 2, while most Palestinians, at least insofar as local news is concerned, watch PATV.[9]

In Israel, the political-economic pressures of the core-directed post-Fordist globalization engendered from the 1980s a gradually expanding process of privatization and deregulation of the economy. This was evidenced in the field of mass communication in the move from a central Israeli Broadcast Authority (IBA) with one single television station tightly controlled by the government and maintained through an imposed tax on all citizens holding televisions,[10] to the slow legislation of laws instituting the Committee for Cable and Satellite Broadcasting in 1986 and of the Second Television and Radio Authority in 1990, which led to the eventual concession of broadcasting licenses to private companies that could broadcast commercials to fund their activities. This led to cable network broadcasts and the institution, after a seven-year "trial period" that already began in 1986, of the independent commercial television network Channel 2 in 1993 (following which, IBA television assumed the title Channel 1). However, the ensuing swift proliferation and commercialization of television broadcasts in Israel evidences the threatened situation of the ruling elites in the government-dominated statutory committees erected to supervise and regulate the private commercial broadcasts, particularly the news broadcasts. In sum, although privately owned and commercial, the mainstream news broadcasts of Channel 2 are highly regulated and mostly differ from the government-regulated Channel 1 in their presentation of Israel's official point of view in commercial "infotainment" guise.[11]

While the economic-political trajectory followed by mainstream Israeli television broadcasts moved from single to multichannel regulated broadcasts, the Palestinian mainstream broadcasts moved from nonregulated multichannel broadcasts to their regulation by the Palestinian Ministry of Information following the institution of the Palestinian National Authority (PNA) and its official television station (PATV) in 1993. Hence, PATV began operating amid other television broadcasters including local stations and pan-Arab satellite channels such as Al Jazeera, often illegally rebroadcasted on local channels. The PNA began to regulate local broadcasts through different measures such as the institution of compulsory licensing. In a survey conducted in 2002 there were forty-three (!) private television stations operating under the PNA jurisdiction, thirty of which where licensed by the Ministry of Information. These stations, funded through local advertisements, broadcasted only a few hours per day and offered very limited coverage of events. Nevertheless, and despite the overt position of the PNA concerning freedom of information, these stations were perceived as potentially destabilizing venues, as indicated in the insistence of Radwan Abu Ayyash, the Palestinian Broadcasting Corporation chairman, on "Broadcasters' Obligations towards Their Audiences in Times of Crisis."[12] Thus, while the proliferation of local private television stations and pan-Arab satellites were indices of post-Fordist globalization, the licensing and regulation instituted by the PNA, along with the clear propagandistic mission of PATV, are indices of the threatened situation of the PNA. This is also evidenced in Abu Ayyash's favorable description of the Ramallah-based private Watan TV founded in 1996 and supported by advertisements and nongovernmental organizations. The fact that Watan television was instituted under the auspices of the PNA and that its self-description as a patriotic station whose reporters' mission is to be "eye-witnesses to Israeli crimes," implies that it relayed PNA elite ideology along the lines of the PATV.

OPPOSING ISRAELI AND PALESTINIAN MAINSTREAM TELEVISION NEWS MACRO-FRAMES

Israeli mainstream television news and its opposing Palestinian Authority Television news evidence in their macro-frames the threatened peripheral states' double-talk ideology. This is symptomatic of the respective Israeli elites and the opposing Palestinian core-dependent ruling elites' weakened legitimacy and bargaining power brought about by the political economy of globalization.

This double-talk is aimed at enlisting the superpower to their side (despite the detrimental effects of globalization) while also reinforcing their national ideology so as to overcome competing subnational and supranational contesting trends. Hence, both parties' mainstream television news counters CNN's global-to-local abstract perspective by audiovisual ideological strategies emphasizing the territorial and the concrete. Their ethnocentric, internal-external perspective counters CNN's macro-frames of simultaneity, synchronicity, and sterile detachment through digital aesthetics, with frames of linearity, diachrony, and warm attachment through close looks. It evokes linearity and diachrony in macro-frames that attempt to generate flow through narrative audiovisual cinematic strategies and through micro-frame dramatic verbal narrative articulations, conveying a notion of their telling a unique story resonating previous endemic cultural themes pertaining to each nation. Hence, IBA's latest dominant promotion bit, revealing its cinematic macro-frame orientation, consists of slow, flowing, yellowish and brownish shots of a cinematic "sound stage." Their dominant micro-frame headline shots often convey close, warm communality or close, suffocating tension, through tightly framed shots of groups (of families, friends, and soldiers on Israeli TV or mass demonstrations and groups of stone-throwing kids on Palestinian television). These reports, in their style and format, contrast the stations' newsroom CNN look-alike styling, characterized by computer-graphic-generated turning globes, and by television and computer flickering screens. However, a closer look reveals these studios to be more warm colored, the anchors are closer to the camera and to each other, and the rendering of news is not neutral but rather patronizingly warm (IBA), panic arousing (Channel 2), or enticing (PATV). This contrasts the "cooler" digital look of the studio.

The IBA *Politica* (Politics) debate program is a good example of double-talk. The program, while quoting CNN styling and moderated-debate format (embedding first-world democratic ideology), generates a peculiar communal atmosphere. The show includes six to eight main guests and a moderator, seated at a round table, each presenting multidirectional opposing political views on current events (e.g., a right-wing settler, a left-wing secularist, an Orthodox Jew, and an Israeli Arab debating fund allocation to West Bank Jewish settlements). The guests are surrounded by a live audience allowed to applaud or question the guests and by large screens through which additional guests from around the country are invited to comment on the ongoing debate. This format, rather than clarifying opposing stands or illuminating the issue from different angles, always generates mutual multidirectional heated arguments and bickering, perceived as characteristic of Israeli communal "argumentativeness" and embedding a variant of Israel's nationalist unifying strategy whereby "we're all in the same rocking boat together." Likewise, PATV often uses MTV clip styling (embedding postmodern nonlinear empty self-referentiality)[13] in various song-typed transitional pieces. However, rather than evoking through digitized image layering a labyrinthine intertextuality, the dreamlike suturing of the fragmented flow references the images to Palestinian's dispersed existence (fragmentation) yet common dream of state and territory (dreamlike flow). Salient is one of the trailers to the Palestinian Authority Television news program. Accompanied by emotive, agitating Western music, whose flow sutures the images, we see a series of brief slow-motion shots, dissolving into each other, of agitated youths using slings to throw stones at Israeli tanks, Israeli soldiers dragging the body of a Palestinian, the back of an old man holding a club and facing flames, and a young man running along a borderlike fence defiantly waving the Palestinian flag. The trailer culminates in a shot of a young child raising his fingers to signal victory, superimposed by a caption reading "We Will Never Forget. We Will Never Forgive." Hence, these transitional pieces, rather than disjunction, imply a suturing attempt aimed at consolidating out of the spatial-temporal dispersion a unity of struggle for independence.

CONCLUSION

This chapter analyzes the overall macro-frames of CNN and of Israeli and Palestinian mainstream television news, arguing that they convey respectively the U.S. core-elite ideology and the double-talk opposing dominant ideologies of the Israeli and Palestinian core-dependent peripheral elites. The next part considers how each of the discussed networks covered through a variety of micro-frame reports the escalating reciprocal terrorist and constitutional nondiscriminatory violence that came out from the al Aksa Intifada and from al Qaeda and the U.S.-led "War against Terror." The close analysis of these various micro-frame reports reveals the specific ideological audiovisual frames developed by each network in its coverage of these conflicts.

NOTES

1. Daya Kishan Thussu, "Live TV and Bloodless Deaths: War, Infotainment, and 24/7 News," in *War and the Media: Reporting Conflict 24/7*, ed. Daya Kishan Thussu and Des Freedman (London: Sage, 2003), 122.

2. See in particular such claims as they relate to CNN as a U.S. core-elite agent of war propaganda in Robert E. Denton Jr., "Television as an Instrument of War," in *The Media and the Persian Gulf War*, ed. Robert E. Denton Jr. (London: Praeger, 1993), 27–42; George Gerbner, "Persian Gulf War, the Movie," in *Triumph of the Image: The Media's War in the Persian Gulf: A Global Perspective*, ed. Hamid Mowlana, George Gerbner, and Herbert I. Schiller (Boulder, Colo.: Westview, 1992), 243–265; Bruce Cumings, *War and Television* (London: Verso, 1992).

3. Ingrid Volkmer, *News in the Global Sphere: A Study of CNN and Its Impact on Global Communication* (Luton, U.K.: University of Luton Press, 1999).

4. Volkmer, *News in the Global Sphere*, 1–2.

5. Roland Robertson, "*Glocalization*: Time-Space and Homogeneity-Heterogeneity," in *Global Modernities*, ed. Mike Featherstone, Scott Lash, and Roland Robertson (London: Sage, 1995), 25–44.

6. Volkmer, *News in the Global Sphere*, 2–3.

7. Susan L. Carruthers, *The Media at War* (New York: St. Martin's Press, 2000), 205–229; Steven Livingston, "Beyond the 'CNN Effect': The Media-Foreign Policy Dynamic," in *Politics and the Press: The News Media and Their Influence*, ed. Pippa Norris (London: Rienner, 1997), 291–318; Steven Livingston and Todd Eachus, "Humanitarian Crises and U.S. Foreign Policy: Somalia and the CNN Effects Reconsidered," *Political Communication* 12 (1995): 413–429.

8. Michael Gurevitch, Mark Levy, and Itzhak Roeh, "The Global Newsroom: Convergences and Diversities in the Globalization of Television News," in *Communication and Citizenship: Journalism and the Public Sphere*, ed. Peter Dahlgren and Colin Sparks (London: Routledge, 1991), 195–212.

9. According to the Israeli Audience Research Board (www.midrug-tv.org.il/), the majority of Israelis watch the news on Channel 1 and Channel 2, while Palestinians participating in a 2002 survey testified that they watch PATV, particularly the news bulletins and other news programs, and that it functions as their main source of local news. See Radwan Abu Ayyash, *Broadcasters' Obligations towards Their Audience in Times of Crisis (The Palestinian Intifada as an Example)* (master's thesis, Center for Mass Communication Research, Leicester, U.K.: Leicester University, 1992), 80.

10. The IBA began its television broadcasts only in 1967, after the government,

earlier fearing it would not be able to control information, realized that Israelis were watching Arab stations. Symbolic of the government's approach to television as propaganda at the time was the opening of broadcasts with the live coverage of the army parade celebrating the Israeli 1967 war victory. See Oren Tokatly, *Communication Policy in Israel* [in Hebrew] (Tel Aviv: The Open University of Israel, 2000), 86.

11. See also Noam Yaron, *Channel 2: The New Statism* [in Hebrew] (Tel-Aviv: Fetish, 2001).

12. This is the title of Ayyash's MA thesis written on Palestinian media. Ayyash, *Broadcasters' Obligations.*

13. John Fiske, "MTV: Post-Structural, Post-Modern," in *The Postmodern Presence*, ed. Arthur Asa Berger (London: Altamira Press, 1998), 166–175.

II

MICRO-FRAME CASE STUDIES

In the following chapters a comparative micro-frame analysis is conducted of the differing cohering headline shots and contained associational editing in CNN, Israeli, and Palestinian television news that framed the salient violent events pertaining to two conflicts: al Qaeda terror and the U.S.-led "War against Terror"; and the al Aksa Intifada. As mentioned, the coverage of these conflicts has been chosen because they exhibit a direct core-periphery conflict (U.S.–al Qaeda) and an indirect one (the al Aksa Intifada). As will be seen, the comparative analysis of the frames developed by the parties in their coverage of each conflict not only reveals their dominant ideologies but also the difference in the coverage of direct or indirect core-periphery conflicts, differences that evidence the overall global divide-and-conquer U.S. core strategy.

SOURCES

The analysis is of reports using the same audiovisual material (where available) and of reports using the exclusive audiovisual material gathered by each party.

CNN

Beyond my own recordings, I have relied on CNN's web archive, which can be accessed through the CNN website.[1] Another source, detailing all CNN reports on the subjects dealt with here can be found at the Vanderbilt University Television News Indexed Archive.[2]

Israeli Channel 1 & 2

The reports taken from Israeli Channel 1 & 2 television news consisted mostly of my own and my research students' recordings. I received additional recordings from the Film and Television Department Archive at Tel Aviv University.

Palestinian Authority Television (PATV)

Beyond my own and my research students' recordings from PATV television and website broadcasts, I relied on some (scant) analyses of PATV broadcasts offered by Palestinian and non-Palestinian researchers and on the raw, unedited recordings made by the Middle East Media Research Institute (MEMRI), which monitors the Palestinian Authority television around the clock. I have also relied on MEMRI's and other Israeli and Palestinian monitoring agencies' selected materials and translations from the Arabic language.[3]

SELECTION OF REPORTS

The selection of reports was event oriented and was focused on salient media coverage of specific violent events[4] or by recurring media coverage of categories of violent events.[5] This is because in the coverage of violent events, the audiovisual overwhelms verbal narration and commentary, and because it is in such televised crucial reports that prevailing verbal biased ideological decoding fails. Therefore I have watched almost all of the coverage directly related to and dominated by the specific events mentioned or by the categories of events mentioned. This has left out secondary or indirect reports on chosen events or of categories of events.

APPROACH

This study deals with overall trends decoded from in-depth qualitative detailed analyses of reports on salient events rather than from "neutrally" statistical and quantitative-based analyses.[6] It is based on an interpretation of the reports oriented by my general comprehension of the ideologies presumed to be informing these reports, and on an understanding that formal qualities bear the brunt of any ideological work (see chapter 3 above). Although the interpretation of formal tropes is based on intertextual and semiotic studies of visual and aural configurations, it places most emphasis on immanently meaningful headline shots and the formal or thematic associational interrelations between shots (see chapter 3).

TROPES ANALYZED

While I have dealt with each report as an enclosed entity, since the particular meaning of a report inheres in the particular dominant interrelation of its sounds and visuals, I have derived this enclosed analysis from the figuration and recurrence of various formal and thematic aspects across reports, which provide the general meaning informing the specific variation exhibited in each report. The recurring tropes analyzed were:

Established historical, generic, or specific intertextual references either through the use of archival material or through formal allusions. For example, framing the 9/11 attack within the context of the Pearl Harbor attack; presenting the hunt after bin Laden as a wild west–styled hunt; showing a dead Palestinian in a cruciform posture.

Immanent references. For example, the recurring figuration of the Twin Towers collapse gathered a particular immanent meaning having to do with a unique, huge disaster.

Formal semiotic decoding.[7] For example, the general meaning imparted by a close-up, which presents spatial proximity, may often create intimacy with the selected image, or may be used for symbolizing such, since it detaches it from its surroundings.[8] However, these initially attributed general meanings, which anchor a particular report, often shift within it, so that the meaning of the same figuration may change or even be reversed within the context of a specific editing of a report (e.g., whereas one close-up among many long-shots may impart a feeling of intimacy, a report consisting of sequential close-ups with only one long shot inserted may impart a claustrophobic feeling). Such general meanings were initially attributed to the following formal tropes:

Relative length of shots
Type of camera angle used (high angle, low angle, eye level, oblique angle)
Shot distance (long shot, medium shot, close-up)
Camera movements (static, panning, zooming, tracking, hand-held shooting)
Shot composition (balanced/imbalanced, orderly/chaotic)
Shot toning (e.g., bluish, greenish, reddish)
Day or night scene
Recurrence of shots within a report or across reports
Editing pace (slow, rapid, accelerating)
Type of transition (cut, dissolve, superimpositions, fades, etc.)
Type of graphics (e.g., maps, lists, quotes)
Logic of shot sequencing (chronological, associational, verbal dependent, etc.)
Type of reporter intervention and positioning (voice-over, voice off, syn-

chronized voice and image of reporter, reporting while standing or while walking, etc.)
Type of interviewer-interviewee interaction (monological, dialogical)
Aural tone of the reporter (calm, agitated, dramatic, inciting, patronizing)
Format of the report (e.g., personal story, summary account)
The type of image selection and focus (e.g., groups, individuals; scenery; type of nature framing; etc.)

In the presentations that follow, each analysis is preceded by a factual account of the reported events and is followed by an analysis of the frames evolved by each network in respect of the events covered.

NOTES

1. A list of websites referenced in this study appears in the bibliography.

2. For CNN go to edition.cnn.com/. For example, for 9/11 go to edition.cnn.com/ SPECIALS/2001/trade.center/multimedia.invest.html; for Vanderbilt go to tvnews .vanderbilt.edu/TV NewsSearch/TVNsearch.pl?SID = 20040906992767333&UID = &CID = 24022&auth = &code = TVN.

3. For a fuller description of these monitoring agencies and their websites see, in chapter 6, the subsection "Israeli and Palestinian Coverage: The Incitement Frame."

4. E.g., the 9/11 attack, the initial bombing of Afghanistan, the killing of the child Muhammad al Durra in the crossfire between Israeli soldiers and Palestinian militants; the lynching of two Israeli soldiers in Ramallah; the Israeli army incursion into Jenin.

5. E.g., the hunt for bin Laden in Afghanistan; the global hunt after al Qaeda; the bin Laden tapes; Palestinian suicide bombings; Palestinian funerals; Israeli army incursions; Israeli targeted killings.

6. For a good survey of qualitative approaches see Thomas R. Lindlof and Bryan C. Taylor, *Qualitative Communication Research Methods*, 2nd ed. (London: Sage, 2002).

7. The general semiotic and intertextual comprehension of the formal tropes listed mostly derives from the following studies: Roland Barthes, *Mythologies* (Paris: Seuil, 1957); Roland Barthes, *Image, Music, Text* (New York: Hill and Wang, 1977); Christian Metz, *Film Language: A Semiotics of the Cinema* (Chicago: University of Chicago Press, 1990); Christian Metz, *The Imaginary Signifier* (Bloomington: Indiana University Press, 1982); Julia Kristeva, *Desire in Language* (New York: Columbia University Press, 1980); Stuart Hall, "Encoding/Decoding," in *Culture, Media, Language: Working Papers in Cultural Studies, 1972–1979*, ed. Stuart Hall, Dorothy Hobson, Andrew Lowe, and Paul Willis (London: Hutchinson, 1980), 128–138; Stuart Hall, "The Determination of News Photographs," in *The Manufacture of News: Social Problems, Deviance, and the Mass Media*, ed. Stanley Cohen and Jock Young (London: Constable, 1981), 176–190; John Fiske, *Television Culture* (London: Methuen, 1987); Arthur Asa Berger, *Media Analysis Techniques* (London: Sage, 1988); Mieke Bal, *On Meaning-Making: Essays in Semiotics* (Santa Rosa, Calif.: Polebridge

Press, 1994); Jonathan Bignell, *Media Semiotics* (Manchester, U.K.: Manchester University Press, 2002); John Fiske and John Hartley, *Reading Television* (London: Routledge, 2003).

8. On the semiotics of the close-up, see Yuri Tynyanov, "The Foundations of Cinema," in *Russian Formalist Film Theory*, ed. Herbert Eagle (Ann Arbor: Michigan Slavic Publications, 1981), 81–101.

5

Reports on al Qaeda Terror and the U.S.-Led "War against Terror"

THE 9/11/2001 ATTACK

On the morning of September 11, 2001, suicide terrorists hijacked four passenger jets. They crashed two of them, American Airlines flight 11 and United Airlines flight 175, along with their passengers, into the World Trade Center Twin Towers in Manhattan, New York. The third plane, American Airlines flight 77, was crashed into the Pentagon in Washington, D.C., and the fourth, United Airlines flight 93, crashed in Somerset County, Pennsylvania, due to the actions taken by some of its passengers against the hijackers. The Twin Towers collapsed, and a wing of the Pentagon was damaged. Over three thousand people were killed in these acts of suicidal terror.

CNN Coverage

Most reports on the event by CNN can be classified into four main categories: reports on the actual attack (planes hitting the buildings, interviews of eyewitnesses, rescue efforts); reports on family members of the victims (interviews, personal stories, gatherings); public statements by or interviews with U.S. politicians and army, police, and firefighter commanders; and reports on official ceremonies (funerals, memorials, etc.).[1]

The immediate main dominant headline shot of CNN's coverage of the event consists of a distant view from across the river of the Twin Towers engulfed in smoke, with the Statue of Liberty in view between the camera position and the World Trade Center (WTC). The shot is lengthy and stable and is accompanied by the calm monotonous voice-over of CNN reporter Aaron Brown in the quiet morning. It offers a spectacular and beautifully

73

framed bluish image of the towers engulfed in smoke. The second immediate dominant headline shot is that of the second plane's slow approach from screen left to the towers and its crash into one of them. This shot is also, relative to the event covered, long in duration, distant, and silent, projecting a sense of quiet detachment. These headline shots accentuate by association the calm and emotionally detached portions figuring in nondominant reports, undervaluing the incidental images and sounds of chaos and disorder.[2] Particularly memorable is a shot of hundreds of sheets of paper slowly and quietly swirling in the dusty air. Except for a couple of long-shot images of a person diving to his death from the building, in all of the reports scanned there are no images of dead bodies on the scene or of them being evacuated, and there are very few and bloodless images of the wounded.[3] Most images of the survivors are of people fleeing the scene, some of them covered with dust.

Likewise, the CNN reports accentuate the orderly, calm, and efficient actions and movements of police, firefighters, or paramedics through stable panning shots of rows of ambulances, police cars, or fire trucks on their way to or from the WTC. There are some "warmer" hand-held tracking shots of firefighters as they walk amid the dust, smoke, and debris toward or from the crash site (e.g., the September 14 report by CNN's Deborah Feyerick). These shots consolidate a rather detached symbolic heroization of firefighters by CNN, a heroization that forms part of an overall orderly patriotic rallying. Emblematic of this heroization are two reports: one covers the funeral for the New York Fire Department chaplain killed in the WTC attack (September 15), focusing on and culminating in a close-up of his white helmet (the firefighter's helmet became one of the event's leading icons). The other shows President Bush embracing a firefighter on top of a pile of debris at the WTC on a sunny day, as happily cheering firefighters and other rescue workers gather around him (September 14).

In several reports on official ceremonies, such as that on the memorial ceremony held in the Yankee Stadium on September 25, the main emphasis is on the orderly conduct of the audience and on the U.S. flag, constantly shown waving, usually in slow motion, in different sizes and from different angles. Another major category of reports concerns the families of victims of the event. These usually include an interview with the family members in their house as they describe their loved ones and how they died, shots from the crash sites, and family photographs of the victims. The general tone of these reports is relatively calm and monotonous in contrast to the emotionally laden subject matter. This is due to the recurring standardized formation of the reports and the overall articulate and contained voices and presence of the interviewees (with occasional but quickly restrained sobbing).[4] Other reports are about relatives seeking their missing loved ones. Most of these reports seem less staged than the reports on victims and are held outdoors in the street, while photographs of the missing relatives are inserted. However, these interviews are also relatively restrained, as exemplified in CNN's Paula Zahn's interview with New Yorker Chris Mills, who is searching for his girlfriend (September 13). In this report we see the two sitting on a bench across the river with sunny Manhattan in the background, while Mills calmly and articulately describes what seems to have happened. Along with the interview the photograph of his missing girlfriend appears over a blue matrixed screen, which is also the dominating background for two very small screens, one showing the interviewee and the other showing the crash site.

The reports on families of the victims seem to deliberately select victims from different social classes (e.g., a lawyer, a window-washer), ethnic origins (e.g., Mexican American, African American, Anglo-Saxon), religions (e.g., Christian, Jew, Muslim), and locations (mostly from different U.S. states but also from around the world). As implied in the reports' uniform formation and occasional commentary, the variety is aimed at both unifying the country around the event and at framing the event as a global attack on the free world at large, since it includes foreigners; but also since Americans originate from different parts of the world and what unites them is their freedom. In general the CNN reports of the event are in line with the messages delivered by President Bush, New York Mayor Rudolph Giuliani, and other U.S. officials who addressed the nation through CNN and other networks, whereby America (or New York) is strong, things are under control, and uncompromising retaliation will soon follow.

Emblematic of the government and of CNN's detached, patronizing framing of the event is an interview held on September 11 by CNN's reporter Mary Slobogin with Dr. Jeffrey Mitchell, a trauma expert, on how parents should behave in front of their children in the face of the atrocity. The interview is conducted in the living room of Dr. Mitchell's country house (we see his blossoming garden in the background). The room is bathed in light and he is dressed casually. Dr. Mitchell quietly suggests that parents remain calm, tell their children that in open societies, as opposed to police states, these things can happen, but that open societies prevail in the end. He tells the reporter that parents should block their children from watching television reports of the event. The interview is interspersed with shots showing the planes crashing into the Twin Towers. The deliberate attempt of the report is to sooth the impact of the traumatic images through encompassing them within the overall calm ambience of the interview. This general approach was still evident a year or so after the event, when two other headline shots took the lead. One shows a tilted smoke-blackened part of a wall of one of the towers over a pile of rubble, imparting a sense of a ghost-like location, reminiscent of World War II images of the ruins of Berlin. The other shows two firefighters trying to straighten a tilted pole bearing the U.S. flag while a third firefighter looks up at the flag. This headline shot conveys the patriotic resurrection of the Flag and the Nation, reminiscent of the famous Iwojima photograph taken by Joe Rosenthal. Both of these headline shots reference the official U.S. symbolization of World War II, and through such swift symbolization they elevate and distance the event. Another interesting point is that during the ceremonies commemorating the 9/11 attacks a year later (2002), CNN hardly showed any images of the planes crashing into the towers or of their collapse.

In general, the CNN reports are characterized by avoidance, detachment, and aesthetic sterilization of the horrific event.

Israeli Television News Coverage

The extensive news coverage of the event by Israel's Channel 1 and Channel 2 television stations in the days that followed the event (September 11–18, 2001) mostly used material gathered by CNN and other networks insofar as the crash of the planes into the buildings is concerned. However, these materials were then edited according to the two stations' fashioning of suicide bombings in Israel (see following chapter). Thus, their headline shot was one that caught from an oblique low angle the moment of the plane approaching and crashing into the building, accentuating the instant of impact. This recurring shot was edited with various other shots showing this moment from different angles. This editing is aimed at creating a shocking and panicking effect. Israeli television also showed several times shots of people jumping out of the Twin Towers windows to their death. Other reports gathered together snippets of hysterical reactions by survivors or onlookers and of the few wounded and burned victims who were filmed by other networks. It also selected from the various tracking shots the few hand-held and unstable portions. These shots, figuring survivors, policemen, firefighters, and paramedics running, were edited together so that shift in direction and locale was emphasized, aimed at creating troubling disorientation and a sense of chaos. Another series of reports were exclusive to Israeli stations, achieved through their correspondents in the United States. These longer reports, while covering the general grieving, focus on the Jewish and Israeli families and communities who suffered loss of relatives or of friends. In these reports emphasis is on gatherings of people mourning together, lighting candles, and crying (CNN also had several such reports, but they are brief and often bracketed as personal or poetic impressions). Most of these reports were shot at night in dimly lit streets, conveying a feeling of anxiety. They were often fashioned like travelogues, whereby the hand-held camera wanders the streets showing gatherings of people. These reports, like the editing of those on the crash itself, also resemble news reports in Israeli television in the aftermath of suicide bombings in Israel. This formal resemblance is replicated in the reporters' commentaries, which often mention their feeling of déjà-vu and emphasize that now Americans are experiencing for the first time what Israelis have been experiencing for a long while. There is also a sense of patriotic comfort, patronization, and even cynicism in their words, as if the novice terror-experience of the Americans will breed sympathy and respect in the United States for terror-ridden Israel. The Israeli coverage usually omitted from its audiovisual rendering of the event correlations to images of suicide terror events in Israel. Such correlation however was made in the formal framing of the event, and as such replicated the explicit correlation made in the studio by the experts' commentaries and in the official reaction of Prime Minister Ariel Sharon, who reiterated that terror is terror and that the terror in the United States as well as those who perpetuate this terror are one and the same as the terror and those who perpetuate it in Israel. Furthermore, Sharon's reaction echoed George W. Bush's own statement that these terror acts are attacks on the free world by an axis of evil. Bush thus coupled Palestinian terror with global Islamic terror and placed Israel on the side of the "free world."[5]

This overall panic-arousing report, formally projecting on the event Israel's siege-type audiovisuality, attests to Israeli television double-talk, whereby Israel's situation is posited as both unique but also as forming part of the global divide between the forces of evil and the free world.

Palestinian Authority Television (PATV) News Coverage

The relatively scarce coverage of the event by PATV in the days that followed the event (September 11–18, 2001) mostly used material from CNN. Similar to the Israeli TV editing of this material and in accordance with its own fashioning of reports on violent events, Palestinian television accentuated the moment of impact compiled from various brief shots taken from different angles and positions. However, what stands out in the PATV coverage is that the event is given minor importance and is constantly related to reports on Israeli military deployments and movement in the West Bank and Gaza Strip. This emerges in the use of two adjacent frames, a smaller one showing in a loop the crash of the airplanes into the Twin Towers and a larger frame showing movements of Israeli tanks and the demolition of Palestinians' houses by Israeli bulldozers. The two frames often run parallel images of debris at the WTC site and in the Palestinian Authority–held territories. The parallelization becomes clear once we see that, rather than images of the crumbling of the towers, the PATV chose as its main headline shot of the WTC event images of the debris of a low-rise building with bulldozers clearing the debris; a shot that appears compositionally similar to the images of debris of houses destroyed by Israeli bulldozers. This audiovisual parallelization is fictive, insofar as the WTC bulldozers were clearing the debris created by terror attacks, whereas Israeli bulldozers were creating the debris.

This presentation of the events offers a generalized, abstract image of destruction and violence, detached from the specific causes and origins of each image. However, for those Palestinians sympathizing with al Qaeda and who rejoiced at the WTC attacks, this parallelization could also imply that the images of the WTC debris were a retaliation for the U.S.-backed Israeli destruction of Palestinian houses (clearly articulated by bin Laden in his tapes, particularly in the tape aired by Al Jazeera television on October 30, 2004).

This general audiovisual rendering of the event was in line with the official reaction of the PA president Yasser Arafat and of the Palestinian spokeswoman Hannan Ashrawi, who sent their condolences to the American people while repeatedly claiming that what happened in New York is similar to the violence and state-terror of Israel toward the Palestinians. This was accompanied with a warning that Israel was already using the WTC event to conduct further acts of aggression against the Palestinian people. However, it was also in line with the widespread support of Palestinians for al Qaeda's attack as an act of retaliation for Israel's behavior toward the Palestinians. This audiovisual double meaning attests to PATV's double-talk.

THE WAR AGAINST TERROR

The U.S.-led response to the September 11, 2001, terrorist attacks, termed by the Bush administration as a "War against Terror," consists of a series of ongoing military, intelligence, diplomatic, and financial operations worldwide, whose primary objective is to unearth and destroy the radical Islamist terrorist organization of al Qaeda and its affiliated groups, and to topple or deter any state from hosting or supporting them. It also involves security measures within the United States that eventuated in the establishment of the Department of Homeland Security. The department is divided into four divisions: Border and Transportation Security; Emergency Preparedness and Response; Chemical, Biological, Radiological, and Nuclear Countermeasures; and Information Analysis and Infrastructure Protection. Existing agencies placed under the department's authority are the U.S. Coast Guard; Customs Service; Immigration and Naturalization Service and Border Patrol; the Animal and Plant Health Inspection Service of the Department of Agriculture; the Transportation Security Administration; and the Secret Service.

The major military operation within this "War against Terror" was initially assigned the name Operation Infinite Justice but was soon changed to Operation Enduring Freedom (following concerns that the first name might offend the Muslim community, as Islam teaches that Allah is the only one who can provide infinite justice). President George W. Bush, in his September 20th address to a joint session of Congress and his October 7th public address, stated that the military objectives of Operation Enduring Freedom included the destruction of terrorist training camps and infrastructure within Afghanistan, the capture of al Qaeda leaders, and the elimination of terrorist activities in Afghanistan. The operation commenced on October 7, 2001, with "early combat operations [including] a mix of air strikes from land-based B-1, B-2 and B-52 bombers; carrier-based F-14 and F/A-18 fighters; and Tomahawk cruise missiles launched from both U.S. and British ships and submarines."[6] In late September, CIA forces entered Afghanistan to organize existing Afghan anti-Taliban forces (primarily the loose coalition of groups called the Northern Alliance). As the war progressed, the U.S. advance teams were joined by army special forces and special forces units from the navy and air force, and ultimately by regular army ground troops and units from coalition partners such as the United Kingdom and Australia. Since December 2001, the U.S.-led coalition's primary military focus has been on locating remnants of the Taliban and al Qaeda that did not surrender but fled into remote areas of the country. Coalition operations have included investigative and intelligence-gathering components aimed at locating or uncovering threats to the United States and other coalition members as part of the global campaign to disrupt the worldwide operations of al Qaeda. Since the fall of the Taliban government in late 2001, small- and medium-scale operations have focused on Taliban or al Qaeda military positions, such as caves and bunkers, usually in remote rural areas.[7]

CNN Coverage

Out of the salient reports on the event by CNN I have focused on four main categories: reports related to the air strike campaign in Afghanistan; reports on tapes by bin Laden; reports on the bin Laden hunt; and reports on the global hunt for suspected al Qaeda members.

Reports Related to the Air Strike Campaign in Afghanistan

The emblematic headline shot of the air strikes figures "surgical" bombs being launched and their targets shown as precisely hit through the missiles' monitoring camera. These images are replicated in shots of F-18 jets at the moment of take-off from the deck of an aircraft carrier, a similar shot of a Tomahawk missile being launched from a missile cruiser, and the apparent result of these launches in the form of greenish night-shots of the sky with occasional explosions and of the "before and after" black-and-white aerial shots of bombarded sites provided by the Pentagon in its briefings on the war.[8] The launching shots emphasize power, speed, and high technology while the shots on the results of the attacks emphasize firepower (the night shots) and precision (the "before and after" shots). The overall framing of the air strikes is based on a *centering-on* coverage, a motif recurring in the reports and comments made by Secretary of Defense Donald Rumsfeld, White House press secretary Ari Fleischer, and General Richard Myers, chairman of the U.S. Joint Chiefs of Staff. This approach is audiovisually achieved through recurring images that zoom in to center on the perpetrators. These include maps targeting bin Laden's compounds in Afghanistan,[9] and inserts of bin Laden's defiant video released a day after the attacks began. This targeting approach reaches its zenith in aesthetic-ideological framing of military preparations enhancing the military might of the U.S.-led coalition being built. Characteristic of these preparations is the digitally supported figuration of high-tech equipment with a global reach.[10] The overall framing of the air strikes is akin to the compilation of science-fiction and western film genres as found in films such as *Star Wars*. This military-might centering-on approach also entails the calculated reconfiguring of headline shots within macro-frame aesthetics, establishing a correlation between the perpetrator and world instability. Hence, in CNN's airing of a Pentagon briefing, the shots of the missiles' monitoring cameras are superimposed on the bottom part of the screen with the online live fluctuation of the stock market expressed in digitized figures. These targeting aesthetics abstract the attack, and isolate and decontextualize bin Laden by pinpointing through animated maps and satellite images his presumed "exact" location.

Reports on the Bin Laden Tapes

Since the September 11 attacks, several video and audio taped messages from bin Laden or his close associate Ayman al-Zawahiri have been aired. The tapes contain warnings on future attacks and ideological rationalization for past and future attacks. These addresses often distinguish between the U.S. government (termed "heathen" or "crusaders") and its allied governments in core states or in core-dependent Arab states whom it blames for the wrongdoings done to Muslims, and between the peoples in these states to whom it explains that al Qaeda's acts are retaliations for the wrongdoings done in their name to Muslims, based on "an eye for an eye" rationale. Bin Laden calls on these peoples to topple their governments if they want to avoid future attacks. There are also addresses to Iraqis and Palestinians, encouraging them to resist the attacks on them and the occupation of their lands. Another source of videotapes dated from before the 9/11 attack was found by CNN correspondent Nic Robertson in Afghanistan and reported by CNN on August 19, 2002. From these al Qaeda internal tapes CNN showed excerpts that focused on al Qaeda guerrilla/terror training, instruction tapes on how to devise explosives, experimentation with chemical substances on dogs, al Qaeda's relations to other radical Islamist groups, and al

Qaeda's use of high-tech equipment.[11] In most externally aimed tapes we see bin Laden alone or with a couple of his associates in medium shot sitting or crouching in front of the camera while delivering their message. The camera is usually static, as are the speakers. The background is often a bare cave wall. Bin Laden preaches in a monotonous, calm, and contained manner, half-raising his arm and his index finger to accentuate a point. The overall lack of audiovisual information as to where the speakers are or when the message was taped, along with the static and monotonous speakers, conveys a sense of floating detachment. Beyond the obvious need to hide their whereabouts, the deliberate obliteration of any background seems to be aimed at concentrating attention on the words spoken and the person delivering them as if they are being delivered from "above" (there is one video where bin Laden is shot from below against a blue sky). This is in contrast to the taped messages of suicide bombers before they set out on their mission or of kidnappers sending their ultimatums, usually with the victims crouching up-front, where despite the need to obliterate any hint of the location of the terrorists there is usually a background with information about the group or the individuals involved. These floating messages seem to attest to bin Laden's global-aiming reach.

CNN's coverage [12] excluded serious attention to bin Laden's ideology. The excerpts shown from the tapes are exclusively about threats he makes toward the United States or its allies. Focus on the early bin Laden messages is mostly on whether he hinted at or claimed responsibility for the September 11 attacks or for other attacks. The audio tapes usually elicit a discussion of whether the speaker is indeed bin Laden, concluding that it probably is him. The video tapes are mostly discussed in respect to when the tape was recorded in that this could give an indication of when he was still alive; on whether his whereabouts can be determined from the tape (not really)[13]; on assessing his physical condition (e.g., in one tape one of his arms does not move; in another tape rumors of his having kidney problems are mentioned; his fatigue or aging are discussed in other tapes, etc.); on identifying coded verbal or audiovisual messages he might be conveying (e.g., does he carry a weapon or not; what is the meaning of the Yemen-styled dagger at his waist?)[14]; and on identifying other persons figuring in the tapes. The commentaries often mention bin Laden's "boasting" about the success of his attacks.[15] However, the audiovisuals themselves do not support the experts' later comments. In all the tapes bin Laden seems calm, detached, and composed, and his tone is monotonic, making it hard to read his particular physical condition or any boasting into his speech. The self-presentation of bin Laden in the tapes and the thrust of the commentary on him boil down to a headline shot of bin Laden as "Most Wanted." In several reports summarizing past appearances of bin Laden and his associates the "Most Wanted" frame is made explicitly manifest, as in CNN's Mike Boettcher's report from

October 8, 2001, a day after the U.S. air strikes on Afghanistan started, where he introduces bin Laden and some of his closest al Qaeda advisors, namely al-Zawahiri and Mohammed Atef. The report shows the three of them together in some of their taped appearances. As each is introduced by the commentary he is audiovisually singled out by having his head circled in whiter tones, as if he were a target. The report then cuts to a blue matrixed screen with a close-up photo of the encircled man in the top left portion of the screen while beneath the photo appears a list of his presumed terrorist activities. This shot then cuts to brief images of the destruction caused by the group's alleged terror acts.

While most of these reports are based on the tapes prepared by bin Laden for broadcasting to the world, the tapes found by Nic Robertson seem to be interorganizational and aimed at internal viewing, as explained on CNN by Rohan Gunaratna, an expert on al Qaeda and the author of *Inside al Qaeda*, who comments on these tapes throughout Robertson's reports on them. Robertson prepared a series he called "Terror on Tape," which is based on these tapes and consists of five reports entitled "Chemical Tests," "Roots of Hatred," "In Training," "Explosive Force," and "Face of Evil."[16] The reports detail chemical gas experiments on dogs, lessons on making explosives, training of terrorist tactics, the organization's use of the Internet to communicate, and previously unseen images of bin Laden and his top aides. The overall audiovisual frame forwarded by Robertson in his reports is that of a film-noir thriller whereby we follow an investigator trailing the evildoer. The images are a tightly knit and quick-changing collection showing explosions, fire, shooting, men bursting into houses, and men chanting religious slogans. In an accompanying report to the series Robertson details how he procured the tapes at great risk to himself. Crouched on a stool, bathed in film-noir shadowy-styled lighting with a red-bricked dilapidated wall behind him that connotes "Afghanistan," Robertson confides to the camera, almost in whispers, the tale of how he was approached by one of his informants about the tapes, how despite the possible treachery he went on a seventeen-hour drive from Kabul through treacherous terrain to a remote part of the war-torn country to view the tapes, and how, having seen the tapes, he realized that he had invaluable incriminating material on bin Laden and al Qaeda.

The commentary on the tapes and their editing consists mostly in presenting the guerrilla and terror training of al Qaeda fighters as extremely threatening; in presenting their widespread contacts with other terror groups around the world; in presenting their instructional videos on how to prepare bombs as having reached an unprecedented, dangerous degree of sophistication; and in presenting the disturbing images of the dying moments of a dog exposed to poison gas as the ultimate, menacing evil (Robertson remarks about the laugh of one of the executioners). The experts interviewed comment throughout on how this material is instructive in regard to the organization's level of sophistication, evil nature, vanity, and global threat, with particular recurring emphasis on the chemical experiments and the use of the Internet to communicate. While this may indeed be the case, the audiovisuals used to support these claims fall short of conveying the threat ascribed to them. The collection of tapes more resembles a home library with scratched, half-torn, and scrabbled stickers. The training segments do show highly skilled maneuverings, but these are performed by a very small number of participants; the segments on al Qaeda's global reaching connections with other radical Islam groups show two small groups of militants from Eritrea and Burma walking in the woods, shouting slogans or having a swim in a river[17]; the instructional segments and detailed sketches on how to prepare bombs resemble home-made cooking recipes and home-video cooking programs; the segments used to support the claim on al Qaeda's high-tech communications show a caption in Arabic and one computer screen with a video of bin Laden preaching; the segments used to frame bin Laden's "vanity" deduce this without clear reasoning from the hidden cameras he used to record the interviews conducted with him by foreign correspondents, and from recordings of CNN's broadcast of the 9/11 attacks; the chemical experimentation with dogs, while horrifying in their presentation of a puppy dying in agony from gas poisoning, show an impoverished environment rather than the sophisticated laboratory that would be expected from the verbal account accompanying them.[18] Hence, it is hard to accept the reporter's conclusion that we are facing a highly sophisticated, global reaching, and dangerous enemy. In fact, contrary to the verbal reports and commentaries, the images selected and their editing together frame the image of an evil yet poor, low-tech, and small organization.

What mostly stands out in this collection of reports (as well as in the overall approach to the event by CNN) is the investigative attitude of the reporter and the commentators in their search for clues to the whereabouts of the events shown. The frame of investigation is dominant in CNN's approach. Another, consequent frame is that of amplification, based on the deductive-based rhetoric following the investigation frame and leading to an audiovisually unsupported amplification of the group's capabilities. Hence, there is an evident discrepancy between the audiovisual framing of bin Laden and al Qaeda as a poor and small organization and the verbal commentary that presents the group as a highly sophisticated, far-reaching, and large terror organization. This discrepancy seems to me both to legitimate the U.S.-led coalition use of immense firepower and troop deployment against one of the world's poorer nations (hence the verbal amplification of the group's size and sophistication) and to reassure viewers that al Qaeda will be easily destroyed (hence, its audiovisual presentation as a poor, small group).

Reports on the Bin Laden Hunt in Afghanistan

The seeming poverty, smallness, and "backwardness" of al Qaeda vis-à-vis coalition forces is enhanced in the presentation of the military ground operations conducted by the special forces in their hunt for bin Laden and the remnants of al Qaeda and the Taliban in the hills and caves of Afghanistan. Hence, on the one hand we see the impersonal professionalism and efficiency of the coalition ground forces,[19] all geared up with high-tech equipment, while on the other we see the barren and desolate mountainous terrain being searched by them. Here, too, there is a discrepancy between the commentary and simulations used, and the documentary images. Hence, while the commentary offers descriptions of an underground, highly sophisticated chain of interconnected caves, often simulated through 3D animation, the documentary images show an impoverished and backward environment.[20] In an emblematic report by CNN's Matthew Chance in which he visits the rubble of camps in Darunta, eastern Afghanistan, we see several panning shots of barren land, some with small piles of mud bricks, remnants of the walls of small houses that the reporter calls "buildings," in which he claims that hundreds of al Qaeda terrorists trained, and in which they performed their terrible chemical experiments on dogs. The report then focuses on the subject of chemical weapons and the reporter's Afghan guide is seen lifting a torn nylon bag described as the remains of a chemical container. Hence, the pathetic and dramatic reporting on the dangerous and chemical-weapon-experimenting evil group is supported by images of a bare land with piles of mud bricks and some torn nylon bags. These images, rather than presenting a highly sophisticated organization, are reminiscent of a wild west movie scene from which the outlaws have fled, and the reporter along with his Afghan (i.e., Indian) aides are part of a posse on the hunt. This intertextual framing of Afghanistan as the wild west conforms to George W. Bush's constant claim that he will "smoke out" bin Laden from his caves. The wild west posse frame is the leading one in most reports showing U.S. special forces on the hunt for al Qaeda in the hills and caves of Afghanistan. It complements the "most wanted" frame found in framing of the tapes by bin Laden, and together with the investigative frame they isolate and decontextualize bin Laden and al Qaeda from the sociopolitical and geopolitical context of their activities, recontextualizing them within the wild-west posse-outlaw framework.

Reports on the Global Hunt for al Qaeda

The *Star Wars* cum wild west investigation framing of al Qaeda, decontextualizing bin Laden from the region, was simultaneously complemented by an investigative *spread and shift* frame, recontextualizing him within an abstract "global" decentered sphere. Within this frame CNN presented al

Qaeda as elusive, with potential appearance anytime and anywhere. This supported the U.S. government's imperative for national and personal security measures and for a global coalition against a global intruder. For example, in CNN's Bill Delaney's report (October 1) on the increase in gun sales, gleaming guns on shelves are shown along with neon-lit shooting galleries, where ordinary citizens are shown shooting at targets. One interviewee explains that he bought a gun because despite CIA and FBI efficiency, these agencies cannot watch up for every individual twenty-four hours a day/seven days a week, whereas terror can strike anywhere and anytime. The report also shows a photo of bin Laden being used for target practice. This elusive national and global threat also frames the series of reports on whether civil liberties should be curtailed, in which the dissenting voices are made irrelevant due to their constant intercut with images and sounds of the 9/11 attacks, as in CNN's Candy Crowley's report (September 24) and in the many reports showing excerpts of U.S. Attorney General John Ashcroft talking (with the U.S. flag invariably in the background) about the tremendous terrorist risks facing Americans.[21]

CNN's replication of the government's trailing of al Qaeda often focuses on the peripheral states' crackdown on illegal financial activities. In all these reports the emphasis is on the ease with which money can go undetected in these states (despite the fact that bin Laden's money was trailed to West European core states such as Britain, Belgium, and Germany). Thus, CNN's Lisa Barron reported on Asian nations enacting tougher financial laws in an effort to crack down on their black-market banking (such as the tighter monitoring and freezing of suspected assets in offshore financial sites in the Philippines and other nations), acts presented by an interviewed economist as "the best way" to wage war against the terrorists (October 3).[22] These series of reports legitimated the core U.S. government's pressuring of dependent peripheral states to cooperate with the core in the monitoring of the global flow of money.

In CNN's Kitty Pilgrim's report dealing with the global "synchronized" decline of the world economy following the 9/11 attacks, we see a high angled shot showing Manhattan in twilight with intermittent shifts to interviewed economists around the world and diagrams of eastern states' economic decline. While the commentary emphasizes that the cost of decline is heavier for "the East," the images of a darkening Manhattan and the audiovisual arrangement of peripheral locations centering on Manhattan indicates the decline in the core (October 11). As can be seen in this report, CNN's enhancement of the globalization of the al Qaeda threat was aesthetically framed through the station's macro-frame strategy of simultaneity and synchronicity. Hence, through shifts to CNN's "globally" spread reporters, a global communication net was woven, isomorphic to al Qaeda's presumed terror net. Hence, the reports that followed the investigation within the

United States, by backtracking the cell members that bombed the Twin Towers through shifting among U.S. locations, soon turned to cover a world-wide hunt after al Qaeda and related radical Islamist dormant cells around the world, through reports coming in from Britain, Belgium, the Nether-lands, France, Germany, the Philippines, Pakistan, Morocco, Lebanon, Kenya, Russia, South America, and so forth.[23] These reports framed the notion of an unsealed America open to borderless, spreading terror, and legitimated the U.S. government's policy of a tightening national and world-wide surveillance. For example, CNN's Eileen O'Connor's report from Sep-tember 20 gathers incidental images of the hijackers taken by a hidden camera positioned above an ATM machine and by an airport camera, as well as images of a crowded sidewalk, insinuating the difficulty of finding a ter-rorist once he or she has entered the country.

These reports on "the murderers among us" found response in a series of reports on the need to tighten security, as in CNN's David George's report on an Iceland airport's use of new biometric technology based on facial rec-ognition. In it, a series of shots shows relaxed passengers in airports lending their eye, their finger, their palms, or their face to high-tech recognition devices, intercut with images of the collapse of the Twin Towers on 9/11 (September 27). The notion of borderless terror was also framed through dominant headline shots of world maps on which crisscrossing arrows trace the terrorists' movements across the globe, as in CNN's Sheila MacVicar's reports from October 3 on the case of one Jordanian terror suspect, where the disparity between the Jordanian court decision that the suspect had no links to al Qaeda and that of Western intelligence sources' claims that he did, is resolved in favor of the intelligence sources primarily through maps of the globe crisscrossed by arrows and dollar signs ("the money trail") that move back and forth from Jordan, to Europe and the United States. Similar in approach in this respect is CNN's Brent Sadler's report consisting of an exclusive video of Ziad Samir Jarrah, provided by his family, which they claim shows that he could not have been living a "double life as a terrorist" (September 18), where we see a map with an arrow pointing to the Ba'aka Valley in Lebanon, from which the report cuts to a home video of the sus-pect dancing at his wedding with his face incriminatingly circled in white, thus audiovisually undermining the family's claim of his being innocent and offering the images of further potential suspects. Finally, there is CNN's Maria Ressa's report from September 19, on Philippine officials who had uncovered a plot to attack the United States six years before 9/11. In it we also see a map of the world with arrows showing the movements of the sus-pects across the globe along with grainy black-and-white police videos of apartments being searched, images of the WTC destruction, and close-ups of the suspects, distorted to lend them an evil look.

The dominant audiovisual framing of these reports, legitimating the above-mentioned interests, use styling that recalls televised figurations of international espionage and televised science fiction thriller/horror series about aliens and biological or chemical weapons (e.g., *Nikita, The X-Files,* and lately, *24*). Hence, these reports, particularly those on core states, usually start with stable images and natural sounds of nice, quiet, and well-kept urban or suburban neighborhoods, slowly focusing through oblique angles on the location where the suspects stayed, showing the entrance door (dramatically emphasizing the number on the door), and moving with hand-held cameras, as if breaking in, into the interior, where rooms in disarray and found documents are shown. Many of these reports include night shots of unidentified wet and dimly lit streets with police car lights flashing and official agents carrying metallic suitcases or dusting for fingerprints behind curtained windows.

Furthermore, in a series of reports focusing on suspected biological and chemical substances found in such apartments, there is frequent use of the glowing green, pink, red, purple, and yellow colors associated with such substances, and the reports include shots of laboratories and enlargements of photos taken through microscopes.[24] This styling can be seen, for example, in CNN's Susan Candiotti's report on how the FBI identified two hijack suspects from evidence gathered in south Florida. The report is dominated by night scenes showing the reporter in the street under a somber dark-blue sky surrounded by reddish street lights (September 12). Such styling is further enhanced in her report on another suspected hijacker, Marwan al Shahidi, where she starts with bright day images of a quiet Florida town, commenting on the fact that the suspect led a normal life. The screen then focuses on a large black dumpster where flight manuals were found, followed by a filtered darkening of the screen showing among other things FBI agents dusting for fingerprints behind a curtained window, a low angled close-up of the number 12 on the suspect's apartment door, and recurring images of the menacing black dumpster (September 19). This format reiterates CNN's Betina Luscher's report from September 18, where she explains how German officials were unaware that their country was host to three suspected terrorists in the attack on the United States, by showing beautiful and peaceful images of Hamburg in the sunset, cut to an agent holding two metallic bags and climbing steps, and then to a fast series of oblique close-shots of the door, the bell, and the evocative opened mail-slot in the door of the apartment of Mohammed Atta and two other of the 9/11 hijackers, from which a beam of light reminiscent of *The X-Files* series erupts.[25] Several lead-ins to these reports enhance the international spy genre intrigue frame in their inclusion of digital composite bluish and greenish enigmatic "title sequences" figuring condensed images of the cell members, airplanes, money, Islamic symbols, and passports. These maps, diagrams, and styling, suggesting a spreading, borderless terror, imply that whatever the historical and regional context for the rise of bin Laden or al Qaeda, it is advisable to eradicate them in order to reach a solution in face of the spreading threat to the globe.

Israeli and Palestinian Coverage

Although Israeli mainstream television coverage of the U.S. "War against Terror" exceeded somewhat the almost total lack of coverage by Palestinian mainstream television, the reports by both sides were highly ethnocentric and therefore minor and disengaged. The Israeli coverage relied almost exclusively on reports by CNN and Sky News, which it basically rebroadcast, including the transliteration of the latter's commentary and their "global" detached view of the events. What mostly stood out in the commentary offered by Israeli reporters was unfettered praise and admiration for the efficiency of the U.S. Army and for the resoluteness of the U.S. administration and of President Bush in their widespread and multileveled globally expanding approach to terror. Overall, Israeli television tried to import CNN's framing of that war into its coverage of Israel Defence Forces (IDF) incursions into Palestinian towns, as will be detailed in the following chapter. This transposition embedded the Israeli government attempts to equate Yasser Arafat and the Palestinian suicide bombing attacks to bin Laden and al Qaeda, in order to legitimate its own "War against Terror," as evidenced in Israel's framing of Operation Defensive Shield on April 2002 (see following chapter). Hence, following Arafat's condemnation of suicide bombings on December 16, 2001, Channel 1's Arab-affairs analyst Ehud Yaari strangely compared Arafat's position to bin Laden's in Tora Bora. He commented that Arafat, under intense international diplomatic pressure, and military pressure from Israel, was desperately appealing to Hamas and Islamic Jihad to restrain suicide bombers.

More interesting, however, is the Palestinian television network's deliberately scant coverage of the "War against Terror." This was due to the widely popular support for the radical Islamic Hamas and Holy Jihad movements' position in favor of bin Laden and against the U.S. attack on Afghanistan. The PNA (Palestinian National Authority), seeking to enlist the United States to its side, feared that such anti-Americanism would totally side the United States with Israel and ease Israel's reoccupation of the territories under PNA control, leading to the dismantling of the PNA, while also fearing that pro–United States coverage of the war would lead to its internal delegitimating and would empower the radical Islam movements. Hence, the Palestinian Authority television network almost entirely refrained from covering the war. Emblematic of this overall approach was the PNA barring of television journalists from filming the October 2001 clashes between the PNA security forces and pro–bin Laden and anti-American demonstrators coming out of the Islamic University in Gaza, in protests that spread to universities in Bethlehem and Nablus. Likewise in a later incident the Associated Press reported that Palestinian authorities had told journalists not to report on the bin Laden posters and slogans ("Our dear bin Laden, hit Tel Aviv") used in a funeral procession for a Palestinian killed in the West Bank town of Hebron. There are several quotes from Arafat and other PNA core-dependent officials expressing their troubled position in face of bin Laden's expression of support for the Palestinians (in one of his videos he says, "Neither America nor the people who live in it will dream of security before we live it in Palestine"). Hence, Palestinian Information Minister Yasser Abed Rabbo was quoted in the *Chicago Tribune* on October 9, 2001, as saying that while the Palestinians were victims of "continuous crimes and killings . . . this does not justify or give cover for anyone to kill or terrorize innocent civilians. We don't want any crimes committed in the name of Palestine." Arafat, too, in an interview with *The Sunday Times* on December 15, 2002, at his Ramallah headquarters said, "Why is bin Laden talking about Palestine now? Bin Laden never, not ever, stressed this issue, he never helped us, and he was working in another completely different area and against our interests." Likewise, Ahmed Abdel Rahman, an aide to Arafat, quoted by Jamie Tarabay (Associated Press) on December 15, 2002, said,

> The Palestinian Authority and other Palestinian groups have all declared that they are fighting the occupation of the land of Palestine and not anywhere else. . . . We are not fighting the entire world, civilization and people. . . . We don't want our just cause to be used as a cover by Sharon and his government to continue their escalation—as though if the U.S. is fighting al Qaeda in Afghanistan, so Israel is fighting al Qaeda in Palestine.

This powerful show of opposition against the PNA led the PATV on October 9, 2001, to call for calm and unity, warning of a complete breakdown of the social order. In the evening it aired a special program during the main news broadcast, "The Regrettable Events in Gaza," in which representatives of all major factions stressed that their main enemy was Israel and called for national unity.

NOTES

1. The leading CNN headline for the reports on the 9/11 attacks was "World Trade Center and Pentagon Bombings," which later, after George W. Bush in his public address described the attack as an act of war, turned into "America Under Attack." The overview of the analysis offered above is based on CNN reports of September 11–21, 2001. These include the following recurring live video and video footage: smoke from collapsed WTC towers; efforts of rescue workers; pictures of

debris; pictures of Osama bin Laden; the planes approaching from left and right of screen in regular or slow motion followed by the camera as they hit the towers; distant views and closer ground-level views of the collapse of the towers; Dr. Mark Heath's video; President Bush's address to the nation; Pentagon fire; excerpt from Donald Rumsfeld's statement; excerpt from Taliban ambassador to Pakistan Abdul Salam Zaeff's statement; public statements, notably by New York City Mayor Rudy Giuliani, Hillary Clinton, New York Governor George Pataki, and Secretary of State Colin Powell; interviews, notably of former CIA director Robert Gates, former State Department spokesman James Rubin, Pennsylvania State Police officer Frank Monoco, Aviation Security Intl. spokesman Philip Baum, EU international affairs minister Javier Solana, spokesman from St. Vincent's hospital, director of the Center for the Study of Terrorism Magnus Ranstorp, and interviews with family members of victims such as Cathy and Alice Hoglan, mother and wife of Flight 93 passenger Mark Bingham, and Jim Ogonowski, brother of the pilot of Flight 11.

2. These are mostly found in footage taken by CNN affiliates and aired on CNN (WABC, WAV, etc.).

3. There is one exceptional interview held by CNN correspondent Dr. Sajay Gupta on September 17 with burn victims in a hospital where we see their slightly burned and scarred faces. There are also images of dead bodies covered by the U.S. flag but these appear within retrospective poetic reports such as a retrospective poetic and cinema-styled report on Rudolph Giuliani's performance during the event. This type of retrospective uses slow motion, dissolves, and dramatic sad music to convey the grief and heroism of the rescue workers rather than the horror, chaos, or massive death within the buildings. It should be pointed out that within reports dealing with the investigation of suspected terrorists we do see brief, dramatic images of the event taken by amateur cameras or other networks, but these images of the atrocity are framed within the context of the intensive and effective search for the perpetrators.

4. E.g., CNN's Thelma Gutierrez on the Bolourchi family (September 18); CNN's Kathy Slobogin on the Falkenberg family in Maryland (September 25).

5. In his address to the Israeli parliament's "Special Solidarity Session" from September 16, 2001, Ariel Sharon said, "Last week, the empire of terrorism struck at the heart of our courageous friend, the greatest democracy on earth—the United States of America. We have assembled here today in Jerusalem, the capital of Israel, the capital of the only democracy in the Middle East, in order to bow our heads in sorrow and deep mourning over the deaths of innocent citizens in New York and Washington. . . . The criminal massacre of innocent citizens was designed to cause the demoralization—and loss of security—of U.S. society in the country that is the exemplar of the rule of law and order. . . . The issue of terrorism—to my regret—is not new to us. The State of Israel has been fighting Arab, Palestinian and Islamic fundamentalist terrorism for over 120 years. Thousands of Jews have been murdered in terrorist attacks. . . . The pain of the bereaved American people is familiar to us—very familiar to us. The war against terrorism must be an international war, a war by a coalition of the free world against the forces of terrorism. . . . This is a war between good and evil—between humanity and those who thirst for blood. . . . We know this. We have been in this war for many years. . . . We were not surprised by Arab, Palestinian and radical Islamic terrorism. Arafat chose a strategy of terrorism and established a coali-

tion of terrorism. Terrorist actions against Israeli citizens are no different from bin Laden's terrorism against American citizens. Terrorism is terrorism and murder is murder. . . . And we must remember: It was Arafat who—dozens of years ago— legitimized the hijacking of planes. It was Palestinian terrorist organizations who began to dispatch suicide-terrorists. . . . I congratulate President George W. Bush on his decision to create a coalition against terrorism. This coalition must fight against all terrorist organizations, including those belonging to Arafat: the Presidential Guard, Force 17, parts of Arafat's security services that are collaborating in terrorism, the Tanzim and Fatah, who are causing a great part of our losses, as well as their partners to Arafat's coalition of terrorists—the Islamic Jihad and Hamas, Hizbullah and the PFLP. If we are invited, we will join, and in the meantime, the President of the United States has warmly thanked us for the help that we have already provided. If we are invited, we will join because we are already fighting terrorism in any case."

6. The website of the Global Security Organization at www.globalsecurity.org/military/ops/enduring-freedom.htm.

7. This was compiled from different sources, in particular the Human Rights Watch report found at hrw.org/reports/2004/afghanistan0304 and the website of the Global Security Organization.

8. See, for example, CNN's Kyra Phillips' visit to a pilot training center in Fallon, Nevada (September 19); CNN's Jeanne Meserve's reports from the *USS Theodore Roosevelt* battle group as it headed toward the Mediterranean Sea (September 20); CNN's Kyra Phillips's report on a U.S. Navy helicopter unit's training for combat (September 19); CNN's Catherine Callaway's report on Fort Rucker, Alabama (October 3) showing pilots ready, night bombardments, various helicopters and their firepower; an F-18 launched from the deck of an aircraft carrier (October 7); a low-angle shot of a Tomahawk missile launched from an aircraft carrier in the night with the U.S. flag waving (October 7); CNN's Jamie McIntyre's report (October 8) on the Pentagon reviews of the first night of air strikes in Afghanistan and General Richard Myers's assessment of the damage to some Afghan targets (October 9); CNN's Walter Rodgers's report from the *USS Carl Vinson* in the Arabian Sea (October 9) poetically portraying in bluish images jets launched over the sea and reddish images of the jets in their hangars on board the ship; CNN's Brian Nelson's mystifying report on the B-2 Stealth bomber, in which he tells that many of the bombs it dropped carried the names of firefighters who died in 9/11 (October 11); Defense Department video of Tomahawk missiles being launched from a missile cruiser (October 12); video of explosions in Kabul, Afghanistan, at night (October 27); or CNN's Frank Buckley's report on the war "through a pilot's eyes" (November 9).

9. See, for example, CNN's Miles O'Brien's report based on computer animation showing some of the military targets in Afghanistan. The animation is of B-52 planes followed by a virtual camera as they fly toward their targets, whose written names (Kandahar, Kabul) float over the animated terrain (October 7).

10. See CNN's Kathy Slobogin's report (October 1) on a Washington university studying new ways to fight wars using new technologies and ways of thinking, where computer images and hardware exemplify notions of simultaneity of information, speed of headquarters-to-ground relations, satellite monitoring, and so forth; or see CNN's Steve Young's report on how spy satellites are helping the Pentagon with the war in Afghanistan (December 20).

11. Following is a timeline of these airings, their broadcasting circumstances, and some of the main messages included in them (compiled from timelines offered by CNN's web page entitled "Timeline: Terror on tape, bin Laden messages," the *Union Tribune* website at www.signonsandiego.com/news/nation/terror/20040415-0720 -binladentape-glance.html, and by my own tracing of the tapes' broadcasts):

October 7, 2001—On the day the United States began dropping bombs on Afghanistan, a video of bin Laden is broadcast by Al Jazeera. In it bin Laden praises the September 11 attacks. The tape shows him seated in a cave next to Ayman al-Zawahiri and Sulaiman Abu Ghaith. Bin Laden demands that "every Muslim must rise to defend his religion. The wind of faith is blowing."

November 3, 2001—Bin Laden in a videotape broadcast on Al Jazeera condemns U.S. air strikes in Afghanistan and claims the United States is targeting civilians. He says that true Muslims celebrated the attacks on 9/11.

December 13, 2001—The U.S. Defense Department releases a videotape in which Osama bin Laden is shown at a dinner with associates in Kandahar, Afghanistan, on November 9, 2001, saying that the destruction of the September 11 attacks had exceeded even his optimistic calculations and that he knew of the September 11 plan several days before the attacks. The tape was found in a private residence in Jalalabad, Afghanistan.

December 26, 2001—Al Jazeera broadcasts excerpts of a videotape of bin Laden in which he accuses the West of hating Islam and says, "We say our terror against America is blessed terror in order to put an end to suppression, in order for the United States to cease its support for Israel."

January 31, 2002—Despite Al Jazeera's objections, CNN airs an interview that Al Jazeera conducted with bin Laden in October 2001. In it bin Laden says in respect of the 9/11 attacks that, "if inciting people to do that is terrorism, and if killing those who kill our sons is terrorism, then let history be witness that we are terrorists."

April 15, 2002—Al Jazeera broadcasts a videotape showing Osama bin Laden with Ayman al-Zawahiri, who says, "The great victory that has been accomplished can only be attributed to God alone. . . . Those 19 brothers who went out and gave their souls to Allah almighty, God almighty has granted them this victory we are enjoying now." The tape also includes a September 11 hijacker giving a farewell message.

August 19, 2002—CNN's Nic Robertson reports on a large archive of al Qaeda videotapes obtained by him in Afghanistan. The archive is said to include sixty-four videotapes that span more than a decade. Nearly all the tapes predate the September 11 terror attacks, but one tape includes recorded segments from televised news reports of the attacks on New York and Washington, including CNN coverage. The portions shown include images of chemical gas experiments on dogs, lessons on making explosives, terrorist training tactics, and previously unseen images of bin Laden and his top aides.

October 6, 2002—Al Jazeera broadcasts an audiotape of bin Laden, in which he says, "That's why I tell you, as God is my witness, whether America increases or reduces tensions, we will surely answer back in the same manner, with God's blessing and grace, and I promise you that the Islamic youth are preparing for you what will fill your hearts with horror, and they will target the centers of your economy until you stop your tyranny and terror."

November 12, 2002—Al Jazeera broadcasts a brief audiotape in which bin Laden warns of future attacks against U.S. targets and praises the terror attacks in Yemen, Kuwait, Bali, and Moscow, Russia. It warns U.S. allies, saying, "Just like you kill us, we will kill you."

February 11, 2003—bin Laden calls on Iraqis to defend themselves against a U.S. attack and to carry out suicide attacks against Americans. He adds that any nation that helps the United States attack Iraq, "[has] to know that they are outside this Islamic nation. Jordan and Morocco and Nigeria and Saudi Arabia should be careful for this war, this crusade, is attacking the people of Islam first." The tape was broadcast by Al Jazeera.

February 13, 2003—In an audiotape obtained by Al-Ansaar news agency bin Laden reads a poetic last will and testament saying he wants to die a martyr in a new attack against the United States.

April 7, 2003—In a twenty-seven-minute audiotape obtained by the Associated Press in Pakistan, bin Laden calls on Muslims to rise up against Kuwait, Saudi Arabia, and other governments he claims are "agents of America," and calls for suicide attacks against U.S. and British interests.

September 10, 2003—Al Jazeera, on the eve of the anniversary of the September 11 attacks aired a video where bin Laden is shown walking through rocky terrain with al-Zawahiri while two taped messages accompany the video. In one, bin Laden praises the "great damage to the enemy" on September 11 and mentions five hijackers by name. In the other tape, al-Zawahiri threatens more attacks on Americans.

October 18, 2003—Al Jazeera airs an audiotape of bin Laden where he threatens to launch suicide attacks against the United States and any countries that assist it in Iraq. He says that most Americans are "a mob with no trace of good morals," and that, "We will continue to fight you as long as we have weapons in our hands."

January 4, 2004—bin Laden says on an audiotape broadcast on Al Jazeera that the U.S.-led war in Iraq is the beginning of the occupation of the Gulf states for their oil. He calls on Muslims to keep fighting a holy war in the Middle East and says, "There is no dialogue except with weapons."

April 15, 2004—bin Laden offers a "truce" to European countries that do not attack Muslims, saying it will begin when their soldiers leave Islamic nations. The tape gives the countries three months to start pulling out their troops. It vows revenge against the United States for the Israeli assassination of Hamas founder Sheik Ahmed Yassin (who was killed March 22 in an Israeli targeted helicopter attack in Gaza City).

May 6, 2004—In an audiotape message bin Laden posted on an Islamic website, he offers twenty-two pounds of gold to anyone who kills Coalition Provisional Authority head Paul Bremer, top U.S. military officers, and UN officials. The message suggests that the bounties are being offered in response to rewards that the United States is offering for wanted figures in Afghanistan and Iraq, including bin Laden.

October 29, 2004—In a videotape aired on Al Jazeera four days before the U.S. presidential elections, bin Laden addresses the American people saying, "Your security is not in the hands of Kerry or Bush or al Qaeda. Your security is in your own hands. Any nation that does not attack us will not be attacked." He also said the attacks of September 11, 2001, were the result of U.S. foreign policy in Arab lands, specifically referring to Lebanon and the Palestinians.

12. CNN posted this introduction to its timeline on bin Laden's tapes: "Several controversial videotapes recorded by Osama bin Laden were made public after the September 11 attacks on the United States. The Bush administration has cautioned U.S.-based media against airing 'prepared propaganda tapes' from bin Laden. Administration officials suggest the recordings, provided by bin Laden to the Al Jazeera network, might contain coded messages to so-called terrorist 'sleeper cells.' U.S. officials are balancing their concern with protecting intelligence sources with the goal of building the public case against bin Laden."

13. See, for example, CNN's David Ensor's report (November 17), or CNN's Wolf Blitzer's report (December 27) on the possible location of Osama bin Laden.

14. See, for example, Islam expert Bernard Haykel's interview with CNN's Paula Zahn, in which he is requested to analyze potential signals that Osama bin Laden and his al Qaeda organization may be sending followers (October 10).

15. These emotionally driven characterizations of bin Laden are reminiscent of President Bush's and other officials' statements after the 9/11 attacks, which they described as "cowardly."

16. See edition.cnn.com/SPECIALS/2002/terror.tapes.

17. There are other videos aired prior to the invasion into Afghanistan that show terrorist training camps, but these are self-promotional and probably aimed at recruiting fighters. These pre-9/11 tapes can be seen, for example, in CNN's Satinder Bindra's report (September 20) on an unidentified radical Islamic group (perhaps called "Al Bader" from the insignia on one of the walls). Within this tape 120 training camps in Afghanistan and Pakistan are mentioned by a former radical Islamist who promotes the idea that these camps are to be destroyed if terror is to be eradicated. In another tape shown several times (e.g., September 21) CNN's Mike Boettcher comments on an al Qaeda recruiting tape claimed to have been shot in Afghanistan, which includes images of the terror attacks in Kenya, Tanzania, and Yemen ascribed to al Qaeda, as well as training in commando tactics. In one image bin Laden is shown firing a machine-gun and in another a person is seen shooting at a large screen showing President Clinton (who ordered the shelling of training camps in Afghanistan in 1999). These earlier aired videos do show a larger and more dangerous organization. Viewed in retrospect and in relation to the airing date of Robertson's videos, there seems to be a progression from an earlier representation of al Qaeda as a potent, dangerous group that has to be eradicated through retaliation against Afghanistan, to the latter videos aimed at diminishing the dangerous potential of the organization following the invasion of Afghanistan and the hunt for bin Laden.

18. In October 8, anchorwoman Paula Zahn interviewed CNN terrorism analyst Peter Bergen, who said that Osama bin Laden's chemical experiments were amateurish. Nevertheless, Bergen slowly turned the description into a dangerous game with spreading dangerous global consequences by reiterating that there is evidence that bin Laden, while technologically deficient, is actively searching for chemical and nuclear weapons and thereby poses a major global threat. This amplification of the group's chemical and biological experimentations echoed the hysterical coverage of the anthrax scare in the United States, to which CNN devoted an unprecedented number of reports, which were audiovisually framed along the science-fiction style developed in series such as *The X-Files*. I will deal with this framing further on.

19. See CNN's Bruce Burkhardt's report on a visit to STRICOM, an Army unit that uses a variety of simulated war environments to train soldiers for battle (November 15, 2001); CNN's Ann Kellan's report on how Hollywood's high technology helps the U.S. military train for combat (December 15); CNN's Steve Young's report (December 18) on how U.S. Special Forces hunting Osama bin Laden are being assisted by state-of-the-art technology; CNN's Thelma Gutierrez's report on a military training center in the Sierra Nevada, California, that is similar to the Afghan mountains (October 6), where simulations of the terrain and of fully high-tech-geared soldiers are seen in greenish-looking night-activity images shot with a night-vision lens; CNN's Walter Rodgers's report on U.S. Marines in Afghanistan geared up to battle the weather as well as remaining Taliban resistance (December 1); CNN's John Vause's report on U.S. Marines on the hunt (January 1, 2002).

20. CNN's animation of the presumed sophisticated chain of caves appears in its Special Report website on Afghanistan, under the heading "Caves of Afghanistan." But see also CNN's Nic Robertson's report in which he shows and says how so far there is little evidence of the presumed super caves of Osama bin Laden (December 24).

21. E.g., in an interview with CNN's Larry King (September 18) or in CNN's Susan Candiotti's report (October 30), where Ashcroft states that the county should be on the highest alert for possible attacks.

22. See in particular the series of reports by CNN's Allan Dodds Frank on the money trail that may lead to Osama bin Laden, which emphasizes the need for governments to cooperate in order to follow the money that funds terrorism (e.g., September 21; 25), focusing particularly on peripheral, predominantly Muslim states, such as in his reports on evidence found of Osama bin Laden's involvement in a Sudanese bank (September 26) and on the diamond-trade funding of guerrilla and terrorist operations (November 16). See also CNN's Maria Ressa's report on how Osama bin Laden's money trail may be being channeled through welfare societies in the Philippines and aiding the Abu Sayyaf terrorist group (September 27); and CNN's Rym Brahimi's report on the search for the terrorists' financial backers in Dubai (October 23).

23. E.g., CNN's Sheila MacVicar's report on how a British court denied bail to Lofti Raissi, suspected of helping to train some of the September 11 hijackers (October 5); CNN's Catherine Bond on the investigation developing in Kenya after a letter sent from the United States contained anthrax (October 19); CNN's Betina Luscher on a Morrocan student suspected of managing the Hamburg bank account of one of the World Trade Center attackers (November 28); CNN's Harris Whitbeck on intelligence sources' claims about a triborder area in South America that serves as a safe haven and money source for terrorists (November 8); CNN's Diana Muriel on a terrorist cell operating in Brussels that may have been connected to the assassination of Afghan leader Ahmed Shah Masooud (November 27); CNN's Robin Oakley on the antiterror laws enabling Britain at the time to detain eight foreign nationals on suspicion of involvement in terrorism (December 20); CNN's Jim Boulden on the Dutch authorities' investigation of Richard Reid's stay in the Netherlands (December 29).

24. See, for example, CNN's Sheila MacVicar's report (December 7) on two retired

Pakistani nuclear scientists under investigation for possible links with al Qaeda; CNN's Jeanne Meserve's report (September 27) on American cities that have no planned response to possible terrorist attacks, where staged antiterrorist drills are shown with "victims" wounded by biological, chemical, or nuclear substances and aided by personnel in glowing green, red, and yellow uniforms; and the large number of reports following the anthrax scare, such as CNN's Thelma Gutierrez's report on how people submitting substances to be checked for anthrax has doubled the workload at health departments (October 11), and in which purple gloves, fluorescently lit laboratories, and pink microbes feature; or CNN's Gary Strieker's report on a government project designed to determine how easily biological weapons can be built (October 27).

25. See also Sheila MacVicar's reports on the movements of Mohamed Atta (September 24) and her report on shoe-bomb suspect Richard Reid (January 11, 2002), focusing in the latter on the European investigators' belief that he was part of a terrorist network that might have had ties to al Qaeda (Reid, by the way, is usually shown in MacVicar's reports with either a stupid or an evil look on his face). See also the styling of CNN's Deborah Feyerick's reports on the Moussaoui arraignment (January 2); CNN's Mike Boettcher on some of the people taken into custody and on the clues in the intensive search for the hijack ring (September 14).

6

The al Aksa Intifada

TIMELINE OF THE AL AKSA INTIFADA
THROUGH ITS MOST SALIENT EVENTS

On September 28, 2000, Israeli opposition leader Ariel Sharon visited the Temple Mount (called *Har HaBayit* in Hebrew and *Al-Haram Al-Sharif* in Arabic) in the Old City of Jerusalem, the holiest site for Judaism and the third holiest site in Islam. Sharon's thirty-four-minute visit was heavily guarded by the Israeli police force (some fifteen hundred policemen). His visit was loudly protested by Palestinian youth, who shouted slogans condemning Sharon's desecration of the site while Sharon's public address on the site proclaimed the area as eternal Israeli territory. During that day there were limited disturbances, but Palestinian violence and Israeli retaliation erupted the next day following the Muslim Friday prayers. Large riots broke out around East Jerusalem and spread into all of the occupied territories. Two events that occured close to the outbreak of this Intifada and were covered by television crews came to symbolize its tragic and violent nature. The first was the killing of the twelve-year-old boy Muhammad al Durra on September 30. The killing was covered and broadcast around the world. The coverage shows images of the boy and his father caught in the crossfire between Israeli soldiers and Palestinian combatants, attempting to hide behind a concrete water barrel before being shot dead.[1] In another highly publicized event that occurred on October 12, 2000, two Israeli reservist soldiers who entered Ramallah were arrested by the Palestinian Authority (PA) police. Because the soldiers were dressed in civilian clothes and one was reportedly wearing a Palestinian headdress, they were suspected of belonging to an undercover Israeli assassination squad. An agitated Palestinian mob stormed the police station, beat the soldiers to death, and threw their mutilated bodies into the street. In response Israel launched a series of retaliatory air strikes against the Palestinian Authority. The violent year that followed was characterized by an escalation of suicide bombings on the part of Palestinian organizations, which reached its peak in the first months of 2002, during which time more than 135 Israeli civilians were killed (in attacks mainly carried out by the radical Islamist groups Hamas and Islamic Jihad, as well as by the secular Fatah's military branch Al Aqsa Martyrs' Brigades).[2] These attacks elicited a large-scale military operation that Israel termed Operation Defensive Shield, launched in April 2002, twenty-four hours after the March 27 suicide bombing at the Park Hotel in the city of Netanya during the Jewish Passover celebration in which thirty people were killed. The goals of the operation as stated on April 8, 2002, to the Israeli parliament by Ariel Sharon were to

> enter cities and villages which have become havens for terrorists; to catch and arrest terrorists and, primarily, their dispatchers and those who finance and support them; to confiscate weapons intended to be used against Israeli citizens; to expose and destroy terrorist facilities and explosives, laboratories, weapons production factories and secret installations. The orders are clear: target and paralyze anyone who takes up weapons and tries to oppose our troops, resists them or endanger them—and to avoid harming the civilian population.

The IDF (Israel Defence Forces) incursions included the cities of Bethlehem, Jenin, Nablus, and Ramallah. During the operation, strict curfews were placed on the Palestinian cities, often resulting in the denial of medical attention to sick and elderly Palestinians. Moreover, Palestinian ambulances were stopped for checks following the discovery of an explosive belt in a Red Crescent ambulance.

Notable events during the operation were the battle of Jenin, the siege of Fatah militants who sought refuge at the Church of the Nativity in Bethlehem, and the siege of Yasser Arafat's compound in Ramallah. In the Jenin refugee camp fierce battles took place (April 3–15). Approximately thirty-two Palestinian militants, twenty-two Palestinian civilians, and twenty-three Israeli soldiers were killed in the fighting, and many buildings were reduced to rubble. The Palestinians made allegations of a massacre by the IDF in the camp. These allegations were disproven by the UN.[3] Parallel to this operation, from April 2 to May 10, a standoff developed between the Fatah militants who had sought refuge in the Church of the Nativity in Bethlehem, and the IDF. IDF snipers killed seven people inside the church and wounded more than forty. The standoff was resolved by the deportation of thirteen Palestinian militants to Europe, and the IDF ended its thirty-eight-day siege. In Ramallah, IDF bulldozers partly demolished the Mukataa, which is the center of government of the Palestinian Authority, also known as "Arafat's Compound," cutting off Arafat's headquarters from the rest of the buildings in the compound. Operation Defensive Shield was officially terminated on May 10, 2002, although occupations and curfews continued after that time and the deployment of roadblocks was intensified. These roadblocks—designed to weed out militants and limit the ability to move weapons around—divide most Palestinian cities and interconnections between cities and seriously disrupt the daily life of Palestinians. In 2003, following an Israeli intelligence report claiming to prove that Arafat paid $20,000 to the Al Aqsa Martyrs' Brigades, the United States demanded democratic reforms in the Palestinian Authority, as well the appointment of a prime minister independent of Arafat. On March 13, 2003, Arafat appointed the moderate Mahmoud Abbas (Abu Mazen) as Palestinian prime minister. Following the appointment, the U.S. administration posited the "Road Map for Peace" aimed at ending the conflict by disbanding militant organizations, ending the Israeli occupation, and establishing a democratic Palestinian state. The first phase of the plan demanded that the PA suppress terrorist attacks and confiscate illegal weapons, but Abu Mazen was unable or unwilling to confront militant organizations and risk civil war. On August 19, 2003, Hamas coordinated a suicide bombing attack on a crowded bus in Jerusalem, killing twenty-three Israelis, including seven children. Unable to govern effectively under Arafat, Abu Mazen resigned in September 2003. Ahmed Qurei (Abu Ala) was appointed to replace him.

On its side, the Israeli government, headed by Ariel Sharon since his election in February 2001, gave up on a negotiated settlement to the conflict and pursued a unilateral policy of physically separating Israel from Palestinian communities by beginning construction on the Israeli West Bank barrier. Israel claims the barrier is necessary to prevent Palestinian attackers from entering Israeli cities. Palestinians claim the barrier separates Palestinian communities from each other and that the construction plan is a de facto annexation of Palestinian territory. In 2004, as a response to repeated shellings of Israeli communities with Qassam rockets and mortar shells from Gaza, the IDF operated in Rafah, seeking out and destroying ninety tunnels dug by Palestinian militants to smuggle in weapons from Egypt. In this and other incursions Israel destroyed almost the entire southern side of the city, creating a buffer zone and displacing hundreds of people. On February 2, 2004, Sharon announced his unilateral disengagement plan to transfer all the Jewish settlers from the Gaza Strip. The Jewish settler's leadership initiated a heated campaign against such a plan. On March 22, 2004, pursuing Israel's policy of "targeted killings," that is, the assassination of prominent militant leaders and activists, an Israeli helicopter gunship killed Hamas leader Sheikh Ahmed Yassin and on April 17 his successor, Abed al-Aziz Rantisi, was similarly killed by Israel.[4] On November 11, 2004, Yasser Arafat, the legendary leader of the Palestinian people and president of the PNA (Palestinian National Authority), died after having been under IDF curfew in the

Mukataa for over two years. Since the beginning of the al Aksa Intifada, over
a thousand Israelis (around 75 percent of them civilians) have been killed and
around seven thousand wounded. On the Palestinian side over twenty-five
hundred have been killed (around 50 percent of them civilians) and over
twenty-two thousand wounded.

CNN COVERAGE

CNN's coverage of the al Aksa Intifada is mostly framed and evaluated in
terms of the parties' mutual violations of "law and order"[5] or of human
rights, echoed audiovisually in the violation of normative stable framing,
shot angle, and editing (e.g., oblique camera angles), and in the recurring
headline shots of criminal-appearing violence used to represent the sides,
such as the image of an Israeli tank, shot from afar and below as it crushes a
house into rubble, countered by a headline shot from below of Palestinian
black-masked gunmen leading an agitated procession.[6] This mutuality is
achieved through reports that almost always alternate between the two sides,
audiovisually blurring the different positions held by different groups within
Israel and Palestine. Hence, reports on Palestinian suicide bombings almost
invariably include images of damage caused by Israeli tanks or bulldozers in
Palestinian territories, while reports on Israeli military incursions or targeted
killings include images of the results of Palestinian suicide bombings, thus
conveying the notion of a vicious circle.

This alternating frame is particularly evident in most of CNN's Jerald
Kessel's reports, such as that from September 19, 2002, on a suicide bombing
on a bus in Tel Aviv that killed five people and wounded sixty. In it, images
showing shots from the suicide bombing (ambulances, policemen running, a
dead body carried away in a stretcher, a portion of the blown-up bus, people
seen from afar searching for body parts) are cut to a shot of an Israeli tank
driving through a West Bank town. Following this we see the response of
Ra'anan Gissin, Sharon's spokesman, tying the bombing to Bush's "axis of
evil." This is cut to images of an earlier suicide bombing in the Israeli Arab
village of Um El-Fahm, where only the suicide bomber died, from which the
report cuts to images of Israeli tanks and bulldozers rumbling over rubble in
the Palestinian town of Abu Dis in the West Bank, showing the huge damage
caused following the IDF's destruction of the house of a suicide bomber's
family and its surroundings (an action considered illegal by international
law). This is cut to Palestinian Authority cabinet member Ghasan Khatib's
response to the suicide bombing, in which he mentions Israel's killing of
seventy-five Palestinians during the past month and condemns the violence
on both sides. From this the report cuts to Kessel in front of a large map of
the Middle East region, abstractly placing the conflict within the context of

the larger regional and global U.S.-Iraq conflict (and distancing the viewers from the specific events reported).[7]

A similar alternating frame can be seen in reports on Israeli incursions or targeted killings. Emblematic is CNN's Sheila MacVicar's retrospective report from May 4, 2002, on the battle in the refugee camp of Jenin[8] during Israel's Defensive Shield Operation, where intense fighting followed Israel's entry. The report opens briefly with images from the suicide bombing in the Park Hotel in Natanya following which Operation Defensive Shield started. It focuses on a burned Bible. It then cuts to an interview held with Lt. Ron, a reservist in the IDF, conducted in his warm and soft-lit apartment, while in the background we see "Middle Eastern" items such as an oriental coffee-pot. Lt. Ron describes how his platoon entered the camp on foot. The report then cuts to an Israeli tank destroying a house wall, followed by shots of a large agitated gathering of Palestinians waving flags. From this the report cuts to an interview held in an Israeli jail with Thabet Mardawi, a Palestinian Islamic Jihad fighter in Jenin, who eventually surrendered. Despite the location, Mardawi is also shot in warm colors and soft lighting, equalizing his look to that of Lt. Ron. He tells MacVicar that there were around a hundred fighters in the camp expecting the Israeli invasion. The date April 2 appears over a black screen followed by a series of shots showing damage to a hospital in Jenin and an interview with a doctor telling the story of a twenty-seven-year-old nurse who was brought to the hospital after being shot in the heart. From here the report cuts back to Lt. Ron's interview, where he describes how, suddenly, immediately after they had started walking into the camp, his commander was shot dead. This is cut to the smiling face of Thabet Mardawi, who says he could not believe the soldiers had entered on foot, that he had been waiting his entire life for this and that "it was like hunting."[9] MacVicar then details how many IDF soldiers were killed and how the army brought in tanks, then Apache helicopters, and finally bulldozers into the camp. This is illustrated by showing tanks rumbling down a street in the camp and two helicopters in the air. The report returns to Lt. Ron stating that the incursion was carried out with the uttermost sensitivity. This sentence is cut to an image of a Jenin resident sitting helplessly on top of a pile of debris and to images evidencing the tremendous destruction to the camp by the Israeli bulldozers. In what follows we see alternating images showing Jenin residents in the streets and within their ruined houses detailing in word and gesture how they had been used as human shields by the Israeli army; Lt. Ron admitting this practice (which is a war crime); and an Israeli army spokeswoman denying this practice as well as the Palestinian allegation that there had been a massacre in Jenin.[10] Interspersed within these alternating images is an interview that MacVicar held with Peter Bouckhardt from the Human Rights Watch (HRW) organization, whose report concluded that there had not been a massacre but that other war crimes had been committed by the IDF such as the use of civilians as human shields. Later MacVicar mentions that the HRW report also blamed the Palestinian militants for their booby-trapping of streets and houses within the refugee camp. This interview diverges from the others in that it is conducted within an unspecified, peaceful, lush, green forest, connoting that it is outside the region. The report ends with images of the ruined refugee camp.

What stands out in this report is the divergence between the reporter's attempt to offer a dramatic narrative of the events (e.g., through its commentary, which offers a consecutive mentioning of dates, or through the opening of the report with the suicide bombing that preceded the incursion and its conclusion with images of the camp's destruction), and the alternating audiovisual construction of the report, which shifts back and forth in time and location and which promotes the notion of a vicious circle of violence. This viciousness is enhanced through its alternating editing structure focused on the two parties' mutual aversion and cynicism (such as the cut from Lt. Ron's story about how his commander was shot to Mardawi's smiling face, or the cut from Lt. Ron's claim that the incursion was conducted with the highest sensitivity to images of the terrible destruction of the refugee camp). The delegitimating of both parties, the mutual neutralization of the atrocities that occurred during this incursion, and the distancing from the events, is enhanced through the spatial and temporal detachment of the interview with the Human Rights Watch representative.[11] Finally, this alternating frame also comes across when CNN introduces a politician, a commentator, an expert, or an eyewitness to explain the situation. Whenever such a commentator belongs to one of the parties he or she is always countered by a similar person from the other side, resulting in the positioning of the CNN anchor or interviewer as the honest broker in-between the debating parties.[12]

Apparently contradicting this alternating frame, but ultimately complementing it, is a multicultural-styled frame, whereby each side's cultural norms and ideologies are respected (from a distance) in an unqualified manner, irrespective of their underlying motivations and their violent results. This is found for example in reports dealing with the way suicide bombers perceive themselves or are perceived by their supporters.[13] This comes across in CNN's Mike Boettcher's report from September 27, 2001, headlined "An Inside Look at Suicide Attacks." In this report Boettcher obtained an "inside look at the tactics that some call suicide—but that its practitioners call martyrdom." The report opens with a video made by Hizbolla's Al Manar television[14] featuring Ali Ashmar, a twenty-year-old suicide bomber, as he is followed by the camera walking along a green meadow and talking about his joyful expectation to give his life and reach paradise. Over this image Boettcher, in a dramatic voice-over, says that we are watching a man readying himself toward his last day on earth. This is followed by a series of slow-motion shots accompanied by melancholic Arabic music dissolving into each other, showing the man preparing the explosive belt, strapping it around his body, praying, bidding good-by to the camera, and running to blow himself up among an Israeli armored patrol. The report cuts to an interview conducted by Boettcher with Munif Ashmar, the suicide bomber's father, seen bathed in soft amber lighting in his quiet living room while saying how proud he is of his son. Following this we see posters of suicide bombers on billboards along modern looking main streets in Beirut, Lebanon's capital. We then return to the Hizbolla video showing rows of suicide bombers in army uniforms pledging allegiance to their cause. This is cut to a segment inserted after the recordings in Lebanon were made, where we see Boettcher in a CNN studio standing beside a large screen showing the previous rows of Hizbolla suicide bombers, on which Boettcher informs us that the report was made in July (that is, before the 9/11 attack), and explains that Hizbolla may have ties to al Qaeda. After this clear audiovisual separation and distancing of CNN and its reporter from Hizbolla, the original segments continue with an interview Boettcher held with Karsem Aleik, head of the Hizbolla's Martyr's Association. Aleik details how the association takes care of the families of suicide bombers/martyrs, whereby we see a series of shots showing happy looking people in day care centers, factories, and health care facilities. Aleik goes on to explain to Boettcher that the martyr attack tactic is an effective resource to fight the sophisticated Zionist army backed by a superpower (i.e., the United States) and that the reason westerners cannot understand the martyr's act derives from their materialism and loss of faith in God. This is followed by an interview with Ali Ashmar's wife and son sitting in what seems to be their comfortable and carefully decorated living room, with a large photo of her husband beside a nicely arranged vase of flowers. The woman, dressed in traditional black dress and head covering, quietly and kindly tells Boettcher how she supported her husband's decision to become a martyr, while the son says shyly in English that he wants to follow in his father's footsteps and meet him in paradise. This is cut to Hizbolla's Al Manar television station, where we see the editing and broadcast of reports on martyrs and their suicidal missions, followed by Boettcher's interview with the station head, who explains that their propagandistic magnification of the attacks constitutes a powerful weapon in the war. In the report's final segment Boettcher visits a Hizbolla museum devoted to the martyrs' attacks, where he interviews a Lebanese return visitor to the museum, who tells him enthusiastically that those who kill themselves in their attacks against the Zionists are not committing suicide but are rather heroes who value life, and that their acts are the highest expression of humanism and devotion to their people. In the background of this open-air interview we see beautiful images of the Lebanese landscape and of a clear blue sky.

Salient in this aestheticized report conveying in unqualified manner Hizbolla ideology, is the abstraction of this floating cultural expression from the real economic-political grievances that drive the suicide bombers and the gruesome results of suicide bombings, particularly when innocent civilians are killed.[15] This strange omission attests to the multicultural approach whereby all cultures are equally legitimate (evidenced in the reporter's attentive listening to Aleik's "explanation," which suggests it is lack of faith that obscures the westerner's understanding of suicide bombers). This multicultural strategy often reaches ridiculous proportions in the reporters' rendering of events being shown in terms of allegations attributed to one of the parties, such as when a suicide bombing shown is presented as an Israeli allegation that it is a suicide bombing, or when an Israeli army bulldozer shown demolishing a house is reported as a Palestinian allegation that the house is being demolished.

Through such complementing frames each side's violation of the other's law and order or human rights is presented from without through the reporter's alternation or multicultural exclusion and through overall detached, distant shots, evoking a fatalistic deadlock. These balancing strategies frame the conflict under an equalizing perspective whereby the ultimately incomprehensible subjectivist perceptions and actions of both parties are equally illegitimate. This equalizing strategy neutralizes the horror of the specific deeds carried out as well as the need for intervention, since the conflict in its exclusive mutuality is contained, and since no party is in the right. In a sense, CNN suggests in its neutralization that two wrongs make a right, the right being CNN and, by extension, the U.S. elites it represents.[16] It suggests that whatever the conflict's reasons and history it is advisable that the parties themselves reach a solution in the face of mutual suffering, or be left to their ongoing mutual struggle.[17]

A recurring audiovisual explanation offered by CNN to the violent encounters reported, consists of bringing to notice, where relevant, the coincidence between the violent acts undertaken and the international diplomatic efforts to bring the parties to negotiate peace, framing these acts as evidencing the perpetrators' unexplained rejection of such initiatives.[18] In such cases the "explanatory" framework, the equalizing alternating frame, and the lack of serious consideration of the interests and rationale driving both parties' violent acts, overvalues an explanation based on irrational mutual vengeance and antipeace stupidity as the driving force behind both parties' actions. It offers rather a moral divide-and-conquer strategy portraying the CNN and by extension the U.S. elites, which it represents as rational and morally superior to both parties.[19] Moreover, the horrific terrorist and constitutional violence emanating from the Israeli-Palestinian conflict is seen, through an overall digital aesthetic of avoidance and a "multicultural" approach, from without and from "above" as a local but bearable disturbance to global calm.[20]

Hence, when shots of atrocities are presented (usually in material taken from local stations) the more graphic portions are either cut out or framed and overloaded with overlapping multimedia information rendered in bluish, reddish, or greenish digital aesthetic coloring, resulting in the viewer's distraction and distancing from the horror. Such is, for example, CNN's minor coverage of the killing of the child Muhammad al Durra in the crossfire between Israeli soldiers and Palestinian militants as well as of the lynching of two Israeli reserve soldiers by an agitated Palestinian mob who also mutilated the soldiers' bodies. These two tragic and horrific events, whose uniqueness lies in their being caught live by news cameras, were hardly mentioned by CNN, which showed only once a highly censored and brief version of the events, further diminishing their import by concentrating on the conflicting allegations made by each party concerning the event. Thus, in the case of Muhammad al Durra's killing, only portions of the video showing how he died are shown, and the commentary emphasizes the Israeli allegations that he was shot by bullets coming from the Palestinian militants. Likewise, in the case of the lynching in Ramallah the commentary emphasizes the Palestinian claims that the Israeli soldiers were suspected of being undercover and on the way to a targeted killing, showing only brief portions of the live-video coverage and offering instead two reassuring archive ID photos of the two victims when they were still alive (October 12).

Again, in the coverage of suicide bombings, there are deliberate attempts to block the disturbing images of the dead and wounded. This can be seen, for example, in CNN's Jason Bellini's report from April 12, 2002, on a suicide bombing at a Jerusalem bus stop near a busy market that left six people dead and over sixty wounded. Bellini and his crew were half a block away at the time of the blast so that they had an opportunity to catch the event firsthand. Indeed, the report shows a hand-held shot of the event taken by the cameraman as he runs toward the site of the blast, while people move in the opposite direction, including a woman whose face is bleeding. As they near the site the crew slows down, while we see a bystander in front of the camera telling them repeatedly to follow him and approach the place of the blast. The crew, however, refuses to go any further. While this may indicate their fear of approaching any further the heart of the disaster, it is also emblematic of CNN's avoidance of traumatic images.

This avoidance can also be seen in CNN's January 5, 2003, report on two bombings in central Tel Aviv that killed at least nineteen people and wounded more than a hundred others. In this report CNN opens with images taken by Israeli television where we see a hand-held camera shot moving among the debris toward the heart of the explosion. However, as the camera tilts down to focus on a victim lying on the street CNN cuts to footage taken by Reuters where, again, whenever images of victims are about to be seen, there is a cut to a different shot. In other cases, the event is distanced in its being shown from "without" and from "above," as in CNN's Jerald

Kessel's report from September 9, 2004, on a suicide bombing outside Tel Aviv that killed eight and wounded fifteen. In it Kessel appears on a large TV screen in Wolf Blitzer's distant U.S. CNN studio and recounts the event. At one point the screen splits in two and images from the event are run parallel to Kessel, who is seen on the other screen. Both screens, however, do not occupy the whole TV screen but are seen floating over a reddish wavering digitalized background, thus splitting the viewer's attention and involvement with the disturbing images taken at the scene of the explosion.

ISRAELI AND PALESTINIAN COVERAGE: THE INCITEMENT FRAME

While the Palestinian Authority Television (PATV) explicitly sees itself as having a role in the Palestinian struggle for liberation, it also claims that it only conveys reality as it is,[21] and while Israeli Channel 1 & 2 television news programs perceive their role as neutral conveyors of reality and watchdogs[22] of democracy, both offer highly biased presentations of the events. As Gadi Wolfsfeld remarked, "The News Media on both sides will probably continue to play their usual role of fanning the flames of hatred."[23] This also becomes evident once we consider the Israeli government's and the Palestinian Authority's mutual perception of each other's mainstream media as effective propaganda tools whose main function in the conflict is to incite against the other party. As Israeli Prime Minister Ariel Sharon said, "The war against terrorism is also a war against incitement, the terrible daily incitement in the official media and in the mosques. It is the incitement that leads to attacks, that dispatches suicide-bombers, that pulls the finger on the detonator trigger."[24] This perception has led the Israeli army to destroy offices of the Palestinian media and to obstruct their functioning in different ways.[25] Moreover, each party has official and nonofficial groups that monitor the other party's media in order to expose its lies, omissions, and what each side perceives as the other's incitement.

The overt leading Israeli governmental monitoring agency is that of the Israeli Ministry of Foreign Affairs.[26] Beyond this official site there are semi-official and independent Israeli monitoring groups such as the Palestinian Media Watch (PMW), founded in 1996 "to gain an understanding of Palestinian society through the monitoring of the Palestinian Arabic language media and schoolbooks . . . documenting the contradictions between the image the Palestinians present to the world in English and the messages to their own people in Arabic;[27] the Independent Media Review and Analysis (IMRA), founded in 1992 and awarded credentials by the government of Israel as a news organization, "IMRA provides an extensive digest of media, polls and significant interviews and events";[28] the Middle East Media

Research Institute (MEMRI), founded in February 1998 (by Ygal Carmon, who was the Israeli prime minister's advisor on terror) "explores the Middle East through the region's media;[29] the United Jerusalem Foundation "examines anti-Israel media bias and inaccuracy."[30]

The leading Palestinian National Authority overt monitoring agency is the Media Watch of the International Press Center (IPC).[31] Beyond this official site there are semiofficial and independent Palestinian monitoring groups such as the Palestinian Human Rights Monitoring Group (PHRMG), founded in December 1996, which "documents human rights violations committed against Palestinians in the West Bank, Gaza Strip and East Jerusalem, regardless of who is responsible";[32] the Palestine Media Watch Group of the Palestinian Non-Governmental Network (PNGO), founded in 2000 due to "a real lack of the Palestinian narrative in the media";[33] and the Electronic Intifada (EI) whose Media Section "offers a quick window on the latest articles added to the Role of the Media, Coverage Trends, Journalists in Danger, and EI in the Press feeds."[34]

This mutual monitoring has been very instructive here, both in what it reveals about each side's ideological perception of the other and about its own self-perception. The following analysis of the respective coverage of the al Aksa Intifada by each party's mainstream television news owes a great deal to these monitoring groups.

Israeli Television Coverage

The coverage of Israeli Channel 1 & 2 television news[35] of the al Aksa Intifada offers a double-talk framing of the conflict. On the one hand it employs a siege-determined framing that is highly ethnocentric and revengeful, audiovisually framing the events as resulting from an irrational persecution of Israeli Jews, demanding vengeance. On the other hand it frames the conflict as being between the law-abiding, ordered, democratic Israeli people and government, and the lawless and brutally violent Palestinian people represented by a criminal Palestinian Authority.

Emblematic of the siege framing are reports on suicide bombings. These are characterized by an overall chaotic presentation of the event consisting of self-defeating attempts to "make order" of the chaos, overwhelmed by lengthy looped audiovisual unsettling and panic arousing configurations. Hence, reporters try to "make order" not only through orientation maps showing the location of the blast, but more particularly through incessant verbal speculations concerning the exact location within the area where the bomber exploded, how the event might have occurred, what were the type, amount, and weight of the explosives used, and the estimated number of victims. These "ordering" attempts are self-defeating, however, since much of the information is irrelevant and/or clearly unreliable (e.g., beyond the actual location, it is irrelevant whether the blast occurred near the second left-hand table of a restaurant or the third right-hand table close to the bathroom. Moreover, this information is often hypothetical and mistakenly detailed, since the reporter usually cannot approach the exact location within the area). And, each speculation tends to be discarded swiftly in favor of a different one. This hypothetical rhetoric is particularly unreliable when it offers estimations of the number of people killed or wounded. The reports usually start with a small number of casualties, which gradually increases. These self-defeating, nervous, incessant ordering attempts, accompanied by the distressing sounds of ambulance and police sirens, add to rather than control the overall sense of chaos emanating from the traumatic-styled audiovisuality of the event.

Hence, suicide bombings are invariably rendered in shaky compositions and jumpy disorienting editing of unstable hand-held camera movements surveying the site or zooming in to close shots of mutilated bodies, scattered body parts, and confused or stunned victims. Many shots search and follow the wounded as they are hurriedly carried away on stretchers or escorted to ambulances. Emphasis is also given to soldiers, policemen, paramedics, and stressed witnesses running around in despair. The usually lengthy and looped broadcasts of these audiovisual configurations convey claustrophobic and Sisyphean notions.[36] This can be seen for example in Guy Peleg's and Gur Tsalal Yachin's report for Channel 1 and in Gal Gabai's and Yoram Binur's report for Channel 2 on the suicide bombing that killed two Israelis and wounded thirty-seven at a pedestrian mall in Rishon Letzion on May 22, 2002. Both reports include a map of the site aimed at orienting the viewers, but are followed by a totally disorienting rendering of the event that loops a collection of night-shots showing stunned faces, close shots of the wounded being carried away, close-ups of people crying, and a lengthy shot of a dead body lying covered on the sidewalk.[37] Over these images the reporter's soon-to-be-discarded speculations are raised concerning the exact location and timing of the blast, and the number of people hurt. Both channels conducted studio discussions with experts and reporters on the event. For example, Ya'acov Ahimeir, the Channel 1 anchor, discusses the event with its military affairs reporter, Ron Ben-Yishai. In this interview, Ben-Yishai mentions the hypothesis that the attack was in retaliation to the IDF's targeted killing earlier in the week of Mahmoud Titi, the leader of the Al Aqsa Martyrs' Brigades, in the Balata refugee camp near Nablus. Ben-Yishai, however, discards this assumption, offering instead a variation on an ongoing claim by Israeli authorities whereby there is no causal connection between what Israel does and Palestinian suicide bombings, since the latter's long-standing agenda is that of destroying Israel. Mentioning how frustrating this attack is in its coming only a week after Israel's ending of Operation Defensive Shield, whose aim was to stop such attacks, Ben-Yishai reiterates another long-standing claim whereby, although it is impossible to totally stop suicide bombers by military means, there are still other "physical measures" (as opposed to political) that can be deployed to avert such operations, beyond the closures, incursions, the barrier fence, and the segmentation of Palestinian territories. Although, by way of negation of the efficacy of military means, Ben-Yishai insinuates that political measures may offer a solution, this vague proposition is meaningless given the overall presentation of terror organizations as motivated by sheer hatred and by their aiming at the total destruction of Israel, and given the conception that the Palestinian Authority (i.e., the only possible political partner) turns a blind eye and even supports terror organizations.[38] What stands out in this commentary and complements the audiovisual rendering of the report is the total lack of any explanation for the horrendous deed, along with an emphasis on the ultimate lack of prospects concerning the possible frustration of further attacks. The chaotic audiovisual patterning of suicide bombings along with the denial of any motive other than blind hatred, or indeed of any solution to suicide bombings, recurs in all of the Israeli television reports covering these attacks.

This ethnocentric siege-typed rendering of suicide bombings is further elaborated in reports that frame these as attacks on specific Israeli groups or communities. This classification, irrelevant to the motives of the attackers (who seem to blow themselves up in places where there are as many people as possible), aims at uniting Israeli society. These classifying frames are often generated during the live coverage of the attacks. Hence, the attack on the Rishon Letzion promenade is quickly generalized into an attack on the community of elderly Russians who commonly visit the area to play chess and backgammon (a frame consolidated by the leading Channel 1 anchor Haim Yavin); while the Petah Tikva attack, in which a one-year-old baby and her grandmother were killed, is generalized into an attack on young babies and their mothers. These reports enhance shared familial or communal suffering, often by means of group shots of the family or community affected, either at their houses, at funerals, or at the site of the bombing, where people often gather to commemorate the victims. These group shots usually fill the frame with emotionally overtaken relatives, friends, or bystanders conveying a claustrophobic feeling.

As noted by David Witztum,[39] the reports on the suicide bombing during the Passover meal in the Park Hotel in Natanya and the attack on the Orthodox Jewish neighborhood "Beit Israel" in Jerusalem were framed as religious-based anti-Semitic attacks, emphasizing images of the remains of burned religious items, resonating past images of pogroms against Jews. Hence, reports on the Natanya bombing repeatedly showed burned Hagadda prayer booklets and the remains of the unleavened bread. Channel 1's Yuli Ofek interviewed Ya'acov Tzintzantos standing among a crowd of protesters in front of the Park Hotel, who correlated the suicide bombing to both religious anti-Semitism and the Holocaust. On the other hand, as Witztum observes, the coverage of suicide bombings at the Café Moment in Jerusalem, at various shopping malls, and at the Sea-Food restaurant in Tel Aviv, was framed as an attack on the lifestyle of secular Israelis, emphasizing the suicide bomber's obstruction of Western-type Israeli secular entertainments. Likewise, the various bus bombings and the suicide attacks at open-air markets, such as the Machaneh Yehuda market in Jerusalem, were framed as attacks aimed at the lower classes in Israel; the attack at the Dolphinarium discotheque in Tel Aviv, in which several young Russian immigrants to Israel were killed, was framed as an attack against an alienated community whose victims should legitimate and ease its absorption into Israeli society; and the attack on the Arab-Israeli owned Matsa restaurant in Haifa, frequented by Israeli Jews, was framed as an attack on Jewish-Arab coexistence within Israel.

This overall siege-typed framing of suicide bombings has a complementary double function: first, it promotes the unification of Israeli society, which suffers from acute religious, ethnic, class, and political divisions, by emphasizing that Israelis are killed indiscriminately just because they are Israelis, echoing the dominant Israeli framing of the Nazi-perpetrated Holocaust whereby Jews of any walk of life or inclination were murdered simply because they were Jews. This framing evokes the long history of persecution of the Jewish people, an ongoing theme in Israeli culture.[40] Second, it presents the suicide bombers' motives as deriving from an irrational, blind, and incomprehensible anti-Semitism and anti-Zionism, which has apparently nothing to do with Palestinian self-interests. It thus promotes and legitimates acts of retaliation whose underlying motive is revenge. This call for vengeance is implicitly endorsed by Israeli television in its coverage of suicide bombings. Hence most reports include shots of the reporter speaking directly to the camera, seemingly undisturbed by the people gathered around him in the background calling for revenge. The retaliation motive also surfaces repeatedly in interviews of eyewitnesses and official representatives at the site of the blast. This can be seen, for example, in the Channel 2 Gal Gabai's coverage of the April 4, 2002, suicide bombing in Tel Aviv, where the crowd around the reporter is shouting out "Death to the Arabs," and in the interview conducted on the site with Gideon Ezra, the deputy minister of Internal Security at the time, who says that the "unconventional attacks of these human animals have to be met with unconventional countermeasures."

This vengefulness can also be seen in reports on targeted killings conducted by the Israeli army, where very graphic images of the results of the killing are shown, including the shattered bodies of the targets.[41] The revengeful motive for such images is further clarified by the fact that available graphic images of innocent Palestinians killed during such actions or during Israeli incursions into Palestinian territories and broadcast around the world are almost never shown.[42]

This overall framing of suicide bombings is directed at internal recruitment, by representing the particular interests of Israel's elite in Jewish, security-oriented national unification as pertaining to all Israelis, and is aimed at obtaining the internal legitimating of harsh retaliation against the Palestinians by eliciting a sense of vengeance.

However, despite its apparent inclusiveness, the siege-typed chaotic framing of suicide bombings and their support of vengeful retaliation shifts when dealing with suicide bombings against Jewish settlers in the occupied territories of the West Bank and the Gaza Strip. This divergence becomes particularly evident in the contradiction between the explicitly verbally reiterated articulation by interviewed settlers of the dominant siege ideology[43] (that audiovisually frames suicide bombings within Israel), and the nonsiege audiovisual rendering of suicide bombings in the occupied territories. Hence, in these reports, the verbal commentary and the camera usually cover the event in a contained and orderly manner, offering detailed diagrams of the way the attack was carried out while emphasizing the efficiency of the army and the rescue forces in their dealing with the event. The focus in these reports is often on the security breaches brought about by the settlers' disregard for their own security that has allowed the Palestinian infiltration, and on the settlers' disrespect for and complaints against the army, despite the heavy burden that the securing of these settlements places on it. This can be seen, for example, in the coverage by Channel 1's Menachem Hadar and Amir Bar-Shalom, and by Channel 2's Ilan Leizerowitch of the attack at the West Bank Jewish religious settlement of Alon Moreh on Mar 28, 2002, where several members of the Gavish family were murdered by a Palestinian who infiltrated their home and opened fire on its inhabitants, murdering the parents Rachel and David, the grandfather Yitzhak Kanner, and an older brother Abraham. The other children present in the household fled the attacker by escaping from an upstairs window. The terrorist was eventually killed by the security forces (Hamas claimed responsibility for the attack). Channel 1's Bar-Shalom's report features a series of diagrams of the house showing the phases of the attack, which are inserted into night shots showing army vehicles and soldiers all around with very few civilians on sight. In the other Channel 1 report, by Menachem Hadar, the fact that the settlement was unfenced for ideological reasons is commented on and generalized to other settlements. Likewise, in Channel 2's Ilan Leizerowitch's report the event is recreated with a hand-held camera that follows the attacker's movement toward the house and his entrance into it. This is followed by images of the blood-stained places where the family members were murdered and by an outside shot showing from where the children on the upper floor had managed to escape. Despite the fact that the attack was on civilians, the overall framing of the event is that usually used in the coverage of Palestinian attacks on Israeli military posts, perceived more as planned military operations rather than chaotic terror attacks. Menachem Hadar's report also covers the funeral in the synagogue where the mourners are gathered. Differing from the coverage of funerals within Israel, the settlers' funeral is framed as a political event. Thus, the coverage focuses on the quiet restraint of the gathering and the political critique voiced against the retaliatory measures presented to the mourners by the right-wing minister of education Limor Livnat, perceived by the audience as minor and ineffective.

The divergence of this coverage from the chaotic coverage of suicide bombings within Israel insinuates that the occupied territories are a war zone contested by both Israelis and Palestinians. This diverging coverage evidences how the dominant siege ideology is contested by both the settlers and the mainstream media embedding the elite interests. This ideology has thereby lost some of its currency for the Israeli state elites given the settlers' attempts to capitalize on it and incorporate it into its messianic religious dictum to hold onto the whole "promised land" irrespective of geopolitical configurations, while accusing any government that considers handing out territories as betraying God's will. Therefore, in the coverage of suicide bombings and terror attacks in the occupied territories the mainstream media audiovisually contradicts the settlers' constant appropriation of the siege ideology to justify their messianic territorial interests.

These attempts by the Israeli mainstream media at reappropriation of the siege ideology include their implicit legitimating of calls for revenge and retaliation when coming after suicide attacks within Israel, and their implicit delegitimating of such calls when coming from the settlers. This can be seen, for example, in a Channel 1 report from May 24, 2002, on an abortive car bomb attack by the Al Aqsa Martyrs' Brigades on a popular Tel Aviv nightclub (Studio 49). In the report, the security guard Eli Federman who aborted the attack is differentiated by the anchor (David Witztum) from the actions of his brother, Noam Federman, a well-known radical settler who has repeatedly broken the law through his many unprovoked attacks on Palestinian civilians. However, Witztum's differentiation comes after Eli Federman's disturbing description of his otherwise commendable act whereby "I fired one bullet at him. He fell out of the car and blew up. After the blast, I shot him twice in the head, and then moved closer and emptied the rest of the clip into his head." Thus, Eli Federman's revengeful description, implicitly supported by Witztum, puts into question the latter's differentiation between Eli Federman the hero and his brother the villain, revealing how the siege ideology and its underlying call for revenge is legitimated when voiced within Israel yet rejected when voiced by Jewish settlers in the occupied territories.

This type of divergence however, does not conform to the settlers' own critique of the mainstream media, as can be found, for example, in A. Goren's article "Stepsons and Spoiled Sons in the Israeli Media." In it, Goren claims that mainstream media present the Jewish settlers "as zealots, lunatics . . . law-breakers and anti-democratic."[44] While this may indeed be a rather accurate description of the movement's leadership and its grassroots supporters, it is certainly not the way the movement is portrayed by the Israeli mainstream media, which but for a few exceptions still treats this subnational opposition movement as legitimate, despite its longstanding law-breaking behavior and antidemocratic orientation.[45] Hence, on July 7, 2001, Channel 1 reported that "in the wake of shooting incidents at Israeli targets, a group of settlers attacked several Palestinian-owned houses in Hebron city. As a result, some windows were smashed." While the said news was being broadcast, a picture of a Palestinian shooting in the air appeared on the screen rather than pictures of the settlers' damage to Palestinian property.

This divergence from the siege-typed presentation of suicide bombings and terror attacks on civilians when covering such events in the settlements within the occupied territories, does not affect however the dominant presentation of Palestinians as inhuman or barbaric, and of their leaders as criminals. A most salient example of this generalized dehumanization is found in the recurring broadcast by Israeli television of the Italian crew coverage of the horrific lynching of two Israeli reserve soldiers by an agitated Palestinian mob in a Palestinian Authority Police Station in Ramallah on October 12, 2000. While the deed was indeed barbaric, Channel 1 & 2 nonetheless omitted the information about a Palestinian police officer injured while attempting to stop the crowd, and exploited the event to the maximum through its frequent broadcasting. In particular it framed as one of its Intifada headline shots the picture of a man standing at the second-floor window of the room within the police station where the lynching took place, with his bloody palms raised in the air as he is cheered on by the aroused mob in the street (who are later seen striking the bodies of the soldiers thrown from the window into their hands). The framing reflects Israeli government claims that Palestinians in general are an inhuman, murderous people.

Another headline shot recurs in the coverage of funerals of Palestinians killed during clashes with the Israeli army, where emphasis is placed on Palestinian masked gunmen shooting in the air. In a particular case, Channel 1 reported on May 1, 2001, on the collective funeral procession of Hassan Alqadi, killed by an Israeli targeted shelling the day before, and of two children who were killed along with him.[46] Rather than commenting on the problematic and immoral killing of the children, Channel 1 focuses on pictures of Palestinian gunmen and on a man waving the Iraqi flag during the funeral procession.

The focus on gunmen shooting in the air during Palestinian funerals forms part of a wider dehumanizing frame implying that Palestinians do not care for human lives, including their own. Within this framing another Israeli governmental accusation amplified and disseminated by the Israeli main-stream media concerns the Palestinian organization's use of Red Crescent ambulances to carry militants or smuggle explosives under the guise of car-rying sick people to hospitals. Hence, Channel 1 & 2 broadcast several times a video shot by the Israeli army and provided to Israeli television by the foreign affairs office, presumably showing fake patients being taken out of an ambulance by an Israeli army patrol and the consequent discovery of explosives within the ambulance. The tilting, unfocused, rough black-and-white, hidden-camera documentary style of these images criminalized the act.[47] While deception forms part of war tactics, and despite the counterpro-ductive nature of such acts, which have been used by the Israeli army to jus-tify its blocking and searching of Red Crescent ambulances, the implication made by Israeli television in reporting these events is that the Palestinians use even the helpless in their overall incomprehensible and inhuman struggle against Israel. Finally, beyond the usual lack of explanation for the acts of suicide bombers, or the overall contempt and ridicule of the Palestinians' religious rationale for such acts (i.e., martyrdom, or Shahada), emphasizing the sexual undertones of the promise that the suicide bomber will enjoy seventy-two virgins upon reaching paradise,[48] the major focus of this dehu-manizing frame revolves around the accusation that Palestinian leaders and Palestinian television criminally manipulate and encourage their children to die in suicide operations against Israel. Hence, on July 19, 2001, Channel 2 broadcast a video on one of the summer camps in Gaza city, opening the report with the claim that "the Islamic Jihad movement is supervising a sum-mer camp, with the knowledge of the PNA, in which it trains children on how to carry out suicide operations." However, it is difficult to deduce from the video images and sounds that the children are being encouraged to com-mit such acts rather than being trained for battle, and there is no support for the claim that this is done with the knowledge of the PNA. Moreover, in another reiterated and rebroadcast video, Yasser Arafat is interviewed on PATV encouraging children to become shahids (martyrs).[49]

While the incitement of children to become martyrs in the struggle against Israel is problematic,[50] the main intention of Arafat or of the Palestinian tele-vision is not for them to become suicide bombers but rather to take an active part in the struggle, mostly through demonstrations, stone-throwing, and the like. Israeli television however, either disregards altogether or verbally dismisses as deceptive rhetoric the many instances in which Arafat and other PNA officials have condemned suicide bombing operations. In an interview given to Amir Bar-Shalom from Channel 1 on the site of the suicide bomb-ing in Petah Tikva on May 22, 2002, Uzi Landau, the internal security minis-ter at the time, said Israel should completely choke the Palestinian terrorists, and that Arafat should be deported since he educates children to go out and blow themselves up on Israelis. Hence, reiterating governmental rhetoric, Israeli television has reduced the complex concept of martyrdom, which refers to a wide span of voluntary activities, including humanitarian ones for the sake of the Islamic community, to the sole phenomenon of suicide operations, implying that the Palestinian television and the Palestinian Authority incites, encourages, and sends its children to commit suicide operations against Israel.

The Israeli governmental and televised criminalization of the PNA focused particularly on its president Yasser Arafat, who was often presented as "Most Wanted" (using CNN's framing of bin Laden)[51] and as a murderous crook through a combination of hatred, despisement, and ridicule.[52] Out of many examples I cite the Channel 1 & 2 airing of CNN's Christiane Amanpour's telephone interview with Arafat on March 29, 2002, when Arafat spoke from within his besieged compound in Ramallah in the midst of the Israeli operation that was using tank fire and bulldozers to destroy most of the buildings in the compound. The interview ended after Arafat abruptly hung up the phone following Amanpour's question of whether he would rein in his militants as demanded by Colin Powell. While Amanpour in her closing remarks explained Arafat's reaction as stemming from the intense pressure he was under, Israeli television omitted most of the interview, including Amanpour's closing remarks, leaving only the segment where Arafat shouts at what he perceives to be her insolence and hangs up the phone. This was followed by sarcastic comments on Arafat's manners and delusions of self-grandeur, such as the one by Amnon Abramowitz, one of Channel 1's most prominent commentators, and by the other reporters in the studio (and see also Moshe Cohen's introduction of this conversation on Channel 2).[53]

This dehumanization of the Palestinians, which forms part of the siege-derived revenge-retaliation frame aimed at enlisting Israelis in support of their elites, also functions to enlist the U.S.-led core-elites to their side and against the Palestinians. This is pursued by combining the siege frame with the core-elite law and order frame. It consists primarily in representing the conflict as being one between the Israelis' humane approach and their law-abiding democratic constitutional order, as against the inhuman, brutal, and violent lawlessness of the Palestinians and of the Palestinian Authority, a conflict presented as replicated in the global sphere (i.e., Arafat is like bin Laden). Hence, Israeli television has adopted a CNN-styled "due process" rhetoric constantly venerating the Israeli judicial system as well as emphasizing the due process followed by the IDF in its internal investigations and courts.

However, the siege-derived dehumanization and criminalization of the Palestinians, particularly the revenge-retaliation frame, works against Israeli elite interests when used to enlist the core-elites using the latter's law and

order frame, because of Israel's own violations of the internationally
accepted law and order norms. Hence, Israel's West Bank and Gaza Strip
settlements, its claim of sovereignty over the Old City of Jerusalem, and
some of its measures against the Palestinians (such as destroying the houses
of suicide bombers' families and of others, or the preemptive targeted killing
of terrorist group activists and leaders) are considered illegal internationally.
This generates the Israeli television framing of issues concerning Israeli violations of law and order through CNN's law and order-derived frames[54] of
"therapeutic sterilization," "surgical targeting," "scientific-investigation,"
and "balanced coverage," complemented by the siege-derived frames of
"turning the blame around" and "compared to others, we're morally far
better."

CNN's therapeutic sterilization and surgical targeting frame is appropriated, for example, in the coverage of targeted killings. Hence, while some
reports framed along the siege-derived "retaliation-revenge" model show
very graphic images of the results of the killing, including the dismembered
bodies of the activists, most other reports show these targeted killings from
afar, emphasizing audiovisually the high-tech tracking capabilities and precision ammunition used to follow and kill only the targeted person, while
omitting to note the usual accidental killing of by-standers, or expressing
regret for the "miscalculation." The therapeutic sterilization frame is also
evident in the detached presentation of the blowing up of houses belonging
to a suicide bomber's family. The latter headline shot consists of a lengthy
and long-distance shot, accompanied by a dispassionate fact-rendering commentary, where we see the targeted house in its quiet surroundings suddenly
collapsing in a burst of smoke, leaving the area surrounding it apparently
intact.

Particularly interesting in this respect is the overall detached and sterilized
framing of Operation Defensive Shield. It started with a series of reports
framing the incursion into the nearby densely populated Palestinian towns,
reflecting the core-elite's "War against Terror" conception whereby the
Israeli army is seen preparing for an orderly war somewhere far away.
Hence, the Channel 1 main news on the eve of the operation opened with a
report showing images of Palestinian masses and of masked gunmen rallying
in the occupied territories and in Lebanon to protest against Israel. This is
followed by Gur Tsalal Yachin's reports showing Israeli reserve soldiers
being drafted, happily meeting up, kissing their anxious wives or girlfriends
farewell, mounting the night buses heading to the front, and offering comments on camera such as the one made by reservist Menachem Goldberg,
who says while shaving that "force is the only solution." In voice-over the
reporter, almost whispering, tells us that "the air smells like war" and "a
State is mobilized once again."

In reports following the IDF incursions focus is on either night preparations before a particular action, showing the functional, efficient, and quiet movements of soldiers putting on their sophisticated war gear or mounting their tanks, or on the return of weary-eyed soldiers and their resting or reading after a particular operation. The reports on the actual incursions usually consist of early morning shots of one or two tanks and a few soldiers entering a Palestinian town through empty streets. One report by Tsalal Yachin shows Israeli soldiers rallying men for questioning and having each one raise his shirt from afar before he approaches the soldiers so as to make sure he is not carrying explosives. This framing of all Palestinian men as potential suicide bombers is followed by the reporter telling us that a few civilians mistakenly hit by IDF fire were given medical treatment by the Israeli soldiers. Most shots of actual fighting are taken from far away, showing Israeli soldiers shooting or a tank firing and usually omitting the deaths and ruins that resulted from these actions. No omission is made, however, of Palestinian attacks. Hence, in a report by Amir Bar-Shalom from March 30, 2002, on the IDF incursion into Bet Jalla after shots were fired from there on the bordering Jerusalem neighborhood of Gilo, Palestinian militants are shown throwing Molotov-cocktails at an Israeli army jeep, which is seen driving backward to avoid the burning bottle without returning fire. Whenever information is given of casualties resulting from the operation, the images shown are not of civilian casualties and mass destruction of buildings but on a few militants killed and of mostly intact houses. Hence, in reports by Tsalal Yachin (Channel 1) and Roni Daniel (Channel 2) on the incursion into Ramallah and the ruining of buildings within Arafat's compound, most shots are long-distance and almost soundless, showing a slow-moving tank demolishing a wall, an arsenal of found weapons neatly arranged for exhibition, and Arafat sitting in the dark by candlelight surrounded by supporters described as "wanted men." One far away shot in Tsalal Yachin's report shows an Israeli soldier standing over five dead Palestinians in army-green uniforms.

Hence, the overall presentation of Operation Defensive Shield was that of a mild war carried out among overall quiet and empty streets with few casualties or destruction. This presentation of the IDF incursions as entering sparsely populated and empty-street towns contradicts the usual Israeli television framing of these towns. In most reports the same towns and streets are presented as densely populated and constantly crisscrossed by agitated masses throwing stones or marching the streets in funeral processions or protests, and of masked gunmen firing in the air. Particular focus in these reports is placed on Palestinians burning Israeli and U.S. flags or waving posters displaying bin Laden and Saddam Hussein, framing the Palestinians as anti-Israeli and anti-American barbarians.[55]

The combination of the siege-derived "turn the blame around" and "compared to others, morally we're far better" frames with CNN's "scientific-interrogative" and "balanced report" framing is produced by Israeli television when reporting on Palestinian or human rights groups' accusations that the IDF has violated law and order or committed atrocities. The resulting argument in such reports,[56] particularly on allegations that the IDF has killed innocent Palestinian civilians or blown up their houses, is that the blame should be put on the Palestinian militants' own inhuman decision to hide among civilians, leaving the army no choice despite its unrivaled utmost care.

Two emblematic examples are worth detailing: the response of Israeli television to Palestinian accusations that Israeli soldiers had shot the child Muhammad al Durra, and the Israeli television exploitation of the far-fetched Palestinian accusation that the IDF had massacred Palestinians during its Operation Defensive Shield incursion into the Jenin refugee camp.

The broadcast by Israeli television of the September 30, 2002, killing of the child Muhammad al Durra and the wounding of his father in the crossfire between IDF soldiers and Palestinian militants was almost inevitable. The video images caught live by France 2 and broadcast all around the world, the international outrage at this incident, the demands of several human rights organizations within Israel to open an independent investigation of the event, and the station's own self-perception as dedicated to reporting outstanding law and order transgressions, led the Israeli mainstream television news to broadcast these disturbing images.[57]

The coverage of the killing of al Durra began with an initial one-time broadcast of the event by Israeli TV, consisting of portions of the France 2 crew's disturbing images, verbally framed as a human tragedy mistakenly resulting from the crossfire between the army and Palestinian militants, mentioning the army spokesman's apology for the incident. Things changed, however, following the results of the IDF investigation of the event (released on November 27, 2000) and the statement made by the head of the investigation, IDF Southern Commander Major General Yom-Tov Samia, whereby "a comprehensive investigation conducted in the last weeks casts serious doubt that the boy was hit by Israeli fire. . . . It is quite plausible that the boy was hit by Palestinian bullets in the course of the exchange of fire that took place in the area." This IDF investigation led Esther Shapira of the German ARD television station to produce a documentary that was aired on March 16, 2002, repeating the conclusion that al Durra could not have been killed by gunfire from the Israeli outpost and was probably killed by the Palestinian militants' gunfire.

Following the airing of this documentary Yom-Tov Samia told Israel Radio that the army had erred in hurrying to apologize for the boy's death and that "one day, it will be proven that the whole story . . . was one big Palestinian production. And Palestinian propaganda has been riding on this for a long time now."[58] While Israeli television did not officially espouse this far-fetched conspiracy theory, they did interview Yosef Duriel and aired a

CBS *60 Minutes* program with him, where he claimed that al Durra had been killed by Palestinian gunmen, collaborating with the French camera crew and the boy's father with the intent of fabricating anti-Israeli propaganda (Duriel participated in the IDF investigation but was removed from it following these accusations). Israeli TV also re-created the results of the IDF investigation, trying to show through diagrams, arrowed photos of the site, and an analysis of the France 2 crew shots, how it would have been impossible for the Israeli soldiers to have killed the boy. The "scientific-investigatory" framing of these reports diffused the heart-breaking import of the boy's killing. Channel 2 also aired Shapira's documentary and interviewed her on the news on March 20, 2002, where she said that because she was Jewish, reports were already circulating in Germany suggesting that her work had been produced in cooperation with the Mossad, Israel's secret service.[59] Hence, the overall impression conveyed by Israeli TV on the incident was that the Palestinian accusations against Israel in this case were groundless, being sheer propaganda solely motivated by blind hatred and anti-Israeliness, blowing the event out of all reality or proportion.[60]

The other emblematic siege-derived turn-around typed response of Israeli mainstream TV to accusations of atrocities committed by the IDF, can be seen in the overall Israeli televised exploitation of the evidently groundless Palestinian accusation that the IDF had conducted a massacre of over five hundred Palestinians in the refugee camp of Jenin during Operation Defensive Shield.[61] Hence, beyond the original reporting of the event by Israeli television under its CNN-borrowed sterilization frame (see above), as the accusations of a massacre kept piling up, Israeli TV began using this groundless accusation to divert attention away from the actual violations of human rights and the war crimes allegedly committed by the IDF during the operation,[62] and, notwithstanding the retraction of these accusations by official Palestinian spokesmen,[63] framed them within the historical context of anti-Semitic blood-libels against Jews. A salient example of this siege-derived response to the events in Jenin can be found in the 2004 documentary *Massacring the Truth*, produced and directed by Martin Himel for the Canadian Global TV Network. The film was aired on December 2004 by Channel 1 in its prime time program *Proper Disclosure* under the headline "The True Story—Jenin, the Truth about the Massacre." It was preceded and followed by a studio discussion ("neutrally" hosted by the channel's prominent anchor Yaakov Ahimeir) between David Tzangan, an Israeli doctor who was part of the IDF force that had entered Jenin, and Majda al Batsh, a Palestinian reporter who covered the event after the fact. The film's establishing sequences, which consist of graphic shots taken from suicide bomb sites, note the suicide bombing at the Park Hotel in Netanya the night before the incursion and cut to an army helicopter in the air and Israeli soldiers walking in the Jenin allies while in voice-over the reporter tells us that "immediately"

after the Park Hotel bombing that killed twenty-nine Israelis the army
entered Jenin. The cut and the term *immediate* suggest a process of swift,
effective, and necessary retaliation (whereas such wide-scale operations in
fact demand lengthy advance planning). The sequence then informs us of the
ambush by Palestinian militants in which thirteen Israeli soldiers died and
introduces Jonathan Van Caspel, an Israeli reservist who participated in the
incursion, who mourns members of his platoon killed in Jenin and who is
haunted by the false accusations that the IDF forces committed a massacre
in the camp. The film then alternates between camcorder footage taken by
both Van Caspel's unit and by Al Aqsa Martyrs' Brigades fighters, aimed at
showing "what it's like to fight urban warfare . . . it's confusing. You don't
see the enemy. . . . You don't know where the bullets are coming from. It's
scary. No one really knows what's going on."[64]

The confusing images shown, beyond framing the event as unknowable,
are also used to emphasize that Israeli forces encountered severe opposition.
This point is further enhanced later on, when Himel is seen driving through
Jenin following a mysteriously presented black car through back-alleys that
lead him to an unspecified location, where he interviews Muntassar, the Al
Aqsa Martyrs' Brigades commander in the refugee camp. Muntassar, surrounded by men holding machine-guns, proudly tells him about the intense
fighting that went on in Jenin. The overall framing of the Palestinian militants
is that of an outlaw gang that strongly countered the incursion. The opening
sequence thereby implicitly explains away the severe reaction of the army to
the aforementioned ambush, which resulted in the eventual bulldozing of the
camp, an action that elicited the massacre accusations. The film then returns
to Van Caspel's distress at being accused of war crimes. This alternation
between camcorder footage taken by both warring sides and between Van
Caspel and Muntassar offers an apparent "balanced coverage," incorrectly
implying that the fight was between equally potent opponents, yet clearly
presenting the Palestinian fighters as a gang of outlaws fighting a well-
intentioned orderly army that has had no choice but to enter a camp that, as
Himel reports, has produced a large percentage of the suicide bombers and
whose militants were supported by Iraq. This commentary is accompanied
by a Muezzin prayer heard over images of Jenin, converging Islam in general
with terror.

Having "balanced" the fight in Jenin, the film shifts toward the massacre
allegations, showing through an "investigative frame" consisting of enlarged
quotes from newspapers and excerpts from television reports, how Palestinian spokesmen and the world media at large gave vent to the massacre allegations based on hearsay, and on either no evidence at all or on fabricated
evidence. The latter point is made mostly through the film's inclusion of an
Israeli army miniature drone flying over Jenin on Monday, April 28, that
recorded a staged Palestinian funeral in which the "deceased" is seen dis-

mounting the stretcher and walking away, while the reporter reiterates the Israeli army's claim that the Palestinians had deliberately inflated the numbers of their casualties. (It should be pointed out that this widely circulated recording of an event shot from afar and from above, by night, in some backalley and involving five or six Palestinians, does not really provide any proof for the claims made.)

Having established through this "investigative" frame the unfounded massacre allegations, Himel, along with Van Caspel, confronts the various journalists and editors who had made the allegation, as well as Sa'ib Arekat, the highly prominent PNA official who had promulgated it, showing how some of them (notably Sa'ib Arekat) were retracting their allegations while others were saying that they had not used the word *massacre* but simply reported on the atrocious behavior of the IDF in Jenin, a report they would not retract. At this point Himel shifts from the "investigative" frame used to disprove the massacre allegation to a "compared with others we're morally far better" frame, whereby among other comparisons, he offers documentary images of the results of NATO bombings in Kosovo or of the U.S. bombing of Iraq, saying that the results of the IDF incursion into Jenin pale in comparison to these acts. One outstanding shot within this frame, which also involves CNN's sterilizing frame, offers an aerial photo of the whole of Jenin city while encircling in red a small white area, aimed at showing the tiny size of the demolished refugee camp in comparison to all of Jenin (but actually hinting at the massive destruction that had occurred).

After disproving the massacre allegations and presenting the bulldozing of the camp as a tiny, insignificant occurrence within the atrocious record of other nations, the film shifts to a siege-derived "turn the blame around" frame. In this particular case, however, the blame is not turned only toward the Palestinians but also toward the European media. This shift follows an interview with the self-proclaimed anti-Israeli journalist Jamie Di Giovani, who refuses to sit in the same room with Van Caspel, and asks Himel whether he is a Jew. This leads to a disturbing, powerful sequence dealing with the anti-Semitic-based anti-Israeliness of Palestinians and of much of the European media, centered around an interview with Harvard law professor Allen Darshowitz, who forcefully argues against this phenomenon (as evidenced in the ongoing anti-Semitic-based critique of the legitimate democratic practice of the Zionist lobby in America). The sequence includes a Palestinian woman comparing the events in Jenin to the Holocaust, photographs of protesters carrying posters equating Nazism with Zionism, and an anti-Semitic award-winning caricature by Dave Brown published in the British newspaper *Independent*, showing an obese half-naked Sharon eating a Palestinian child's head while blood pours down his fat chin. This caricature sends Himel to review an anti-Semitic drama broadcast by Hizbolla's Al Manar television showing Jews kidnapping a child in order to drink his blood during the Passover celebration. This sequence, while strongly exposing anti-Semitism in the European and Arab media, is somewhat irrelevantly used by Himel to frame the events in Jenin as part of the ongoing blood libel of Jews by anti-Semites.

Hence, Himel's emblematic documentary diverts attention away from the Israeli violations of Palestinian human rights and the alleged war crimes committed during the incursion into the Jenin refugee camp, by exploiting the evidently false massacre accusation through its incorporation into the siege-derived "anti-Semitic turned anti-Israeli" framework. This diversion is continued in the studio discussion that followed the film's airing. Sitting under the banner "The True Story—Jenin, the Truth about the Massacre," Yaakov Ahimeir "balances" the discussion by asking the Israeli doctor and the Palestinian reporter questions focused on the massacre lie, such as what were the reasons for the lie, why do Palestinians promulgate such lies, and so forth. This gives the Israeli doctor an opportunity to continue the diversion (e.g., "the blood libel massacre allegations encourage suicide bombers") and obliges the Palestinian reporter to offer justifications for the promulgation of the lie (e.g., "the IDF closed off all access to the camp so we were fed by hearsay" or, "no, there was no intentional fabrication in order to forge a Palestinian legend but we did want to extol the battle fought by our militants in Jenin, since no such fierce battle occurred in Ramallah or Bethlehem during the operation").

Palestinian Authority Television Coverage

The coverage of the al Aksa Intifada by PATV news also offered a double-talk framing of the conflict. On the one hand it offered a Shahada-(martyrdom) determined framing that was highly ethnocentric, revengeful, and based on the exaltation of death, audiovisually framing the events as resulting from a murderous Jewish imperialistic appetite, aimed at destroying Palestinian homes and towns, and at killing, persecuting, and exiling them from their country, giving Palestinians an opportunity to die in the struggle, kill the killers, and reach paradise. It constantly called on Palestinians to be resolute, to rally behind the potent Palestinian National Authority and its leader Yasser Arafat, and to seek death in their offering of collective and personal heroic sacrifices in order to achieve national liberation. The PATV used an audiovisual terrorizing frame to overtly incite violence; disseminated horrifying images of killed Palestinians; eulogized their dead; and incited Palestinians to inflict injuries on Israelis, to damage holy Jewish sites, and to engage in various forms of struggle against the Israeli occupation, including acts of terror. Many of its messages used religious language, sometimes emphasizing that the conflict is between Islam and Judaism. On the other hand it also framed the conflict as being between a people fighting for their right to self-determination yet facing a genocidal murderous terror state, headed by a criminal prime minister (Ariel Sharon), that victimizes the Palestinians and violates their human rights.

Emblematic are the many Palestinian television reports on mass-attended funeral processions of Palestinians killed by the IDF, characterized by an unsettling excitement and ardor-arousing verbal narrative; by laudatory commentary; and by jumpy editing, with unstable hand-held camera movement focusing through close shots on the excited crowd surrounding the deceased ("martyr") and, whenever available, on his bleeding wounds, all rendered in warm colors and shaky compositions.[65] The same pattern recurs in looped reports on Israeli troop movements and incursions and on clashes with the IDF, edited in a dialectic montage style to show low-angled shots of threatening Israeli tanks firing cut to a blown-up building, of bulldozers destroying houses with (almost elated) Palestinian civilians or militants firing, throwing burning Molotov-cocktails, or throwing stones.[66] These reports, constantly and abruptly interrupting the regular programming schedule, are characterized by an overall chaotic presentation of the events, often shifting among several locations and towns in the West Bank or Gaza, using hand-held tilting and shaking tracking shots accompanied by an often hysterical commentary conveying a sense of an ongoing multidirectional invasion and issuing encouraging urgent calls for collective mobilization and sacrifice in the struggle.[67] The commentary constantly praises Palestinian resistance and often calls Israeli soldiers murderers, war criminals, and child killers, with edited sequences showing Israeli soldiers shooting at ambulances or at Palestinian children.[68] The reports insert horrific pictures of dead and wounded Palestinians on the streets and in hospitals, often showing in close-up burned or mutilated bodies of men, women, and children and of elderly women raising their hands to the sky and pleading for vengeance.[69]

These traumatic, inflammatory scenes, broadcast several times a day, seamlessly glide from documentary-styled reporting to poeticized fictionalization. Hence, the reports are often accompanied by the reading or singing of nationalistic poems or the playing of nationalistic music. Televised funeral processions are replayed in slow motion overlaid by Israeli soldiers firing, and there is constant use of poetic eulogies for the "martyrs," a category applied equally to rock-throwing children, innocent bystanders, firing militants, and suicide bombers. One of the trailers to the Palestinian Authority television news program provides a good illustration. Accompanied by emotive, stirring march-style music, whose flow sutures the separate images, we see a series of brief slow-motion shots dissolving into each other of selected dynamic symbolic images. These include furious youths using slings to throw stones at Israeli tanks, Israeli soldiers dragging the body of a Palestinian, the back of an old man holding a club and facing flames, and a young man running along a border-like fence defiantly waving the Palestinian flag.

The trailer culminates in a shot of a young child raising his fingers to signal victory, superimposed by a caption reading, "We Will Never Forget. We Will Never Forgive."

This poeticized framing of news is aimed at forging powerful emotive symbols through recurring headline shots. Such is the PATV coverage and consequent symbolization of the child Muhammad al Durra killed in the crossfire between Israeli soldiers and Palestinian militants on September 30, 2000. The PATV showed over and over again an edited version of the France 2 crew's live shots of the boy, seen futilely sheltered by his father's arm until the father is wounded and the boy killed. Later, the PATV manipulated the shots to create an edited version wherein pictures of an Israeli soldier shooting were spliced into the original footage. The sequence became a rallying symbol of resistance and rage against Israel. The child's death (and funeral) were broadcast hundreds of times. Portions of the video were inserted into many poetic trailers, and a still photograph from the video was overlaid with varying captions and the Palestinian flag as studio background.[70] From then on PATV labeled the IDF as "Israeli child-killers." Beyond the news, PATV repeatedly aired a song featuring a father singing about his son as a martyr—the son being Muhammad al Durra—and even re-created the event with actors and showed al Durra in paradise urging other children to "follow him" (aired many times, for example, on December 25, 2000). The PATV Shahada-styled presentation of death as desirable was particularly focused on children. Hence, in this segment (as well as in several other music clips and dramatized sequences),[71] children are seen in heaven or shown as longing to die as martyrs. Andrea Levin describes the al Durra videotape: "Death is presented as serene and happy, a place of sunlit green fields and reunion with friends. Mohammed al Durra (is seen) frolicking at a beach, at an amusement park and flying a kite in a tree-lined meadow."[72]

A similar major poeticization and symbolization was performed on news reports on the incursion into Jenin, in line with Arafat's description of it as "Jeningrad." The PATV reported intensively on Jenin and framed the incursion as a "last stand at the Alamo"[73] that ended in a massacre of Palestinians by the IDF. Its framing can best be described by the message posted by WAFA (the Palestinian News Agency) on its website on April 10, 2002, which reads, "The invading Israeli tanks, planes and bulldozers are demolishing the Jenin refugee camp house by house over the heads of their remaining residents . . . the heroic resistance men are still holding out . . . while the Israeli invasion army bulldozers are burying the martyrs in mass graves in order to conceal the massacre." Among the shots recurring in many of the poeticized news segments, and dissolving into each other, are shots of Palestinian militants firing at IDF tanks, bulldozers razing buildings to the ground, grisly corpses being excavated from the rubble, images of women and children trapped in basements, the Palestinian flag waving, and photographs of killed "martyrs" (e.g., June 20, 2002).

The demonization of the IDF, the recurring horrific images showing dead Palestinians and ruined houses, is coupled as mentioned by a Shahada-derived revenge frame characterized by an exaltation of martyrdom and sacrifice through longing for Paradise, often for the sake of revenge and often couched in anti-Semitic language.[74] Hence, several segments include interviews with parents praising their sons or daughters "martyred" in clashes with the IDF and calling for others to follow in their steps,[75] including interviews with parents of suicide bombers.[76] On September 21, 2004, for example, PATV interviewed in its studio Um Taysir, the mother of Hamas suicide bomber Taysir al Ajrami, in which she is seen dressed in black, bathed in soft yellow lighting, and quietly exalting in religious mystical terms her son's death while killing Jews. After she recounts how she has told her youngest grandson Faraj that "Your father killed Jews and achieved martyrdom" and describes Taysir's insistence that "Wherever you go—Mecca, al-Madina, Mina, or Mount 'Arafat—pray that I will be martyred," the interviewer, describing her reaction to Taysir's death as "with cries of joy and the hope that Allah receives him as a martyr," asks her how she came to know about her fifth (!) son's "martyrdom." At this point the mother recounts that "Taysir came to me in a dream. I was standing at the entrance to the house and he appeared, wearing a groom's suit and his face was lit up like the moon. . . . He went straight to his brother's room and knocked on the door, his brother opened the door for him. He hugged his brother, patted him on the back and went on his way. I called out their names, but they both went on their way." The mother's closing remarks are, "We Palestinians are a role model for all the countries. When I watch Arab TV, I see them exclaiming: 'How the Palestinian mother bid goodbye to her son! How the Palestinian mother breaks into cries of joy!' "[77]

This overall terror-trauma Shahada framing formation exalts personal and collective sacrifice while stimulating liberating violence.[78] It also constantly overlays the images with religious and national symbols invariantly present in the design of the news studio. These include photos, digital imaging, or paintings of the al Aksa mosque (also represented on the TV station's logo), of the Palestinian flag, and of President Arafat. The exaltation of death and violence along with the explicit convergence of religious and national symbols appropriates the Shahada ideology originating in the Hamas and Islamic Jihad radical Islam ideology, whose representatives hardly ever appear on PATV and whose terrorist struggle for a regional Islamic nation is hardly mentioned.[79] This appropriation also includes the broadcasting of Arafat's repeated praise of those killed as shahids,[80] deliberately blurring differences between the different circumstances that led to their deaths and thus implicitly incorporating suicide bombers (most of whom were sent by radical

Islamic movements) under this term. In addition, in Arafat's speeches and in the PATV images focus is on the waving of the national flag over the holy Islamic sites in East Jerusalem as the ultimate aim of the Palestinian struggle, blurring the traditional Palestinian claim to all of historical Palestine (maintained by Hamas and Islamic Jihad, and supported by Palestinians demanding the "right of return"), and implicitly endorsing the idea of a Palestinian state besides Israel, with East Jerusalem as its capital.[81]

The appropriated Shahada framing is aimed at internal recruitment by representing as pertaining to all Palestinians the particular interests of the Palestinian Authority elite in attaining an independent Arab-Palestinian state alongside Israel. The Shahada-derived demonization of the IDF and the presentation of Israel as a genocidal colonialist nation victimizing the Palestinians, also functions to enlist the U.S.-led core-elites to the Palestinian side and against the Israelis. This is achieved by combining the Shahada frame with the core-elite "human rights violations" frame. It consists primarily in representing the conflict as being one between a people fighting for their right to self-determination while facing a terror state, headed by a criminal prime minister (Sharon), that victimizes the Palestinians and violates their human rights.

However, these strategies of core-elite enlistment also work against the Palestinian core-dependent elite interests. This is mostly because the exaltation of death and the terrorist forms of the Palestinian struggle for liberation echo the al Qaeda struggle, and works against its human rights violation claim. Hence PATV's reports on the conflict and its escalating violence are often framed through an "external" CNN global look-alike perspective, reserved almost exclusively to portray (in an air of international respectability) what is otherwise presented as the Palestinians' death-wish ideology and their murderous form of struggle. This double-talk can be seen in reports on Israeli aggression, which is covered on the one hand, Shahada-style, as an opportunity for Palestinians to die in struggle, kill the killers, and reach Paradise, while on the other hand it is covered through a CNN-emulating "human rights violation as human tragedy" frame, emphasized through Western-styled melancholic music, slow-motion shots of wretched looking and desperate people, of ragged children running amongst ruined houses or dying as innocent victims, of the human tragedy embedded in an old woman's helpless rage, of the desolation and destitution brought about by destruction of property and resulting in tragic homelessness and poverty, and of the agonizing wounds of innocent civilians lying helpless.

This was complemented by PATV's omission of the atrocities committed by Palestinian mobs, and by CNN-adopted frames offering biased reports on suicide bombings. Thus, the PATV did not broadcast any of the images whatsoever of the torching and desecration of a Jewish holy site known as Joseph's tomb on October 7, 2000, in Nablus, nor of the images caught live and broadcast around the world of the horrific lynching of two Israeli soldiers by a Palestinian crowd in Ramallah on October 12, 2000.[82] PATV also usually omits reporting on suicide bombings. In the few instances in which it does mention these it shows a few CNN-styled sterilized distant shots of the event and reports on the number of casualties, but then quickly turns to a "human rights" framing of the Israeli response.[83]

Another PATV strategy when dealing with suicide bombings consists in using CNN's multicultural framing in its separation of the deed from the praising of the doer by his parents, achieved through interviews with the parents of the suicide bomber in which he is extolled as a shahid who died fighting for his people, without mentioning the fact that he died in a suicide attack or the results of this attack.[84] Finally, in official responses condemning such acts, a CNN-type "balancing" frame is used whereby the PNA regrets the terror killing of innocent civilians on both sides. This is usually coupled with accusations that Israel impedes the PNA's resolve to put a stop to such acts when it attacks the PNA security forces, then "debalancing" the report through following it with images of Israeli tanks and soldiers shooting at Palestinians. Hence, on May 8, 2002, Yasser Arafat, in a televised speech on PATV, condemns suicide bombings after the Islamic militant group Hamas has claimed responsibility for an attack that killed fifteen Israelis, saying, "I gave my orders and directions to all the Palestinian security forces to confront and prevent all terror attacks against Israeli civilians from any Palestinian side or parties." However, Arafat then qualified his statement by calling on "the U.S. government, President Bush, and the international community to provide the support and needed immunity for the Palestinian security forces, whose infrastructure has been destroyed by the Israeli occupation, so that they can carry out and implement their orders . . . to completely stop any terror attempt targeting Israeli civilians or Palestinian civilians, and to prevent using terror as a political way to achieve their goals."[85]

NOTES

1. Muhammad al Durra left home that morning to accompany his father, Jamal al Durra, on a day's outing to shop for a car. On the return trip home, the father and son crossed a main street in the Bureij refugee camp when heavy shooting broke out between Palestinian militiamen and an Israel Defence Force (IDF) outpost near Netzarim junction. Muhammad and Jamal al Durra sought sanctuary in vain between a concrete cylinder and a low cinderblock wall as bullets rained down around them for about forty-five minutes, of which several minutes were filmed. "He stayed close to me, clutching me from my back while I was trying to keep him away from the bullets," said his father. "But one bullet hit him in the leg. I started screaming and crying, hoping that the bullets would stop, but to no avail." Edited television footage showed Jamal al Durra waving desperately, shouting, "Don't shoot!" but Muham-

mad was eventually hit by four bullets and collapsed in his father's arms. Jamal al Durra was also shot and suffered critical injuries but survived after receiving emergency surgery in Jordan. He suffered a permanently paralyzed right arm. "It is the worst nightmare of my life. . . . My son was terrified, he pleaded with me: 'For the love of God protect me, Baba (Dad).' I will never forget these words." An ambulance driver who tried to reach the trapped pair was shot and killed by IDF soldiers. A second ambulance driver was wounded. The killing was captured on film by a France 2 cameraman. The IDF initially admitted that it was "probably responsible" for killing Muhammad al Durra and expressed sorrow at his death. IDF operations chief Giora Eiland announced that a preliminary investigation revealed that "the shots were apparently fired by Israeli soldiers from the outpost at Netzarim." On October 7, 2001, al Qaeda spokesman Sulaiman Abu Ghaith warned President Bush that he "must not forget the video footage of Muhammad al Durra" and promised that violence against the United States would continue until, among other things, the country ended its assistance "to the Jews in Palestine."

2. Following is a partial chronology of major Palestinian suicide bombing attacks on Israeli civilians and military targets (from September 30, 2000, to November 30, 2004):

October 26, 2000—A twenty-four-year-old Palestinian man riding a bicycle died after detonating explosives near an Israeli army outpost in Gaza, injuring an Israeli soldier.

November 2, 2000—A car bomb killed two Israelis in central Jerusalem.

March 4, 2001—Three people were killed and sixty were wounded when a suicide bomber attacked a shopping mall in Netanya. Hamas claimed responsibility. The bomber was a twenty-two-year-old refugee, Ahmad Ayam, from Tulkarem.

May 18, 2001—Five were killed and more than one hundred injured when a suicide bomber attacked a shopping mall in Netanya. Hamas claimed responsibility.

May 25, 2001—Forty-five people were wounded when two suicide bombers drove an explosives-laden truck into a bus in Hadera. Islamic Jihad claimed responsibility.

June 1, 2001—Twenty-one people were killed and at least 120 injured by a suicide bomb attack on the Dolphinarium discotheque in Tel Aviv. Although at first Islamic Jihad claimed the attack, later Hamas said it was responsible.

August 9, 2001—Fifteen people were killed and at least 130 injured when a suicide bomber attacked the Sbarro pizza restaurant on the Jaffa Road in downtown Jerusalem. Islamic Jihad and Hamas issued competing claims of responsibility.

September 9, 2001—Three people were killed and at least ninety wounded when an Israeli Arab committed a suicide bomb attack on a group of soldiers and civilians disembarking from a train at the Nahariya station. Hamas claimed responsibility.

December 1, 2001—Eleven people were killed and more than 130 injured after two suicide bombers set off sequential explosions followed by a car bomb in a pedestrian mall in West Jerusalem. Hamas claimed responsibility.

December 2, 2001—Fifteen people were killed and at least forty wounded by a suicide bomber on a Haifa city bus. Hamas claimed responsibility.

January 27, 2002—One person was killed and more than 111 wounded when a suicide bomber blew herself up in downtown Jerusalem. Wafa Idris, the perpetrator, was the first female suicide bomber. The Al Aqsa Martyrs' Brigades, the militant off-shoot of Palestinian leader Yasser Arafat's Fatah movement, claimed responsibility.

February 16, 2002—Three were killed and more than thirty wounded when an eighteen-year-old suicide bomber attacked a pizza restaurant in a shopping center in the Karnei Shomron settlement. The perpetrator dyed his spiky hair blond, reportedly to be able to blend in. The Popular Front for the Liberation of Palestine (PFLP) claimed responsibility.

March 9, 2002—Eleven people were killed and more than fifty injured when a twenty-year-old suicide bomber attacked the crowded Café Moment in Jerusalem. Hamas claimed responsibility.

March 27, 2002—Twenty-nine people were killed and more than one hundred injured by a suicide bomb attack at the Park Hotel in Netanya during a Passover seder dinner. Hamas claimed responsibility.

March 29, 2002—Two people were killed and at least twenty wounded in an attack at a supermarket in the Kiryat Hayovel district of Jerusalem. The perpetrator was an eighteen-year-old woman. The Al Aqsa Martyrs' Brigades claimed responsibility.

March 31, 2002—Fifteen people were killed and more than forty-four injured when a suicide bomber struck the Israeli-Arab owned Matza restaurant in Haifa. Hamas claimed responsibility.

April 4, 2002—One woman died and more than thirty injured in a suicide bombing in a café in Tel Aviv. The Al Aqsa Martyrs' Brigades claimed responsibility.

May 8, 2002—A suicide bombing in the center of a crowded pedestrian district in a pool hall in Rishon Letzion killed fifteen people and wounded sixty. Hamas claimed responsibility.

May 18, 2002—three Israelis were killed and fifty-six wounded in a suicide bombing in the Israeli coastal city of Netanya. The PFLP and Hamas claimed responsibility.

May 22, 2002—Two died and at least thirty-seven were wounded following a suicide bomb attack at a pedestrian mall in Rishon Letzion.

May 5, 2002—Two died and forty-five were wounded in a suicide attack in Petah Tikva. The Al Aqsa Martyrs' Brigades claimed responsibility.

June 5, 2002—Seventeen people were killed and at least thirty-eight injured in a suicide attack at Megiddo Junction on a bus headed for Tiberias. Islamic Jihad claimed responsibility.

June 18, 2002—Nineteen people were killed and seventy-four wounded in an attack on a bus traveling to Jerusalem from the nearby Gilo settlement. Hamas claimed responsibility for the attack.

June 19, 2002—Seven people were killed and thirty-five wounded in an attack at a popular hitchhiking post in East Jerusalem. The al-Aqsa Martyrs' Brigades claimed responsibility.

August 4, 2002—Nine people were killed and thirty-seven injured in a suicide bomb attack on a bus traveling from Haifa to Safed in northern Israel. Hamas claimed responsibility.

September 18, 2002—A suicide bomber set off a blast on a crowded city bus in downtown Tel Aviv, killing five people and wounding sixty.

October 10, 2002—Two people struggled to subdue a Palestinian suicide bomber before he blew himself up at a bus stop near Tel Aviv, killing one person and wounding twenty.

October 21, 2002—A suicide bomber drove a vehicle loaded with explosives next to a bus packed with passengers in northern Israel and blew it up, killing fourteen people and wounding fifty.

October 27, 2002—A suicide bomber blew himself up near a gas station in the West Bank killing three people and wounding nineteen. The Al Aqsa Martyrs' Brigades claimed responsibility.

November 4, 2002—An explosion set off by a suicide bomber rocked a shopping mall in Kfar Saba, killing two people and wounding twenty.

January 5, 2003—A double suicide bombing in Tel Aviv left twenty-three people dead and more than one hundred injured.

March 5, 2003—A suicide bomber set off a powerful explosion that destroyed a suburban bus in the northern Israeli port city of Haifa, killing fifteen people and wounding forty.

April 24, 2003—A Palestinian teenager blew himself up outside Kfar Saba's new train station, killing an Israeli security guard who had prevented him from entering the station, and injuring fourteen other people.

April 30, 2003—A security guard at a beachfront café blocked a suicide bomber from entering the establishment but the bomber blew himself up at the café door killing three people and wounding fifty.

May 10, 2003—A suicide bomber killed an Israeli couple in a Jewish settlement in the West Bank town of Hebron. Izzedine al Qassam, the military wing of Hamas claimed responsibility.

May 11, 2003—A suicide bomber on a commuter bus killed seven people and wounded nineteen others. Moments later, a second suicide bombing took place nearby in East Jerusalem, but no one was injured other than the bomber.

May 19, 2003—A suicide bomber killed three people at a shopping mall in the northern Israeli city of Afula. Forty-seven people were wounded. The suicide bomber was a nineteen-year-old woman. The Islamic Jihad and the Al Aqsa Martyrs' Brigades claimed responsibility.

June 11, 2003—A deadly suicide bomb attack struck a Jerusalem bus. Sixteen people died and sixty were wounded. Hamas claimed responsibility.

August 12, 2003—Hamas's armed wing, Izzedine al Qassam, claimed responsibility for an attack at a bus stop near the West Bank settlement of Ariel that killed one Israeli and critically wounded two others. The Al Aqsa Martyrs' Brigades claimed responsibility for another attack, a grocery store bombing in central Israel that killed one Israeli and wounded at least ten others.

August 19, 2003—Twenty-two people were killed and 130 wounded on a Jerusalem bus by a suicide bomber who came from Hebron in the West Bank.

September 9, 2003—A suicide bomber detonated a powerful explosive at a bus stop outside a military base near Tel Aviv. Eight people died and fifteen were wounded. Hamas took responsibility.

September 10, 2003—A suicide bomber killed seven people on an outdoor terrace of a popular café in West Jerusalem. Hamas took responsibility.

October 4, 2003—Nineteen people were killed and fifty wounded by a female suicide bomber in a terror attack at the crowded Maxim restaurant in the northern Israeli city of Haifa.

December 25, 2003—A suicide bombing at a major intersection outside Tel Aviv during rush hour killed four people and wounded thirteen. The PFLP claimed responsibility.

January 14, 2004—A female suicide bomber killed four and wounded ten at the Erez border crossing separating Israel and northern Gaza.

January 29, 2004—Ten people were killed and forty-five were wounded when a Palestinian policeman got on a passenger bus in Jerusalem and set off a blast as the vehicle neared the Israeli prime minister's home.

February 22, 2004—A suicide bomber killed eight passengers on a crowded bus in Jerusalem at the height of rush hour. The Al Aqsa Martyrs' Brigades claimed responsibility.

July 11, 2004—An explosion at a Tel Aviv bus stop killed one woman and wounded twenty-two people. The Al Aqsa Martyrs' Brigades claimed responsibility.

August 31, 2004—Two suicide bombers set off almost simultaneous blasts on buses in Beer Sheba, killing sixteen people and wounding ninety-five. Hamas claimed responsibility.

September 22, 2004—A female suicide bomber set off a blast in Jerusalem, killing two border policemen who tried to stop her. For a fuller report on attacks see www.jewishvirtuallibrary.org/jsource/Terrorism/TerrorAttacks.html.

3. *Report of the Secretary-General Prepared Pursuant to General Assembly Resolution ES-10/10.*

4. According to the Palestinian Centre for Human Rights report from April 2003, during the period September 2000 to April 2003 Israel carried out 165 assassination attempts that killed 229 targeted Palestinians from various Palestinian militant organizations and wounded hundreds of others. Following are several cases of Israeli targeted killings of Palestinian militant leaders and activists as reported by CNN:

July 19, 2001—An Israeli helicopter attack in Bethlehem killed Osama Saada from Hamas. Three others were killed in the attack and eight others were injured.

August 21, 2001—Israeli forces shot and wounded Hmad Bsharat, a Hamas militant in Jenin, who managed to escape.

October 14–18, 2001—Abdel Rahman Hamad, a Hamas militant was shot by Israeli forces as he stood on the roof of his house; Iyad al Akhras, a Hamas militant was assassinated by Israel in Rafah; Ahmad Marshoud, another Hamas militant, was killed in a car bomb explosion in the West Bank town of Nablus; Atif Abayyat, a member of the Fatah military wing, was killed along with two other people when a car exploded in Beit Sahour near Bethlehem in the West Bank.

March 2, 2002—Israeli soldiers in Jenin shot dead Amjad al-Fakhouri, a prominent member of the Al Aqsa Martyrs' Brigades.

July 23, 2002—An attack by Israeli F-16 aircraft in the heart of Gaza city killed Salah Shehade, leader of Izzedine al Qassam, the military wing of Hamas. Fourteen others were killed and fifteen were wounded.

August 7, 2002—Ziad Duaa, a member of the Al Aqsa Martyrs' Brigades was killed when an Apache helicopter fired on his house in the West Bank town of Tulkarem. On the same date, at the Khan Younis refugee camp in southern Gaza, Israeli snipers shot and killed Hussam Hamdan, a member of Hamas' military wing, Izzedine al Qassam. Israel had tried to get Hamdan several weeks earlier but killed a colleague of his by mistake.

August 14, 2002—Nasser Jarrar, a regional leader of Hamas's military wing, was killed in the northern West Bank town of Tubas when Israeli troops planted explosive charges around the house he was hiding in, and an Israeli helicopter ignited them. Two bulldozers then destroyed the house.

March 22, 2004—Hamas founder and spiritual leader Sheikh Ahmed Yassin was killed in an Israeli airstrike in Gaza. Seven others were killed and sixteen were wounded.

April 17, 2004—An Israeli helicopter attacked the car of Hamas's new leader Abdel Aziz Rantisi in Gaza City, killing him and two others.

5. Law and order–typed frames are discussed also in Stuart Hall, Charles Critcher, Tony Jefferson, John Clarke, and Brian Robert, *Policing the Crisis: Mugging, the State, and Law and Order* (Bakingstoke, U.K.: Macmillan Education Ltd., 1978); Robin Andersen, "Vision of Stability: US Television Law and Order News of El Salvador," *Media Culture and Society* 10, no. 2 (1988): 236–264.

6. E.g., CNN's John King's report from March 20, 2003, showing these headline shots.

7. See also Jerald Kessel's report from March 5, 2003, on the Haifa bombing that killed fifteen, where he alternates between images of the suicide bomb site and Israeli tanks battling stone-throwing Palestinians.

8. The Jenin camp houses about fourteen thousand people within one square mile. The UN-administered Jenin refugee camp was established in 1953 to house Palestinians displaced during the 1948 war.

9. This references the thirteen Israeli soldiers killed in a single ambush in a booby-trapped courtyard during the battle.

10. This references the Palestinian allegations that the Israel Defence Forces massacred over five hundred Palestinians in Jenin. The UN and the Human Rights Watch concluded that this accusation was groundless and that fifty-two Palestinians were killed during the incursion to Jenin.

11. Other reports that exemplify the "vicious circle" alternating framework are the November 1, 2002, CNN report on the Human Rights Watch report assessing suicide bombing operations as war crimes. This report moves from shots of suicide bombings to shots of Israeli tanks firing and bulldozers demolishing houses. It includes interviews with Hamas leaders reacting to the report and claiming suicide bombings are not suicides but acts of martyrdom. Likewise, CNN's Chris Burn's report from March 17, 2004, on two Israeli missile strikes in a refugee camp in Gaza that killed four Palestinians and wounded eleven others is correlated to the suicide bombing in Ashdod earlier that week. In the report we see Israeli Apache helicopters firing, Palestinian militants running into alleys, and images from the Ashdod suicide bombing.

12. E.g., CNN's Brian Nelson's interview of two experts on the situation or CNN's Gene Randall's hosting of an interview of Israeli and Palestinian diplomats (October 29, 2000).

13. A similar frame is occasionally used by CNN in its reports on the "ideology-driven" settling of "Judea and Samaria" (i.e., the occupied West Bank).

14. Al Manar (the beacon) is the official television station of the Lebanese-based Hizbolla, an Iranian supported Shiite movement that was instrumental in ending the

Israeli occupation of Lebanon through its fighting a guerrilla/terror war against it and which continues its fight both through sporadic attacks on the Lebanese border with Israel and through its support of Palestinian radical Islamist organizations such as Hamas. For a good review of Al Manar, albeit from a highly partisan critical view, see Avi Jorisch, "Al Manar: Hizbullah TV, 24/7" *Middle East Quarterly* (Winter 2004): 17–31.

15. Although this report deals with Lebanese rather than Palestinian suicide bombers, it is emblematic of CNN's multicultural framing of ideologies on both the Palestinian and the Israeli side that result in horrible atrocities. See, for example, the same pattern as that found in Boettcher's report within the following portions from a transcript of a report by CNN's Jerusalem bureau chief Mike Hanna from August 9, 2001, made after a Palestinian suicide bombing of a pizzeria in Jerusalem that left 15 dead and over 130 injured:

The international community has condemned the bombings in strong terms, labeling the bombers as terrorists and murderers. But the view is quite different on the streets of Gaza and the West Bank. There, the young men who carry out the attacks are seen as heroes in the fight against Israel, martyrs for the teachings of Islam, even role models for Palestinian youth. Their likenesses have been painted on walls, even though in some cases, the bombers killed only themselves. . . . Though the Koran teaches against taking one's own life, the suicide bombers are seen as martyrs and are said to be living in the heavens. At bomber Shadi al-Kahlout's funeral, attended by thousands of people, his mother, Subhia al-Kahlout, grieved for the loss of her son, even as she expressed pride in the way he died. "I am a mother and I was sad to lose him," she said. That pain is sometimes hidden under a public mask of stoicism, as explained by Dr. Iyad Sarraj, a psychiatrist. "In this tribal society we have two sets of language—one for the public, which is a language of steadfastness . . . , a language of being macho . . . a language of being proud . . . even of dying," Sarraj said. "Underneath of course we're human beings and we suffer." In a letter left for his parents, Shadi al-Kahlout told his mother to rejoice for him, and told his father, Abdul Rahim al-Kahlout, to be patient, as he would see him in paradise. "We had a feeling that one day Shadi would become a martyr, but we didn't know when." Abdul Rahim and Subhia al-Kahlout have 10 surviving children, and numerous pictures of a dead son. A son they say they think of every hour of the day.

16. The problem with this equalizing "balanced" approach rests not only in its neutralization of economic-political contextualizing but also in its detachment, as evidenced by the critique of CNN from both the Israeli and Palestinian sides, each of which blames CNN precisely for being biased. Although this criticism attests to each side's ethnocentric bias it also indicates CNN's overall insensitivity to their grievances. Hence on June 20, 2002, Reuters reported that Israeli television broadcasters had suggested blocking CNN broadcasts in Israel, citing CNN's founder Ted Turner, who had said, among other things, that the Israeli military was engaged in terrorism against the Palestinians that could be compared to Palestinian suicide bomber attacks on Israelis. Likewise, Michael Brown wrote on the pro-Palestinian *Electronic Intifada* site on December 3, 2003: "Casualties in Tel Aviv. Casualties in Rafah. Where does CNN go? Tel Aviv."

17. The idea of mutual suffering comes strongly across in CNN's Jerald Kessel's report from October 28, 2000, which alternates between funerals on both sides.

18. E.g., CNN's February 28, 2002, report on a Palestinian woman's suicide

bombing at a West Bank checkpoint correlated the attack to Saudi Arabia's initiative to resolve the conflict; CNN's February 9, 2003, report correlated a series of suicide bombings (in Afula, Jerusalem, Kfar Darom, Hebron) and Israeli retaliations (such as closing off Palestinian entry into Israeli territory) to a meeting between Israeli Prime Minister Ariel Sharon and Palestinian Prime Minister Mahmoud Abbas on the "Road Map" initiative to solve the conflict, backed by the United States, the European Union, the United Nations, and Russia.

19. Emblematic is CNN's John King's report from March 20, 2003, on President Bush's efforts to revive the peace talks stalled by Palestinian suicide bombings.

20. While the coverage of this peripheral violence is much more graphic than the coverage of such events within core states, relative to the coverage of the same events by peripheral TV stations it is highly detached and abstract.

21. See Radwan Abu Ayyash, *Broadcasters' Obligations towards Their Audience in Times of Crisis (The Palestinian Intifada as an Example)* (master's thesis, Center for Mass Communication Research, Leicester, U.K.: Leicester University, 1992).

22. Tamar Liebes has shown how journalists in democratic countries "rally around the flag" foregoing their traditional watchdog postures. See Tamar Liebes, *Reporting the Arab–Israeli Conflict: How Hegemony Works* (London: Routledge, 1997).

23. Gadi Wolfsfeld, "The News Media and the Second Intifada: Some Basic Lessons," *Palestine-Israel Journal* 10, no. 2 (2003): 5–12. Wolfsfeld's article is based on a joint study he conducted, along with Mohamad Dajani in 2003, that "examined some of the journalistic routines used by the news media in the two cultures that serve to reinforce hatred towards the other side" (Wolfsfeld, "News Media," 7). Their study, focused on the newspaper coverage of the second Intifada, also revealed demonizing frames. Israeli newspaper distortions and manipulations in reporting events before and during the second Intifada are also discussed by Daniel Dor in his book *Intifada Hits the Headlines: How the Israeli Press Misreported the Outbreak of the Second Palestinian Uprising* (Bloomington: Indiana University Press, 2004). Another important precedent to my analysis of the Israeli television coverage of the al Aksa Intifada can be found in Cohen, Adoni, and Nossek,'s study of the television coverage of the first Intifada. See Akiva Cohen, Hanna Adoni, and Hillel Nossek, "Television News and the Intifada," in *Framing the Intifada People and Media* (Jerusalem: Ablex, 1991).

24. Excerpt from Sharon's address to the Israeli Parliament on September 16, 2001.

25. E.g., On January 19, 2002, the IDF destroyed the Palestinian Broadcasting Corporation building in the West Bank city of Ramallah and on April 3, 2002, Israeli troops destroyed several nonofficial Palestinian broadcasting outlets in Ramallah.

26. See w3.castup.net/mfa/main_menu.htm.

27. See www.pmw.org.il/index.html.

28. See www.imra.org.il/aboutus.php3.

29. See www.memri.org.

30. See www.unitedjerusalem.org/index2.asp.

31. See www.ipc.gov.ps/ipc_e/ipc_e-1/ipc-e_israeli%20watch.html.

32. See www.phrmg.org/monitor.htm.

33. See www.palestinemonitor.org/new_web/mediawatch_archive.htm.

34. See electronicintifada.net/themedia.shtml.

35. By "Israeli television coverage" I refer exclusively to the coverage by Israeli Channel 1 & 2 news programs.

36. Particularly revealing in this respect is Amos Gitai's contribution to the film *11'09"01 September 11* (2002), produced by the French film company Studio Canal, which invited eleven renowned international directors to each create a film lasting eleven minutes, nine seconds, and one frame. Gitai's brief fiction film follows a reporter (Keren Mor) sent to cover a suicide bombing in Tel Aviv coinciding with the 9/11 attack on the Twin Towers in New York. Gitai succinctly describes the utter chaos at the site through the reporter's incessant commentary offering meaningless information and her being sent back and forth by the contradictory orders she receives from different police and army officers. In the background, people are also seen hurrying disorientedly, sporadically reappearing behind the reporter. Gitai strongly conveys in the film the sense of a hectic recursive activity leading nowhere.

37. This type of coverage recurs in all reports on suicide bombings. See, for example, the coverage of the suicide bombing in a Tel Aviv café on April 4, 2002, by Channel 1's Guy Peleg, Gur Tsalal Yachin, and others, and by Channel 2's Gal Gabai, Roni Daniel, Itai Engel, and others. In it the hand-held cameras survey the area, focusing on a man with blood dripping down his forehead, a wounded couple crouching on the sidewalk, people running around in despair, policemen and soldiers trying to disperse the agitated crowds, and so forth. Likewise, in the Channel 1 coverage by Amir Bar-Shalom of the May 27, 2002, suicide bombing in a mall in Petah Tikva we see hand-held camera shots surveying the site, searching around for victims, and focusing on a baby carriage and on blood under a chair, while ambulance sirens and alarms are heard.

38. In the coverage by Channel 1 of the Petah Tikva suicide bombing, Fuad Ben-Eliezer, the minister of defense at the time, reiterated the Israeli government's position that the Palestinian Authority was doing nothing to prevent suicide bombings and that Arafat was "irrelevant."

39. See David Witztum, "The Television Report and History," in *Cinema and Memory: A Dangerous Relationship?* [in Hebrew] ed. Haim Bresheet, Shlomo Sand, and Moshe Zimmerman (Jerusalem: The Zalman Shazar Center for Jewish History, 2004), 169–198. I follow here Witztum's unearthing of this classification though not his conclusions.

40. Nitzan Ben-Shaul, *Mythical Expressions of Siege in Israeli Films* (Lewiston, N.Y.: The Edwin Mellen Press, 1997).

41. E.g., Reports on the targeted killing of Hamas founder Ahmed Yassin and of his successor, Rantisi.

42. One notable exception was the airing of the killing of the child Muhammad al Durra discussed further below.

43. The settlers' continuous explicit framing of Palestinian suicide attacks within the dominant siege ideology is aimed at promoting their religious-territorial clandestine perspective (which tries to delegitimate the elites). Hence, by claiming that these attacks prove that the Palestinians do not differentiate between Jews in the occupied territories and Jews within the "Green Line" (the Israeli border before the 1967 war, a war that led to Israel's conquest of the West Bank and Gaza Strip), it follows that the conflict with the Palestinians is not over the Israeli debated occupation of these territories but over the very existence of all of Israel.

44. Quoted in Witztum, "The Television Report," 175, fn. 16.

45. While Israeli television does portray negatively the "bad seeds" this movement has bred—such as anti-Palestinian terror groups (and see the Channel 1 coverage from September 17, 2003, of the conviction by a Jerusalem court of three Israeli settlers for attempting to blow up an Arab girls' school in Jerusalem, showing the settlers as wild-eyed fanatic zealots offering a close-up on their shackled hands) and the murderer of Israeli Prime Minister Yitzhak Rabin—it treats in a legitimate and respectful manner their dominant religious and political leadership, despite its labeling of the government's disengagement plan as illegal and its calling for active massive refusal from within and without the army to any attempt to evacuate settlers from the Gaza Strip. One rather ridiculous yet disturbing symbolic expression of the settlers' attitude toward the Israeli government has been their wearing of orange Star of David patches, implying that the Israeli government is behaving toward them like the Nazis did toward the Jews in Germany.

46. The report by Channel 1 the day before only mentioned that three people had died in the attack without specifying that two of those killed were children, and avoided airing the distressing images of their evacuation broadcast by BBC and other TV stations around the world.

47. There are several similarly styled videos provided by the IDF to television channels.

48. In a photomontage widely circulated in Israel through the Internet after Yasser Arafat's death, he is seen engulfed in the flames of Hell, wide-eyed and astonished while exclaiming, "What? No virgins?"

49. Aired on PATV January 15, 2002.

50. This incitement does not differ so greatly from the Jewish settlers' encouragement and involvement of their children in their struggle, or from that of the Jewish pre-state organizations' use of children in their struggle for independence (e.g., the inculcation of a saying attributed to Joseph Trumpeldor, one of Zionism's legendary warriors, whereby as he lay fatally wounded he said, "it is good to die for our land").

51. Hence, borrowing CNN's styling of bin Laden as a most wanted man hiding in caves, Israeli television recurrently showed a shot of Arafat (taken during the siege of the Mukataa) sitting in the dark by candlelight and surrounded by his supporters. Despite the fact that this shot was taken in Arafat's office the visuals and commentary on Israeli television connoted his sitting in a cave.

52. This vulgar televised presentation cannot be justified or explained by the Israeli government allegations that Arafat was implicated in terror or had sums of money in banks outside the region. The only explanation is sheer hatred of the man and of what he represented following his tagging by the Israeli government as "irrelevant." Ironically, this demonization of Arafat on Israeli television swiftly reversed his previous, almost glorifying Israeli televised presentation during Yitzhak Rabin's premiership, following Rabin's signing with Arafat of the Oslo Accords and receiving along with him (and with the Israeli foreign minister at the time, Shimon Peres) the Nobel Peace Prize; a glorifying presentation that had itself quickly reversed the previous televised demonization of the man. This quick-shifting presentation of Arafat by Israeli television is very instructive in its evidencing the ideological elaboration by the mainstream media of governmental policies.

53. The height of Israeli television ridicule of Arafat came, however, in the days preceding and immediately following his death, after a lengthy and unknown illness, at a Paris hospital on November 11, 2004, which eventuated in a happy celebration of his demise.

54. An analysis of U.S. television frames of "law and order" can be found in Robin Andersen, "Vision of Stability."

55. For example, on July 17, 2001, Israeli TV broadcast pictures of Palestinians in the West Bank city of Hebron throwing Molotov cocktails at a number of Israeli soldiers, who were passively bearing the attacks. In the same news bulletin, a picture of a massive Palestinian demonstration in the West Bank city of Nablus is shown focusing on Israeli and U.S. flags along with burning posters of Sharon and of an Israeli bus.

56. Many such cases do not get reported at all.

57. There are a few instances in which Israeli television critically reported unlawful acts by Israeli soldiers, usually following internal or external pressure. These include Channel 2's Ilana Dayan's critical reporting in her investigative *Uvda* (Fact) program about the shooting and killing of a thirteen-year-old Palestinian girl who had approached an army outpost. While the night shooting in itself may have been a case of mistaken identity, the fact that the commander had gone down and shot the girl again from close range to assure her death, led to general outrage and to the arrest of the officer. Nevertheless, Dayan's report, harshly critiqued by the army for her "one-sided" and biased presentation, was framed by Dayan herself as aimed at urging the army to review its opening-of-fire procedures rather than focusing on the horrendous act apparently committed by the officer. In another case Channel 1's military affairs reporter Yoav Limor reported on December 4, 2004, on the killing of Mahmud Abd a-Rahman Hamdan Kmel (A-Dab'i), in the village of Raba, southeast of Jenin, by an Israeli elite commando unit. The IDF spokesperson issued a statement saying that Kmel had been killed by soldiers as he fled from a house in which he had been hiding. However, an investigation by Be'tselem (an Israeli human rights group: www.btselem.org) at the site of the incident raised grave suspicions that IDF soldiers had executed Kmel while he was lying injured on the ground and after his weapon had already been taken away from him. Be'tselem's investigation also indicated that soldiers had threatened two Palestinians at gunpoint and forced them to carry the wounded man and search his body. After briefly mentioning the gravity of this act, the reporter hurried on to claim that when he received notice of the affair from Be'tselem he found out that the army was already aware of the incident, had suspended the unit from further activity, and had already opened an external investigation headed by a general from a different unit, thus emphasizing the importance of "due process" for the IDF. Hence, rather than harshly criticizing such an act the reporter chose to focus in his report on the army's responsible reaction to the event prior to Be'tselem's complaint (i.e., the army does not need anybody to tell it what is right or wrong) and on its opening of an external investigation (which is internal to the army but which the army terms external in order to fend off demands that it allow external-to-the-army investigations in what appear to be criminal cases).

58. Quoted in the Israeli newspaper *Ha'aretz* (19 March 2002).

59. On the evolution of the coverage of this event see also David Kupelian, "Who

Killed Muhammed al-Dura?" *WorldNetDaily*, WorldNetDaily.com (accessed December 4, 2000).

60. Notwithstanding Palestinian incitement in this incident (see the following section) and irrespective of whether the IDF inquiry or Shapira's documentary raise serious doubts about the culpability of the IDF soldiers in the killing of the boy (they seem to offer inconclusive evidence), the time alloted by Israeli TV to the broadcast of these versions (as well as to Duriel's far-fetched conspiracy theory), as compared to the one-time airing of the tragic incident in the immediate aftermath of the event, evidence a siege-derived tendency to turn the blame around on the accusers.

61. Several official Palestinian spokesmen accused Israel of a massacre being carried out by the IDF in Jenin (e.g., on April 12, Abdel Rahman from the PNA told CNN's Aaron Brown that " as a matter of principle, everyone in this world knows that Israel committed a massacre in Jenin in the last week, . . . I am saying that there were massacres committed against the Palestinians, 400 to 500 Palestinians, mainly civilians, children, men, and women killed by Israel." See a documentation of these allegations in Yehuda Kraut, "Backgrounder: A Study in Palestinian Duplicity and Media Indifference," Committee for Accuracy in Middle East Reporting in America, at www.camera.org/index.asp?x_article = 217&x_context = 7. Counter to these accusations all three major international reports on the events in the Jenin refugee camp during Operation Defensive Shield, while citing various human right violations and different war crimes apparently committed by the IDF in the camp, did not find evidence to support the accusation that the IDF had massacred Palestinians within the camp. See the *Human Rights Watch Report* 14, no. 3 (E) (May 2002); the *Amnesty International Report*, No. 15/143/2002 (November 4, 2002); and the *UN Report of the Secretary-General Prepared Pursuant to General Assembly Resolution ES-10/10*. Hence, the UN stated in its introduction to section F of its report the following:

43. In the early hours of 3 April 2002, as part of Operation Defensive Shield, the Israeli Defence Forces entered the city of Jenin and the refugee camp adjacent to it, declared them a closed military area, prevented all access, and imposed a round-the-clock curfew. By the time of the IDF withdrawal and the lifting of the curfew on 18 April, at least 52 Palestinians, of whom up to half may have been civilians, and 23 Israeli soldiers were dead. Many more were injured. Approximately 150 buildings had been destroyed and many others were rendered structurally unsound. Four hundred and fifty families were rendered homeless. The cost of the destruction of property is estimated at approximately $27 million.

Notwithstanding the unfounded massacre allegations, the IDF seems to have indeed violated Palestinian human rights and committed war crimes in the camp. The events in Jenin form part of the ongoing media war between Israelis and Palestinians. These include a barrage of newspaper articles and websites (e.g., *The Jenin Inquiry*, at www.jenininquiry.org/articles.htm, as well as several documentary films, notably the Palestinian-oriented film *Jenin, Jenin* [2002] directed by the Israeli-Arab Mohammed Bakri [banned by the Israeli Film Ratings Board for its insinuations that a massacre took place, then cut by the director and consequently allowed to be screened by the Israeli Supreme Court], and the Israeli-oriented film *Road to Jenin* [2003] directed by Pierre Rehov, which was produced in direct response to Bakri's film).

62. The most salient ones being the use of Palestinian civilians by IDF soldiers as human shields against Palestinian militant fire, some deliberate unlawful killings, the

blocking of medical and humanitarian access, and the disproportionate and indiscriminate use of force without clear military necessity. See the *Human Watch Rights Report*, "Jenin: IDF Military Operations" (May 2002).

63. Notably Sa'ib Arekat, for example, interviewed in the documentary film *Massacring the Truth* (Martin Himel, 2004).

64. Himel quoted in *The Calgary Herald*, May 30, 2004.

65. There are almost daily reports on funeral processions. Very graphic shots can be seen in many reports (e.g., August 6 and 20, 2001; September 17 and 28, 2001; October 3 and 7, 2001; February 19 and 27, 2002; March 6, 2002).

66. There are daily clips or reports on such violent encounters (e.g., June 6, 2001; August 28, 2001; July 8 and 9, 2003).

67. On April 1, 2001, Palestinian television offered ongoing reports on Israeli incursions shifting among different reporters stationed in different locations (e.g., Said Ayyad from Bethlehem TV described the situation in Bethlehem for PATV and PATV's Naim Suilam reported from Kalkilya). On October 20, 2000, Israeli Channel 1 rebroadcast the following call aired on PATV: "The Supreme Monitoring Committee of the National Arab and Islamic forces calls upon the masses of our people to immediately assemble in the streets and public squares, in order to express their rage and strong stand against the barbaric Israeli aggression, and their determination to continue the Intifada."

68. These segments, often fabricated, were used even prior to the eruption of the Intifada. Hence, as noted by Ittamar Marcus of the PMW (in his September 11, 2000, Special Report # 30), on July 26, 2000, Palestinian television edited shots from the first Intifada showing an Israeli soldier shooting followed by a shot of girl falling to the ground (implying the girl was shot in the back by the soldier).

69. E.g., July 21, 2001—Pictures of a Palestinian baby killed by Israeli fire that hit his head; August 26, 2001—Horrible pictures of two youngsters killed by IDF fire in the Gaza Strip; September 28, 2001—Images of wounded Palestinians in streets and in hospitals; October 3, 2001—Images of wounded Palestinians following the IDF attack in Bet Lahiya; December 12, 2001—Graphic pictures of wounded children in a Gaza hospital; March 4, 2002—Close-ups of burned body parts of a mother and her three children who died from IDF fire in Ramallah; March 6, 2002—Shots of a wounded Palestinian whose face is burned and of a dead Palestinian killed in an Israeli Apache helicopter attack.

70. Another such still was that of a Palestinian boy standing alone, with a stone in his hand, facing a threatening Israeli tank, reminiscent of the famous Tiananmen Square photo.

71. E.g., "The Farewell Letter," which shows an actor child falling dead on the ground after being shot by the IDF, while in voice-over someone sings the words "How sweet is Shahada when I embrace you, oh! My land"). This videotape, aired hundreds of times (starting May 7, 2001) as well as other PATV-aired Shahada death-praising videotapes, can be seen at the Palestinian Media Watch (PMW) site in its "Ask for Death" section, www.pmw.org.il/AFD.html. The site includes a highly biased Israeli account of these PATV aired videotapes written by Ittamar Marcus, the center's director. Despite its bias, however, the account is well documented.

72. Andrea Levin, "Eye on the Media: Arafat's Incitement, Lies, and Videotape,"

Camera 2001, at www.camera.org/index.asp?x_article = 175&x_context = 8 (accessed June 8, 2001). The videotape can be watched at the PMW site.

73. See Mohammad Dajani, "Press Reporting during the Intifada: Palestinian Coverage of Jenin: The Consequences of Politically Driven Reporting," *Palestine-Israel Journal* 10, no. 2 (2003): 39–46.

74. Anti-Semitic opinions are salient in Friday sermons broadcast live by PATV, such as in Sheik Ibrahim Mudeiris's Friday sermon in a Gaza mosque dated June 25, 2004, where he claims that Israel sent Jewish and other women to Muslim countries to spread abomination, or his constant description of Jews as "pigs and apes." Palestinian historian 'Issam Sisalem too appeared on PATV, where he delegitimized the Jews' religious claims over Palestine, negated the Holocaust, and often used expressions like "The Jews are like eels" (PATV, September 21, 2004). These and other anti-Semitic videos and their transcripts can be viewed at MEMRITV.org.

75. E.g., on September 24, 2000, PATV recorded in a crowded street the mother of a child killed in clashes with the IDF in which she praises her son's death as a martyr, repeatedly saying, "The pride is mine."

76. Frantz Fanon's view whereby a colonized people's brutal and suicidal erupting violence during their struggle for liberation results from their longstanding brutal physical oppression by the colonizer and from the mental oppression of their own myths, offers a compelling explanation for the radical Islam movement's effective manipulation of heavenly rewards in order to channel this accumulated violence toward suicide bombings. Frantz Fanon, *The Wretched of the Earth* (New York: Grove Press, 1968), 53–60.

77. The video of the interview and its transcript can be seen at MEMRITV.org. Praising suicide bomber shahids can also be seen in a May 12, 2002, airing by PATV of a song dedicated to Wafa Idris, the first woman suicide bomber, which includes the words "You chose Shahada, in death you have brought life to our will." The song was performed in a crowded concert hall by a singer accompanied by a large orchestra and chorus.

78. Fanon's explanation and legitimation of the violence characterizing the national liberation movements of the "wretched of the earth," whereby colonialist dehumanization brings about a brutal violent response through which the oppressed rise to humanness, aptly describes the PATV conception of and incitement to violence. See Frantz Fanon, "Concerning Violence," *The Wretched of the Earth*, 35–95.

79. Even in the interview with the mother of a Hamas suicide bomber described above there is no mention of Hamas or of the results of the suicide bombing.

80. E.g., on June 6, 2003, in Arafat's speech before a young audience he repeatedly praises the child "martyr" Fares al Uda killed while throwing a stone at an Israeli tank.

81. E.g., Arafat on Palestinian TV on January 26, 2002, called for millions of shahids for the sake of Jerusalem and prayed that he himself would become a shahid for Jerusalem, hoping "one day a Palestinian child will raise the Palestinian flag above our mosques and churches." Nevertheless there are still some clips where the PATV implies that the aim is the liberation of the whole of Palestine. In this respect it is instructive that a clip repeatedly aired prior to the Intifada (e.g., September 11, 2000) was removed. It showed a group of children building "Palestine" with small figures

of trees and houses, followed by an earthquake tumbling the houses and trees whereby a girl says, "Do you know what happened in 1948? They took everything. They emptied the room, they broke the house, they burned down the forest, they changed the names, changed the names. . . . This is still my country, it is very pretty. My country's name is Palestine." A description of this clip and others appears on the site of the Israeli Palestinian Media Watch organization, in its Special Report # 30 from September 11, 2000, written by Ittamar Marcus, director of the PMW, and entitled "Rape, Murder, Violence, and War for Allah against the Jews: Summer 2000 on Palestinian Television."

82. Ibrahim Milhem, an editorial director for Palestine Satellite Television (the Palestinian Authority Satellite channel), offered an illuminating explanation for not airing these images. He said the PATV did not broadcast these incidents because they represented instances of the PNA's "losing control." See William Orme's article, where Milhem is interviewed, in William Orme, "A Parallel Mideast Battle: Is It News or Incitement?" *Israel Resource Review* 2000, at israelbehindthenews.com/Oct-25-00.htm#PLO7 (accessed October 25, 2000).

83. E.g., in the November 27, 2001, report on two gunmen that opened fire on a crowd near the central bus station of the northern Israeli city of Afula, killing two and wounding dozens, PATV offered a factual brief report of the event inserting a few long shots taken by Israeli television, and moved on to report on the Israeli occupying forces. A similar scant report was aired October 28, 2001, concerning a car bomb suicide attack on October 25 in Hadera injuring more than sixty people.

84. See the PATV interview of September 21, 2004, with Um Taysir, the mother of Hamas suicide bomber Taysir Al Ajrami.

85. It should be noted that the few condemnations of suicide bombings on PATV (as opposed to continuous condemnation, along the same lines, by PNA officials in interviews given to foreign channels) usually followed intense Israeli military pressure threatening to topple the PNA, or mounting U.S. diplomatic pressures resulting from the U.S. interest in suppressing Palestinian and other radical Islam support for al Qaeda (e.g., Arafat's condemnation of suicide bombings on December 16, 2002, following a message by al Qaeda dedicating the attack against Israeli targets in Kenya to the Palestinians).

7

Summary Discussion of Case Studies

The overall difference between CNN's global audiovisual framing of terror events and that of the Israeli and Palestinian national frames can be defined as "open" versus "closed" reports. This methodological differentiation, developed by Itzhak Roeh and Akiva Cohen and applied by Hillel Nossek in his "Qualitative content analysis method" to the verbal coverage of violent events, contends that "open" reports ("stories") are balanced, offering a variety of sources and few historical allusions or emotive labels, whereas "closed" reports offer the opposite. However, this does not mean, as Roeh, Cohen, and Nossek imply, that open reports are less ideologically oriented and vice versa. Hence, while CNN's "open" reports offer more information, their balancing and variety-typed audiovisual framing of violent events neutralizes and distances the viewers from the events, offering a global, distracted, and detached view that replicates the post-Fordist economy, effacing the core-elite interests and their deployment of brutal force to forward these interests. Conversely, while the Israeli and Palestinian "closed" reports offer less variety, balance, and information, their historical allusions and highly emotive framing of violent events reveals rather than effaces their peripheral motivations and the perceptions driving both parties, hence offering a clearer understanding of the reasons that have led to such violent events.

CNN FRAMES

Within its overall global-to-local perspective of a decentered world, CNN has evolved several ideological audiovisual frames in respect to Middle East contemporary conflicts and their escalating reciprocal terrorist and constitutional nondiscriminatory violence. This study has deciphered four major frames. The first was discovered in the coverage of the al Aksa Intifada, a local conflict that did not seriously impede global capital flow, did not pose a direct violent threat to core countries, and did not seriously threaten the dependent peripheral state system. This frame implemented conflict containment through aesthetic strategies that generated the conflict's abstraction and neutralization by a glocal *equalizing* frame. Two other frames were used in cases where capital flow was impeded, serious violent threats to core countries loomed, or core interests in the regional dependence system were threatened. This was revealed in the analysis of the coverage of al Qaeda terror and the U.S.-led "War against Terror." In this case impending and actual military intervention was aestheticized through a global-to-local simulacrum-derived *isolating and targeting* frame complemented by an *investigation-typed spreading and shifting* frame.[2]

These frames enhanced the notion of a decentered world both in their isolation of Afghanistan and in their presentation of a hard-to-trace globally spreading al Qaeda organization. In their decenteredness these frames supported the United States' divide-and-conquer strategy and obscured its forceful approach to integrating the new world order by war and through exertion of economic and diplomatic pressures on peripheral governments (rationalized as a need to investigate terror within each state). However threatening or nonthreatening to the United States conflicts were, their escalating terrorist and constitutional nondiscriminatory violence was dealt with from within a major aesthetic-ideological frame that can be termed *digital aesthetics of therapeutic sterilization*. Its major effects were abstraction, detachment, and avoidance. It was aimed at filtering out the horrific consequences of violence while transmitting a sense of there being control and order wherever the United States was involved within a decentered globe. These frames also enhanced the virtual devaluation of human life inherent in digital and postmodern simulacrum ideological-cultural production. Through these frames CNN both replicated the government's rhetoric and lent it support.

The Equalizing Frame

This ideological aesthetic framing used CNN's global strategy of simultaneity and synchronicity through swift, live, on-air shifts to CNN's "globally" spread reporters in order to emphasize the abstract commonality and lack of concrete history of these separate and apparently unconnected conflicts. These simultaneous spatially dispersed brief reports were audiovisually similarly structured irrespective of the specific local conflict addressed (e.g., centered on the similarly positioned spread reporters, themselves replicating by association the headline shot of the anchor, who commands the shifts from one location to another). Moreover, these conflicts were almost exclusively evaluated in terms of violations of law and order or of human rights echoed audiovisually in the violation of normative stable framing, shot angle, and editing (e.g., oblique camera angles). This framing of reports on conflicts not in need of first-world military intervention (which seem to frame not only the Israeli-Palestinian conflict, but also the Russian-Chechnyan conflict or most conflicts on the African continent), attributed these violations to both parties through balancing strategies alternating between the sides. Moreover, this balancing frame was presented from without through the reporter's voice-over and through overall detached, distant shots, evoking a fatalistic deadlock. These strategies framed the conflicts under a global equalizing perspective whereby the subjectivist perceptions and actions of both parties were presented as equally illegitimate. This equalizing strategy neutralized the need for intervention, since the conflict, in its exclusive mutuality, was contained, and since no party was in the right. Through the ultimate lack of serious consideration of the interests and rationale driving both parties' violent acts, overvaluing an explanation based on irrational mutual vengeance and antipeace stupidity, this frame suggested that whatever the conflict's reasons and history it is advisable that the parties reach by themselves a solution in face of mutual suffering or be left to their ongoing mutual struggle. It henceforth offered a moral divide-and-conquer strategy portraying the CNN, and by extension, the U.S. elites it represented, as rational and morally superior to both parties.

The Isolating and Targeting Frame and the Investigation-Typed Spreading and Shifting Frame

Following the September 11 attack, described by an American businessman in one of CNN's trailers as an unaffordable "black hole in world economy," the aesthetic ideological frame immediately forwarded by CNN was one implying that the whole decentered world was threatened by a single perpetrator (bin Laden). It was implemented through a CNN global-to-local perspective of centering-on coverage, achieved through recurring images that zoomed in to center on the perpetrator. These included maps targeting bin Laden's compounds in Afghanistan, satellite close-up shots of sites evidencing his culpability, and shots of his defiant posture or of al Qaeda's atrocities. This targeting approach reached its zenith in aesthetic-ideological framing of military preparations enhancing the military might of the U.S.-led coalition of the willing being built. An emblematic headline shot of this military-might centering-on approach figured "surgical" bombs being launched and their targets shown as precisely hit through the missiles' monitoring camera. Another strategy entailed the calculated reconfiguring of headline shots within macro-frame aesthetics, establishing a correlation between the perpetrator and world instability. Hence, in CNN's airing of a Pentagon briefing, the shots of the missiles' monitoring cameras were superimposed on the bottom part of the screen with the online live fluctuation of the stock market expressed in digitized figures. Characteristic also was the digitally supported figuration of the high-tech impersonal professionalism and efficiency of the coalition forces, referencing the science fiction *Star Wars* film trilogy aesthetics vis-à-vis the framing of the perpetrator's forces as backward, unsophisticated, and menacing. The latter's backward look was enhanced through referencing the wild west movie scenes depicting the posse-outlaw interaction (as used in the framing of the U.S. special forces' hunt of the "most wanted" bin Laden).[3] The pinpointing of bin Laden, however, decontextualizing the perpetrator from the region, was complemented by an investigative-typed spreading and shifting frame, recontextualizing him within an abstract decentered "global" sphere. This globalization of the threat was aesthetically framed through CNN's strategy of simultaneity and synchronicity. Hence, through swift shifts to CNN's "globally" spread reporters a global communication net was woven, isomorphic to al Qaeda's presumed terror net. Furthermore, in backtracking reports on the cell members that bombed the Twin Towers and in other widespread reports about radical Islamic cells uncovered around the world, the notion of borderless and spreading terror was evoked.[4] This was conveyed through dominant headline shots recalling international espionage television series, science-fiction series, and investigation thrillers (e.g., *Nikita, The X-Files*, and lately, *24*). These images, recalling spies, aliens, and biological or chemical weapons, enhanced the spread of the threat in a decentered world. These frames suggested that whatever the historical and regional context of the rise of bin Laden, it is advisable to eradicate him so as to reach a solution in face of his spreading threat to the globe.

The Digital Aesthetics of Therapeutic Sterilization Frame

Concomitant with the three aesthetic ideological framings described, was the strategy of obscuring and therapeutic sterilization of the horrifying consequences of terrorist and constitutional violence emanating from the conflicts addressed. Through a digital aesthetic of therapeutic sterilization, these conflicts were shown from without and from "above" as local disturbances to global calm. This frame evoked sterile detachment through a distant gaze (long-distance aestheticized shots, digitized maps). When shots of atrocities were presented (usually in material taken from local stations) the frame was framed and overloaded with overlapping multimedia information and bluish, reddish, or greenish digital aesthetic coloring, resulting in the viewers' distraction and distancing from the horror. This frame was applied not only when dealing with the Israeli/Palestinian conflict or with the attacks by U.S.-led forces in Afghanistan, but also when dealing with terrorist attacks on U.S. targets. Emblematic was CNN's aesthetic sterilization of the September

11 Twin Towers destruction. The distanced, balanced, aesthetic filtering of the horrific consequences of violence, coupled with orderly patriotism and symbolic heroization, transmitted a sense of restrained power, control, and order.

PATV AND ISRAELI MAINSTREAM TELEVISION NEWS FRAMES

Israeli and Palestinian respective (and mutually opposed) internal-external double-talk representations developed several frames to deal with reciprocal terror and constitutional violence. I focus on two of the major ones.

The *Analogic Aesthetics of Traumatic Contamination* Frame

This frame offered an "internal" perspective on violence. Its major effects were concretization, engagement, and nonavoidance. It was aimed at enhancing the horrific consequences of the other side's violence and was thus symptomatic of the actual devaluation of human life inhering in volatile peripheral states. It also embedded the internal dominant national ideologies aimed at enlisting their respective peoples. Hence, the Israeli variant embedded Israel's elite dominant siege ideology, seeking internal enlistment by exploiting Palestinian and international terror in order to perpetuate an audiovisual self-image of a besieged victimized collective. The Palestinian variant embedded the Palestinian Authority's core-dependent elite dominant ideology of national liberation through sacrifice and martyrdom (Shahada) by presenting Palestinian collective or individual heroic sacrifice to the national cause.

The Israeli variant consisted of an audiovisuality of siege, characterized by audiovisual unsettling panic arousal configurations. Emblematic were the reports on suicide bombings. Alongside these were found images enhancing shared personal, familial, or communal suffering presented by means of claustrophobic group shots and the classification of the people affected by the attacks into different Israeli communities or ways of life. These audiovisual configurations evoked the long history of persecution of the Jewish people, an ongoing theme in Israeli culture. They were coupled with siege-derived "revenge-retaliation," "turn the blame around," and "compared to others, we're morally far better" frames, all aimed at internal enlistment. The dominant Israeli siege frame was used to represent as pertaining to all Israelis the particular interests of Israel's elite in Jewish, secular and security-oriented national unification, (rather than, for instance, the Jewish settlers' religious-territorial clandestine and oppositional perspective, whose coverage was not siege derived).

The Palestinian variant consisted of a terror-typed traumatic audiovisuality.

Emblematic were Palestinian television reports on funeral processions of Palestinians killed by the Israel Defense Force. The overall terror-trauma Shahada framing formation exalted personal and collective sacrifice. By also constantly overlaying the images with religious and national symbols this framing stimulated liberating violence and symbolic nationhood, an ongoing theme in Palestinian culture. It was aimed at internal enlistment, by representing as pertaining to all Palestinians the particular interests of the Palestinian Authority elite in attaining an independent Arab-Palestinian state (rather than, for instance, the Hamas and Islamic Jihad radical terrorist struggle for a regional Islamic nation).

The *Law and Order* and *Human Rights* Frames

The second major frame used by both parties was aimed at enlisting the superpower to their own side and against the other. Israeli rhetorical strategy of enlistment focused on the superpower's law and order conception by emphasizing Israel's democratic constitution and its rule of law, whereas that of the Palestinian Authority focused on the superpower's human rights conception by emphasizing the victimization of the Palestinians by Israel. However, these strategies of enlistment also worked against the respective elites' interests. Hence, Israeli conduct often violated international law, whereas the Palestinians' terrorist form of struggle worked against its "human rights violation" claim. Therefore, the conflict and its escalating violence were framed by each side through an "external" CNN global look-alike perspective, reserved almost exclusively to portray (in an air of international respectability) each party's atrocious conduct toward the other. Within this perspective, issues were dealt with along core-styled "law and order" (Israelis) or "human rights" (Palestinians) frames. This generated the double-talk characterizing Israeli and Palestinian television news. Hence, Israeli television showed at times the mutilated bodies of targeted Palestinians as part of its siege-derived revenge-retaliation frame while on the other hand it showed these targeted killings along CNN's therapeutic sterilization and targeting frame. Likewise, Palestinian television coverage of Israeli aggression showed it on the one hand, in Shahada-style, while on the other hand it was covered through a core-type "human rights violation as human tragedy" frame.

CONCLUSION

Considering post-Fordism to be the dominant mode of production propelling globalization, and viewing the U.S.-led core-elites' formation of a "new world order" as a further expansion of their capitalist exploitation of the periphery, this study showed how mainstream television news respectively embedded the dominant ideologies of the U.S. core-elites and of dependent peripheral elites in Israeli and Palestine in their coverage of the terror and constitutional violence that emanated from the U.S.–al Qaeda conflict and from the al Aksa Intifada.

The coverage of these conflicts, exhibiting a direct core-periphery conflict (U.S.–al Qaeda) and an indirect one (the al Aksa Intifada), revealed different CNN frames exhibiting variations on a postmodern decentered world ideological conception that supported the overall global divide-and-conquer U.S. core strategy used to subdue the periphery. This strategy was also found to be aided by the double-talk ideological audiovisual frames of Israeli and Palestinian mainstream television news, evident in the ethnocentric coverage by each party of their mutual conflict and in the attendant scant and disengaged coverage of the U.S.-led "War against Terror."

The comparative analyses of the coverage of these conflicts also revealed the high degree of divergence between the different points of view, and the high degree with which the different types of coverage were oriented by the dominant ideologies of the respective elites, making a mockery of widespread claims to "objectivity" in the news. These claims often rely on the "documentary" import of audiovisuals. However, what this study has shown is that audiovisuals are powerful ideological venues.

Nevertheless, the competing news images analyzed also reveal, in their divergences, a very real global violence brought about by the brutal dynamics of the political economy of post-Fordist capitalism.

This study has tried to integrate a broad political economic analysis with a close comparative audiovisual semiotic decoding of ideologies in the news coverage of two specific conflicts by three networks. However, for such an approach to establish itself, more studies need to be conducted that bridge in more detail the various levels analyzed; cover other global and national networks in their interrelations; and focus on more aspects of post-Fordist globalization.

As for the specific conflicts analyzed, it would be interesting to study the new audiovisual frames that have evolved in the PATV coverage of the Israeli-Palestinian conflict after Arafat's death and particularly after the Hamas won the elections for the Palestine Legislative Council in January 2006. Likewise, it is intriguing to discern the Israeli mainstream audiovisual frames evolved after Sharon's disengagement process, his leaving the Likud to form the Kadima Party, his incapacitation following a stroke, and the March 2006 elections in Israel. Also, this type of analysis can be expanded to reveal the audiovisual frames used by different global and national networks in their competing coverage of other core-periphery conflicts. Particularly interesting will be the coverage of the U.S.-Iraq war and its aftermath and of the escalating U.S.-Iran conflict.

NOTES

1. Itzhak Roeh and Akiva Cohen, "One of the Bloodiest Days: A Comparative Analysis of Open and Closed Television News," *Journal of Communication* 42, no. 2 (1992): 42–55; Hillel Nossek, "Our News and Their News: The Role of National Identity in the Coverage of Foreign News," *Journalism* 5, no. 3 (2004): 343–368.

2. In Iraq CNN appears to be using an inspection-typed spreading and shifting frame (in its reports on prewar UN inspections in Iraq and on U.S. inspections during and after the war).

3. Similar framing recurred with Saddam Hussein and his regime before and during the war in Iraq. Of particular interest was CNN's wild west–styled amplification of the U.S. army spreading of the list of "most wanted" Iraqi officials as a pack of cards, the spreading of the photos figuring the dead and mutilated bodies of Saddam's sons, and the framing of Saddam Hussein's capture, showing him as a ridiculous weary outlaw and his hiding site as a cave.

4. A similar spreading and shifting borderless threat frame was used in the coverage of Saddam Hussein's presumed outward threat.

Bibliography

Abu Ayyash, Radwan. *Broadcasters' Obligations towards Their Audience in Times of Crisis (The Palestinian Intifada as an Example).* Master's thesis, Center for Mass Communication Research. Leicester, U.K.: Leicester University, 1992.

Alexander, Yonah. "Terrorism, the Media, and the Police." *Journal of International Affairs* 32, no. 1 (Spring–Summer 1978): 101–113.

Althusser, Louis. "Ideology and Ideological State Apparatuses." In *Lenin and Philosophy*, 127–186. New York: NLB, 1971.

Altman, Rick. "Television/Sound." In *Studies in Entertainment: Critical Approaches to Mass Culture*, edited by Tania Modelsky, 39–54. Bloomington: Indiana University Press, 1986.

Al-Sayyid, Mustapha. "International and Regional Environments and State Transformation in Some Arab Countries." In *The State and Global Change: The Political Economy of Transition in the Middle East and North Africa*, edited by Hassan Hakimian and Ziba Moshaver, 156–178. Surrey: Curzon, 2001.

Amnesty International Report. No. 15/143/2002. November 4, 2002.

Andersen, Robin. "Vision of Stability: US Television Law and Order News of El Salvador." *Media Culture and Society* 10, no. 2 (1988): 236–264.

Anderson, Benedict. *Imagined Communities: Reflections on the Origins and Appeal of Nationalism.* New York: Verso, 1991.

Appadurai, Arjun. *Modernity at Large: Cultural Dimensions of Globalization.* Minneapolis: Minnesota University Press, 1996.

Aruri, H. Naseer. *Dishonest Broker: The U.S. Role in Israel and Palestine.* Cambridge, Mass.: South End Press, 2003.

Axtmann, Roland. "Collective Identity and the Democratic Nation State in the Age of Globalization." In *Articulating the Global and the Local*, edited by Ann Cvetkovich and Douglas Kellner, 33–54 . Boulder, Colo.: Westview, 1997.

Bal, Mieke. *On Meaning-Making: Essays in Semiotics.* Santa Rosa, Calif.: Polebridge Press, 1994.

Bar-Tal, Daniel, and Dikla Antebi. "Siege Mentality in Israel." *International Journal of Intercultural Relations* 16 (1992): 251–275.

151

Barthes, Roland. *Image, Music, Text.* New York: Hill and Wang, 1977.
———. *Mythologies.* Paris: Seuil, 1957.
Baudrillard, Jean. *For a Critique of the Political Economy of the Sign.* St. Louis, Mo.: Telos, 1981.
———. *The Gulf War Did Not Take Place.* Bloomington: Indiana University Press, 1995.
———. *Simulations.* New York: Semiotext(e), 1983.
Benjamin, Walter. "The Work of Art in the Age of Mechanical Reproduction." In *Illuminations,* edited by Hannah Arendt. New York: Shoken Books, 1969.
Ben-Shaul, Nitzan. "Different yet Even: The Effacement of Power in Post-Structuralism: The Case of *Seinfeld.*" *Third Text,* Special Issue 51 (Summer 2000): 75–84.
———. *Mythical Expressions of Siege in Israeli Films.* Lewiston, N.Y.: The Edwin Mellen Press, 1997.
———. "TV News: Visual Ideological Frames and the Coverage of Terror Events." *Third Text* 73, vol. 19, no. 2 (March 2005): 145–153.
Benvenisti, Meron. *The Sling and the Club* [in Hebrew]. Jerusalem: Keter, 1988.
Berger, Arthur Asa. *Media Analysis Techniques.* London: Sage, 1988.
Bhaba, Homi K. "DissemiNation." In *Nation and Narration,* edited by Homi K. Bhaba, 291–322. London: Routledge & Kegan Paul, 1990.
———. *The Location of Culture.* London: Routledge, 1994.
Bignell, Jonathan. *Media Semiotics.* Manchester, U.K.: Manchester University Press, 2002.
Bodansky, Yossef. *Bin Laden: The Man Who Declared War on America.* Roseville, Calif.: Prima, 2001.
Brecher, Michael. *Decisions in Crisis: Israel, 1967 and 1973.* Berkeley: University of California Press, 1980.
Browne, Nick. "The Political Economy of the Television (Super) Text." In *American Television: New Directions in History and Theory,* edited by Nick Browne, 69–80. Langhorne, Pa.: Harwood Academic Publishers, 1994.
Carruthers, Susan L. *The Media at War.* New York: St. Martin's Press, 2000.
Chomsky, Noam. *Fateful Triangle: The United States, Israel, and the Palestinians.* Cambridge, Mass.: South End Press, 1999.
Chomsky, Noam, and Edward S. Herman. *Manufacturing Consent.* New York: Pantheon, 1988.
———. *The Washington Connection and Third World Fascism: The Political Economy of Human Rights.* Vol. 2. Nottingham: Spokesman Books, 1979.
Cohen, Akiva, Hanna Adoni, and Hillel Nossek. "Television News and the Intifada." In *Framing the Intifada People and Media.* Jerusalem: Ablex, 1991.
Cooley, John. *Unholy Wars: Afghanistan, America, and International Terrorism.* London: Pluto Press, 1999.
Crockatt, Richard. *America Embattled: September 11, Anti-Americanism, and the Global Order.* London: Routledge, 2003.
Cumings, Bruce. *War and Television.* London: Verso, 1992.
Curran, James. *Media and Power.* London: Routledge, 2002.
Dajani, Mohammad. "Press Reporting during the Intifada: Palestinian Coverage of

Jenin: The Consequences of Politically Driven Reporting." *Palestine-Israel Journal* 10, no. 2 (2003): 39–46.

Dayan, Daniel, and Elihu Katz. *Defining Media Events: The Live Broadcasting of History.* Cambridge, Mass.: Harvard University Press, 1992.

Delli Carpini, Michael, and Bruce A. Williams. "Terrorism and the Media: Patterns of Presentation and Occurrence, 1969 to 1980." *Western Political Quarterly* 40, no. 1 (1987): 45–64.

Denton, Robert E., Jr. "Television as an Instrument of War." In *The Media and the Persian Gulf War,* edited by Robert E. Denton Jr., 27–42. London: Praeger, 1993.

Derrida, Jacques. "The Law of Genre." *Critical Inquiry* 7 (Autumn 1980): 55–81.

Dessouki, Ali E. Hillal. "The Primacy of Economics: The Foreign Policy of Egypt." In *The Foreign Policies of Arab States: The Challenge of Change,* edited by Baghat Korany and Ali E. Hillal Dessouki, 156–185. Boulder, Colo.: Westview, 1991.

Dobkin, Bethami A. *Tales of Terror.* London: Praeger, 1992.

Dor, Daniel. *Intifada Hits the Headlines: How the Israeli Press Misreported the Outbreak of the Second Palestinian Uprising.* Bloomington: Indiana University Press, 2004.

Downey, John, and Graham Murdock. "The Counter-Revolution in Military Affairs: The Globalization of Guerrilla Warfare." In *War and the Media: Reporting Conflict 24/7,* edited by Daya Kishan Thussu and Des Freedman, 70–86. London: Sage, 2003.

Dowty, Alan. "Impact of the Aqsa Intifada on the Israeli-Palestinian Conflict." *Israel Studies Forum* 19, no. 2 (2004): 9–28.

Elias, Norbert. *The Civilizing Process.* Vol. 2: *State Formation and Civilization.* Oxford: Blackwell, 1982.

Entman, Robert. "Framing: Toward Clarification of a Fractured Paradigm." *Journal of Communication* 43, no. 4 (1993): 51–58.

———. "Framing U.S. Coverage of International News: Contrast in Narratives of the Korean and Iranian Airline Incidents." *Journal of Communication* 51, no. 4 (1991): 6–27.

Esslin, Martin. *The Age of Television.* San Francisco: Freeman, 1982.

Fanon, Frantz. *The Wretched of the Earth.* New York: Grove Press, 1968.

Feuer, Jane. "Melodrama, Serial Form, and Television Today." In *Television: The Critical View,* edited by H. Newcombe, 87–101. Oxford: Oxford University Press, 1984.

Fiske, John. "*Cagney and Lacey*: Reading Character Structurally and Politically." *Communication* 19 (1987), 399–426.

———. "MTV: Post-Structural, Post-Modern." In *The Postmodern Presence,* edited by Arthur Asa Berger, 166–175. London: Altamira Press, 1998.

———. *Television Culture.* London: Methuen, 1987.

———. "Television Polysemy and Popularity." *Critical Studies in Mass Communication* 3 (1986): 391–408.

Fiske, John, and John Hartley. *Reading Television.* London: Routledge, 2003.

Frow, John. "Intertextuality and Ontology." In *Intertextuality: Theories and Practices,* edited by Judith Still and Michael Worton, 45–55. Manchester, U.K.: Manchester University Press, 1990.

Gamson, William A., and Andre Modigliani. "Media Discourse and Public Opinion on Nuclear Power: A Constructionist Approach." *American Journal of Sociology* 95, no. 1 (1989): 1–37.

Gerbner, George. "Persian Gulf War, the Movie." In *Triumph of the Image: The Media's War in the Persian Gulf: A Global Perspective*, edited by Hamid Mowlana, George Gerbner, and Herbert I. Schiller, 243–265. Boulder, Colo.: Westview, 1992.

Gitlin, Todd. *The Whole World Is Watching: Mass Media in the Making and Unmaking of the New Left*. Berkeley: University of California Press, 1980.

Goffman, Erving. *Frame Analysis: An Essay on the Organization of Experience*. New York: Harper & Row, 1974.

Golding, Peter, and Philip Elliot. *Making the News*. London: Longman, 1979.

Gramsci, Antonio. *Selections from Prison Notebooks*. London: Lawrence and Wishart, 1971.

Gurevitch, Michael, Mark Levy, and Itzhak Roeh. "The Global Newsroom: Convergences and Diversities in the Globalization of Television News." In *Communication and Citizenship: Journalism and the Public Sphere*, edited by Peter Dahlgren and Colin Sparks, 195–212. London: Routledge, 1991.

Hall, Stuart. "The Determination of News Photographs." In *The Manufacture of News: Social Problems, Deviance, and the Mass Media*, edited by Stanley Cohen and Jock Young, 176–190. London: Constable, 1981.

———. "Encoding/Decoding." In *Culture, Media, Language: Working Papers in Cultural Studies, 1972–1979*, edited by Stuart Hall, Dorothy Hobson, Andrew Lowe, and Paul Willis, 128–138. London: Hutchinson, 1980.

———. "The Question of Cultural Identity." In *Modernity and Its Futures*, edited by Stuart Hall, David Held, and Tony McGrew, 273–326. Cambridge, U.K.: Polity Press, 1992.

Hall, Stuart, Charles Critcher, Tony Jefferson, John Clarke, and Brian Robert. *Policing the Crisis: Mugging, the State, and Law and Order*. Bakingstoke, U.K.: Macmillan Education Ltd., 1978.

Haraway, Donna. "Manifesto for Cyborgs: Science, Technology, and Socialist Feminism in the Late Twentieth Century." In *Simians, Cyborgs, and Women: The Reinvention of Nature*, 149–181. London: Free Association Books, 1991.

Harkaby, Yehoshafat. *Facing Reality* [in Hebrew]. Jerusalem: Van Leer Foundation, 1981.

Harvey, David. *The Condition of Postmodernity*. Cambridge, U.K.: Blackwell, 1991.

Hinnebusch, Raymond. "The Politics of Economic Liberalization: Comparing Egypt and Syria." In *The State and Global Change: The Political Economy of Transition in the Middle East and North Africa*, edited by Hassan Hakimian and Ziba Moshaver, 111–135. Surrey: Curzon, 2001.

Houston, Beverle. "Viewing Television: The Metapsychology of Endless Consumption." In *American Television: New Directions in History and Theory*, ed. Nick Browne, 81–97. Langhorne, Pa.: Harwood Academic Publishers, 1994.

Human Rights Watch Report 14, no. 3 (E). May 2002.

Huntington, Samuel P. *The Clash of Civilizations and the Remaking of World Order*. New York: Simon & Schuster, 1996.

Jameson, Fredric. *Postmodernism; or, The Cultural Logic of Late Capitalism*. London: Duke University Press, 1991.

Jorisch, Avi. "Al Manar: Hizbullah TV, 24/7." *Middle East Quarterly* (Winter 2004): 17–31.

Khalili, Rashid. *Palestinian Identity: The Constitution of Modern National Consciousness.* New York: Columbia University Press, 1988.

Kimmerling, Baruch. *Politicide: Ariel Sharon's War against the Palestinians.* New York: Verso, 2003.

Korany, Baghat, and Ali E. Hillal Dessouki. "The Global System and Arab Foreign Policies: The Primacy of Constrains." In *The Foreign Policies of Arab States: The Challenge of Change*, edited by Baghat Korany and Ali E. Hillal Dessouki, 25–48. Boulder, Colo.: Westview Press, 1991.

Kraut, Yehuda. "Backgrounder: A Study in Palestinian Duplicity and Media Indifference." Committee for Accuracy in Middle East Reporting in America (Camera), at www.camera.org/index.asp?x_article = 217&x_context = 7 (accessed August 1, 2002).

Kristeva, Julia. *Desire in Language.* New York: Columbia University Press, 1980.

Kupelian, David. "Who Killed Muhammed al-Dura?" WorldNetDaily.com (accessed December 4, 2000).

Lash, Scott, and John Urry. *The End of Organized Capitalism.* Oxford: Oxford University Press, 1987.

Levin, Andrea. "Eye on the Media: Arafat's Incitement, Lies, and Videotape." Camera 2001, www.camera.org/index.asp?x_article = 175&x_ context = 8 (accessed June 8, 2001).

Lewis, Bernard. *What Went Wrong: Western Impact and Middle East Response.* New York: Oxford University Press, 2001.

Liebes, Tamar. *Reporting the Arab–Israeli Conflict: How Hegemony Works.* London: Routledge, 1997.

Liebman, Charles, and Eliezer Don Yehiya. *Civil Religion in Israel.* Berkeley: University of California Press, 1983.

Lindlof, Thomas R., and Bryan C. Taylor. *Qualitative Communication Research Methods.* 2nd ed. London: Sage, 2002.

Livingston, Steven. "Beyond the 'CNN Effect': The Media-Foreign Policy Dynamic." In *Politics and the Press: The News Media and Their Influence*, edited by Pippa Norris, 291–318. London: Lynne Rienner, 1997.

Livingston, Steven, and Todd Eachus. "Humanitarian Crises and U.S. Foreign Policy: Somalia and the CNN Effects Reconsidered." *Political Communication* 12 (1995): 413–429.

Lule, Jack. "The Myth of My Widow: A Dramatic Analysis of News Portrayals of a Terrorist Victim." In *Media Coverage of Terrorism*, edited by A. Odasuo Alali and Kenoye Kelvin Eke, 86–111. Newbury Park: Sage, 1991.

Lutz, James, and Brenda Lutz. *Global Terrorism.* London: Routledge, 2004.

Marantz, Paul, and Brenda S. Steinberg, eds. *Superpower Involvement in the Middle East: Dynamics of Foreign Policy.* Boulder, Colo.: Westview, 1995.

Marcus, Ittamar. "Rape, Murder, Violence, and War for Allah against the Jews: Summer 2000 on Palestinian Television." Palestinian Media Watch (PMW), Special Report # 30, September 11, 2000, at www.pmw.org.il.

Martin, Hans-Peter, and Harald Schumann. *The Global Trap.* London: Zed Books, 1997.

Metz, Christian. *Film Language: A Semiotics of the Cinema*. Chicago: University of Chicago Press, 1990.

———. *The Imaginary Signifier*. Bloomington: Indiana University Press, 1982.

Netanyahu, Benjamin, ed. *Terrorism: How the West Can Win*. New York: Farrar, Strauss and Giroux, 1986.

Nossek, Hillel. "Our News and Their News: The Role of National Identity in the Coverage of Foreign News." *Journalism* 5, no. 3 (2004): 343–368.

O'Brien, Conor Cruise. *The Siege*. New York: Simon & Schuster, 1986.

Orme, William. "A Parallel Mideast Battle: Is It News or Incitement?" *Israel Resource Review* 2000, at israelbehindthenews.com/Oct-25-00.htm#PLO7 (accessed October 25, 2000).

Paletz, David. L., Pewter Fozzard, and John Z. Ayanian. "The IRA, the Red Brigades, and the F.A.L.N. in the 'New York Times.'" *Journal of Communication* 32 (1982): 162–171.

Perry, Nick. *Hyper-Reality and Global Culture*. London: Routledge, 1998.

Picard, Robert. *Media Portrayals of Terrorism*. Ames: Iowa State University Press, 1993.

Pressman, Jeremy. "The Primary Role of the United States in Israeli-Palestinian Relations." *International Studies Perspectives* 4, no. 2 (2003): 191–194.

———. "The Second Intifada: Background and Causes of the Israeli-Palestinian Conflict." *The Journal of Conflict Studies* 23, no. 2 (2003): 114–141.

Robertson, Roland. *Globalization: Social Theory and Global Culture*. London: Sage, 1992.

———. "*Glocalization*: Time-Space and Homogeneity-Heterogeneity." In *Global Modernities*, edited by Mike Featherstone, Scott Lash, and Roland Robertson, 25–44. London: Sage, 1995.

Roeh, Itzhak, and Akiva Cohen. "One of the Bloodiest Days: A Comparative Analysis of Open and Closed Television News." *Journal of Communication* 42, no. 2 (1992): 42–55.

Said, Edward D. *Peace and Its Discontents*. New York: Vintage Books, 1999.

Sakwa, Richard. *Gorbachev and His Reforms, 1985–1990*. New York: Prentice Hall, 1991.

Schmid, Alex P. *Political Terrorism: A Research Guide to Concepts, Theories, Data Bases, and Literature*. New Brunswick, N.J.: Transaction Books, 1984.

Selim, Mohammed E. "The Survival of a Non-State Actor: The Foreign Policy of the Palestine Liberation Organization." In *The Foreign Policies of Arab States*, edited by Baghat Korany and Ali E. Hillal Dessouki, 260–309. Boulder, Colo.: Westview Press, 1991.

Shinar, Dov. *Palestinian Voices: Communication and Nation Building in the West Bank*. Boulder, Colo.: Rienner, 1987.

Strange, Susan. *Casino Capitalism*. New York: St. Francis Press, 1996.

Tessler, Mark. *A History of the Israeli-Palestinian Conflict*. Bloomington: Indiana University Press, 1994.

Thussu, Daya Kishan. "Live TV and Bloodless Deaths: War, Infotainment, and 24/7 News." In *War and the Media: Reporting Conflict 24/7*, edited by Daya Kishan Thussu and Des Freedman, 117–132. London: Sage, 2003.

Tokatly, Oren. *Communication Policy in Israel* [in Hebrew]. Tel Aviv: The Open University of Israel, 2000.

Tomlinson, John. *Globalization and Culture.* Cambridge, U.K.: Polity, 1999.

Tuchman, Gaye. *Making News: A Study in the Construction of Reality.* New York: The Free Press, 1978.

Tynyanov, Yuri. "The Foundations of Cinema." In *Russian Formalist Film Theory,* edited by Herbert Eagle, 81–101. Ann Arbor: Michigan Slavic Publications, 1981.

UN Report of the Secretary-General Prepared Pursuant to General Assembly Resolution ES-10/10.

Van Ginneken, Jaap. *Understanding Global News.* London: Sage, 1998.

Virilio, Paul. *Open Sky.* New York: Verso, 1995.

Volkmer, Ingrid. *News in the Global Sphere: A Study of CNN and Its Impact on Global Communication.* Luton, U.K.: University of Luton Press, 1999.

Wallerstein, Immanuel. *The Politics of the World Economy: The States, the Movements, and the Civilization.* Cambridge, U.K.: Cambridge University Press, 1984.

Weinman, Gabriel. "The Theatre of Terror: Effects of Press Coverage." *Journal of Communication* 33 (1983): 38–45.

Witztum, D. "The Television Report and History." In *Cinema and Memory: A Dangerous Relationship?* [in Hebrew], edited by Haim Bresheet, Shlomo Sand, and Moshe Zimmerman, 169–198. Jerusalem: The Zalman Shazar Center for Jewish History, 2004.

Wolf, Mark. *Abstracting Reality.* Lanham, Md.: University Press of America, 2000.

Wolfsfeld, Gadi. "The News Media and the Second Intifada: Some Basic Lessons." *Palestine-Israel Journal* 10, no. 2 (2003): 5–12.

Yaron, Noam. *Channel 2: The New Statism* [in Hebrew]. Tel-Aviv: Fetish, 2001.

INTERNET SOURCES

Be'Tselem. www.btselem.org.
Camera. www.camera.org/index.
CNN Specials. edition.cnn.com/SPECIALS/2002/terror.tapes.
Intifada. electronicintifada.net/themedia.
Global Security Organization. www.globalsecurity.org/military/ops/enduring-freedom.htm.
Human Rights Watch (HRW). hrw.org.
Independent Media Review and Analysis. www.imra.org.il.
Israeli Audience Research Board. www.midrug-tv.org.il/.
Israeli Ministry of Foreign Affairs. w3.castup.net/mfa/main_menu.htm.
Israelinsider. www.israelinsider.com/channels/diplomacy/articles.
Israel Resource Review. israelbehindthenews.com.
Jenin Inquiry. www.jenininquiry.org/articles.htm.
Jewish Virtual Library. www.jewishvirtuallibrary.org/jsource/Terrorism.
Middle East Media Research Institute (MEMRI). www.memri.org.
Palestinian Authority International Press Center. www.ipc.gov.ps.
Palestinian Human Rights Monitoring Group. www.phrmg.org/monitor.htm.
Palestinian Media Watch (PMW). www.pmw.org.il.

Palestine Monitor. www.palestinemonitor.org/new_web/mediawatch_archive.htm.
Union Tribune. www.signonsandiego.com/news/nation/terror.
United Jerusalem. www.unitedjerusalem.org.
Vanderbilt University Television News Indexed Archive. tvnews.vanderbilt.edu/TV.
WorldNetDaily. WorldNetDaily.com

Index

About the Author

Nitzan Ben-Shaul received his PhD from New York University. He is senior lecturer in the Film and Television Department at Tel Aviv University and former chair of the department. He is the author of *Mythical Expressions of Siege in Israeli Films* (1997); *Introduction to Film Theories* (2000); and *Film: The Key Concepts* (forthcoming). Articles of his on television, film theory, new media, and Israeli cinema have been published in journals such as *Third Text, New Cinemas Journal, Shofar,* and *Journal of Modern Jewish Studies.*